TEN SECONDS OF BOLDNESS

*The Essential Guide to Solving Problems
and Building Self-Confidence*

Shawn Langwell

Copyright © 2022 Shawn Langwell

All rights reserved. No part of this book may be reproduced or used in any manner without the prior written permission of the copyright owner, except for the use of brief quotations in a book review. To request permissions, contact the publisher at shawnlangwellwriter@gmail.com

ISBN: 978-0-9982487-5-2

First paperback edition August 1, 2022

Edited by Jim Baldwin
Cover design by Crissi Langwell
Interior layout by Crissi Langwell

Interior Photos:
Page 356: Alysha Rosly, Madhuri Mohite, Dan Wallace, Kelly McClintock

Author photo by Stuart Lirette

Scriptures taken from the Holy Bible, New International Version®, NIV®. Copyright © 1973, 1978, 1984, 2011 by Biblica, Inc.™ Used by permission of Zondervan. All rights reserved worldwide. www.zondervan.com The "NIV" and "New International Version" are trademarks registered in the United States Patent and Trademark Office by Biblica, Inc.™

This book is also available in hardcover and eBook.

ShawnLangwell.com

Dedicated to my beautiful, kind, loving,
and intelligent wife, Crissi,
and dreamers everywhere.

bold·ness
bōldnəs
> 1. willingness to take risks and act innovatively; confidence or courage.

in·no·va·tive
inə̦vādiv
> 1. introducing or using new ideas or methods.
> 2. having new ideas about how something can be done.

in·no·va·tion
inə'vāSH(ə)n
> 1. a new method, idea, product, etc.
> 2. the practical application of creativity and effort to create new ideas, products, or solutions to problems.

self-con·fi·dence
self 'känfəd(ə)ns
> 1. a feeling of trust in one's abilities, qualities, and judgment.

be·lief
bə'lēf
> 1. trust, faith, or confidence in someone or something.

am·bi·tious
am'biSHəs

adjective
> 1. having or showing a strong desire and determination to succeed.

<u>fear of failure</u>
persistent and irrational anxiety about failing to measure up to the standards and goals set by oneself or others. This may include anxiety over academic standing, losing a job, sexual inadequacy, or loss of face and self-esteem. Fear of failure may be associated with perfectionism and is implicated in a number of psychological disorders, including eating disorders and some anxiety disorders.

Table of Contents

 i My Story i
 ii Why This Book, Now? xxi
 iii How to Get the Most Out of This Book xxxiii

Section I Identify the Problem / Opportunity

 1. Getting Started: Finding Courage to Change 3
 2. Reality Check: You Can Be, Do, or Have Almost Anything By Developing Better Habits 23
 3. Getting Honest With Yourself: Five Truths About Self-Confidence 33
 4. How Do We Tame Our Inner Critics and Become More Self-Confident? 61
 5. Jump! 73
 6. Bridging the Confidence Gap 79
 7. Increasing Your Self-Awareness by Taking a Personal Inventory 93
 8. *Ten Seconds of Boldness*: Finding Courage Within to Start 115

Section II Clearly Decide What You Want

 9. Five Key Questions to Become More Decisive 123
 10. Make a Decision and Don't Overthink or Second Guess It 131
 11. The Five Decisions 145
 12. The Not-So-Secret Power of Prayer, Meditation, and Creative Visualization 167
 13. Building Clarity, Vision, Mission, and Purpose 179

Section III Find Your Why

 14. Finding Your Why 191
 15. Belief: Changing How You Think About Everything 197
 16. Willingness: What Are You Willing to Do to Get What You Want? 209
 17. Love: The Source of All Motivation and Inspiration 219

Section IV Plan Your Work

 18. Keep it Simple 227
 19. Write That Shit Down 243
 20. Shit Happens: Expect It. Plan For It. Deal With It and Be Flexible 249
 21. Manage Your Time or It Will Manage You 253

Section V Start Working Your Plan

22. Getting Into Action 267
23. The Power of Association and Perpetual Curiosity 277
24. Practical Steps 285
25. Progress Not Perfection 291
26. Persistence, Practice, and Patience 299
27. Visualization: Using Your Imagination to Create the Life You Want .. 305
28. Affirmations: Inspiration From the Inside Out 309
29. Building Confidence is a Balancing Act 317
Conclusion – The End is Just a New Beginning 327
Acknowledgements 335
Appendix I – Self-Assessment Sheets 341
Appendix II – *Ten Seconds of Boldness* Productivity Planner 345
Ten Seconds of Boldness – Productivity Planning Sheets: 349
Appendix III – Affirmations 363
Appendix IV – Your Personal *Ten Seconds of Boldness* Agreement 365
Appendix V – Gratitude List 367
Notes 369
About the Author 377

i
My Story

I believe who we are and who we become is a product of five things:

1. Our upbringing.
2. Our experiences.
3. Our environment.
4. Our inner spirit, curiosity, and creativity.
5. What we believe and how we respond to all of the above.

Growing up in the sixties and seventies, I had what I call a normal middle-class hippie upbringing. Dad, a fireman. Mom, a wife, and stay-at-home mother. My brothers and I were loved. Both parents said so often and showed it, too. I loved the times when Dad treated us to ten-cent tacos from Taco Bell or burgers and milkshakes from Foster's Freeze. I especially loved it when Dad would vigorously dry my hair after a bath as a kid or when Mom gave me hugs and kisses good night and always said "I love you" before turning out the lights.

    Wherever we lived, there always seemed to be a steady parade of Dad's friends visiting, mostly on his days off. For hours they would drink and get high while listening to rock and roll, or watching baseball or football, often engaging in deep philosophical conversations about the meaning of life, spirituality, or the Vietnam War. I loved to listen, but mostly, I just wanted to be around my dad.

    Academically, I was a confident kid who loved the recognition I got from my teachers and parents for being a good student. But, at the age of twelve, the spring before I graduated 8th grade as valedictorian, my safe and perfect world was shattered.

Early one morning I awoke to the sound of tires spitting gravel in the driveway outside my room and my mother shouting, "How dare you leave without saying goodbye to your kids!" I yanked the curtains back and watched as my dad sped off in a blue 1975 VW bus without looking back, leaving me, my mom, and two younger brothers to fend for ourselves with no income. I was shocked, confused, angry, sad, and worried how we would survive. That day would forever change and shape the rest of my life. It would take many years for me to fully process my grief.

We Did What it Took to Survive

I was twelve when my dad left us. Mom hadn't worked since high school, but she quickly landed a job as a secretary for a local insurance broker. Her meager paycheck was barely enough to keep food in our bellies and a roof over our head, but not enough for back-to-school clothes. Fortunately, my grandparents on my dad's side were very generous and gave Mom money to buy new shoes, Converse high tops, for us three growing boys.

One day my mom saw me on the floor stuffing cardboard inside them and went ballistic, "What happened to your new shoes?!" she shouted. "I can't afford a new pair." I had worn holes in the soles using them as brakes while skateboarding down steep neighborhood hills with my friends. "Looks like you better get a job if you want new ones," she declared, then turned and walked away.

"Fine," I said, not having a clue of where to look or what I wanted to do.

It didn't take long. By summer I found a dishwasher job at a local café. I hated it, but I saw how much money the waitresses earned from tips and knew I wanted some of that. I hoped to become a busser so I could earn more than the $2.10 minimum wage, but the owner didn't want or need a busser. I pleaded but she wouldn't budge.

As I entered high school, I became reclusive and full of social anxiety. I was smoking pot every day before, during, and after school. Soon my grades started to slip, and the downward spiral continued.

By sophomore year, I quit the café and found work at a yacht club and later a popular Italian restaurant. That was my first taste of success; I often came home with a pocketful of cash—a small fortune for a teenager with no financial responsibilities. I felt on top of the world.

Big Dreams at Seventeen

At seventeen, I started to dream of wealth and riches and making a name for myself. I was determined to be the man I thought my father should have been. I discovered motivational tapes by Wayne Dyer, Brian Tracy, and Earl Nightingale and many others, listening to them over and over. I couldn't get enough. They gave me hope and planted the seeds of a dream: that I would not have to live in poverty and that I was destined to do great things.

In many respects, I thought of these men and several others as surrogate father figures. I trusted them. I became obsessed with personal achievement and goals, devouring any new tape sets or books that came out, like *The Magic of Thinking Big*, by David J. Schwartz and *See You at the Top*, by Zig Ziglar. I wanted to be like them and dreamed of one day becoming a motivational speaker and owning my own business. I also wanted to be the first in my family to earn a four-year college degree. Only there was a problem.

By my senior year of high school, I was making really good money and started drinking and partying a lot. Many of my friends had girlfriends but I was shy and a "late bloomer." While the tapes gave me hope and got me all pumped up, they didn't give me enough confidence to talk to girls. I needed liquid courage for that.

After one semester at a junior college, I packed up and headed to San Diego State University, intending to earn a bachelor's degree in business. I had good intentions but, for the next two and a half years, I was drunk nearly every night. Long story short, by twenty-two, I had become a full-blown alcoholic, and was literally pissing my dreams away.

In the spring of 1986, I had a drunken accident with a soda machine that nearly cost me my right hand.

One afternoon as I sat in the public hot tub, I watched two buff dudes with gorgeous women on their arms show off by shaking a free soda out of the vending machine. A few nights later, after drinking a tumbler full of rum and Coke, I thought I'd give it a go. I grabbed the machine from the back, but it wouldn't budge. No surprise. Back then I weighed a whopping hundred-thirty-five pounds wet, and that machine must've weighed over eight-hundred pounds. Naturally, to feel bigger than I was, I did what any resourceful drunk college kid would do: I climbed on top of it and pushed off the wall with my feet. Not smart. It smashed my right hand, sheering off the knuckle of my index finger and tearing a gash in my palm.

Seven hours, fifty-six stitches, and a steel pin later, I came to. The phone beside my hospital bed ringing. It was Mom. She urged me to get help.

"I'll be okay! I need to get out of here. We can't afford it." I said, still woozy.

A few weeks later she called to tell me I had to come home.

"I got this, Mom," I pleaded.

"You don't get to vote," she insisted.

Like a puppy with its tail between its legs, I came home with good intentions to get sober.

Earlier she had told me that a few family friends were in recovery and urged me to reach out to them, but I was too scared to ask for help. And the pain wasn't great enough for me to want to change. I hadn't hit bottom, yet.

Night after night, I swore to myself that I wouldn't drink again. Inevitably, no matter how strong I thought my will power was, I'd find myself back at a local bar, wasted, unable to stop. My alcoholism was winning. I was consumed by guilt and shame and saw no way out.

Hitting Bottom

After yet another night bar hopping, I got so wasted, I blacked out. Next thing I remember was wandering the hills of Fairfax, California at dawn.

Head hung low in an oversized thrift store suit, I shuffled along a narrow trail, the sound of gravel crunching beneath my feet, and birds chirping in nearby bushes as the sun slowly began to rise. I stepped onto a grassy hill and slipped, tumbling head over heels down the hill before coming to rest on my butt.

Feeling lost and destitute as I picked the stickers from my suit, I put my head between my legs and cried out, "Why? Why me? God, please help me!"

What happened next is inexplicable. In that moment of despair, I vividly recalled the exact location of a nearby recovery meeting from a schedule one of my brother's friends had left on our coffee table weeks earlier. I made my way to the 7:00 a.m. meeting.

Standing there looking like something the cat dragged in, I was welcomed by several happy caffeinated people. It kind of creeped me out, but I went inside anyway.

As the meeting started, someone who appeared to be in charge invited new people to introduce themselves. I could feel my hands shaking, but I took a deep breath, staggered to my feet and for the first time in my life, boldly declared, "My name is Shawn, and I'm an alcoholic."

The rest of the meeting was a blur. When the meeting ended, I made a dash for the exit. Between me and the door stood a short round man with a bald head. He offered his number and to take me to another meeting.

I raised my hand like a stop signal.

"I'm fine. I got this."

He took one look at me and said, "You ain't got shit, kid. If you don't know where your next meeting is, you may not make it back alive."

I stomped away, determined to prove him wrong. *I'll show you,* I thought.

Over the next few months, no matter how hard I tried, I always seemed to end up back at the bar or passed out on the kitchen floor. My mom even threatened to throw me out if I didn't get help. My life was falling apart, and I was only twenty-two.

One afternoon, after repeating more of the same insane, destructive patterns, I woke up and immediately reached for a smoke. On my nightstand next to an ashtray overflowing with cigarette butts was a white envelope with my name neatly written on the outside. Inside was a card. The front depicted a waddle of cartoon penguins standing on an iceberg. In the center, was one lone sunburnt penguin. I opened the card and read:

Son,

*You are one in a million.
I love you too much to watch you die.
Please, get help.*

*Love,
Mom*

Ever since that April when I came home, I was literally drowning in my alcoholism and that card was a lifeline.

Soon after, I finally made the biggest decision of my life. On October 10, 1986, I checked into a treatment program and began the journey of recovery that has made me who I am today. I have not had a drink or drug since. I pray I never do.

The End is Only a New Beginning

After I got sober, I reenrolled in college as a transfer student at San Francisco State University. In 1992, ten years after I started, I finally graduated college, earning a Bachelor of Science degree in Business Administration. That same year, I got married and landed a promising job in media sales.

Shortly after, we bought a home and became parents. I was well on my way to living the American Dream. But, like any good story, there were many more obstacles along the way that soon became painful lessons.

What it's Like Now

Despite all my struggles and the normal ups and downs of life, I have a lot to be grateful for: I am sober, healthy, married, raised three awesome adults, live in a nice home, and have more money than month which allows me to enjoy travel, dine out, and do lots of other fun things. And yet, I never gave up on my teenage dreams. I still have a deep desire to inspire others and own a business. Fortunately, I am well on my way.

Today, however, I am not as obsessed with material wealth and external rewards as I was for most of my adult life. I now place a higher value on building relationships, personal growth, and maturity, and trying to be helpful to others.

> Since starting this book I have been tested and challenged so many times I've often felt like a man overboard, drowning in my own fear of failure while simultaneously trying to write about a five-step life vest for others.

Reflection and Self-Awareness

I came to believe a long time ago that **there are no mistakes in this world.** That **everything happens for a reason.** I believe it is my responsibility to pay close attention to and learn from my personal struggles. To try my best to adapt and make adjustments to improve my attitude, thoughts, or actions so that I may have a different outcome.

What started as a drive to become a better writer and more confident speaker and salesperson evolved into this quest for boldness. To become willing and honest enough to acknowledge my strengths and weaknesses in terms of skill, ability, and habits. And to embrace the ones I like and find the courage to change those I don't.

I began a process of daily reflection and introspection. Some days that included reading something spiritual, others included periods of prayer and meditation. Still others, mostly on weekends, I would clear my head on long hikes along the Point Reyes National Seashore, hoping to find the right thought or inspiration for this book. I would pray, meditate, and ask the universe or God for direction as I put one foot in front of the other along scenic coastal paths to places like Alamere Falls, or Sculptured Beach.

I Found Clarity by Taking Action

My quest for clarity began to motivate me to keep pressing forward. I took on new challenges and learned new skills to support my goal of becoming a best-selling author and inspirational speaker.

To improve my writing, I took critical thinking and creative writing classes over two and half years at a local junior college. To become a more confident speaker, I joined Toastmasters. Two months later, my local club elected me president. The following year, the Board of Directors of the Redwood Writers Club, nominated me as Vice President, then President the following year.

With each new opportunity, I boldly stepped forward not knowing if I would succeed or fail. Eventually I began to believe in myself and ability to lead and inspire others.

Personal Responsibility and Determination

Along the way, I discovered that our struggles do not define us. But how we respond to them can, if we let them. When we identify a weakness or obstacle about ourselves that we want to change, it is our personal responsibility to take the necessary steps. Those steps are the frame for this entire book. They are the work necessary get you from where you are to where you want to be.

Here are the five essential steps:

1. **Identify** the problem or opportunity.
2. Clearly **decide** what you want.
3. Know **why** you want it.
4. Write a clear **plan.**
5. **Start** working that plan.

When We Want Something Bad Enough, We Usually Find a Way to Get it.

I learned a long time ago that my success in virtually any endeavor increases dramatically when I write down my goals. When I finally culled through five years of messy notes and came up with the five key principles, I wrote them down. I played with the order. I questioned whether they were too basic, obvious, or simple. *Did they make sense logically? Were they easy to remember?* And the biggest question, *Will they work?*

When I was happy with the order, I printed, cut, and pasted them to two separate 3" x 5" index cards then pinned them to the wall in my home office. One to my left and the other on my right. At eye level from my desk chair, where I still look at them multiple times a day.

Between them are a white board filled with my goals (both work and personal) for the next quarter, year, five, and ten years, and a corkboard, covered with positive quotes, pictures of my family, and a series of index cards outlining the framing for this book. They are daily reminders to inspire me to keep going especially when I want to give up.

Life Lessons and Making Mistakes

Many of my life lessons have come as a result of making many mistakes and repeating old habits until I became bold enough to change. *Ten Seconds of Boldness* came as a solution to a major problem in my life.

I was in a sales slump at work. Mainly because I got comfortable and complacent and stopped pursuing new business. I knew what the block was, but still kept finding other things to do to feel "busy" and avoid facing my real fear, *rejection*.

Even after decades of sales experience, I still dreaded making cold calls. They were my kryptonite. That phone owned me. No matter how much I prepared and tried to psyche myself up to make unsolicited sales calls, I often felt weak and timid. And I only made them when necessary to hit my sales goal and earn commission. That was my carrot. Not making my goal and possibly losing my job was the stick.

It bothered me that even after decades of experience I had not yet conquered this fear, yet if I was to earn any commission and keep my job, I had to figure it out. I grabbed a Sharpie and scribbled these words on a Post-it note and stuck it on my cubicle wall above the phone: **"Ten Seconds of Boldness."**

A Power Packed Post-it Note

At first, I read it and did nothing. I feared that if I didn't hit my sales goals, my dwindling savings would not be enough to cover my mortgage and, worse, if the slump continued, I could be fired. I was backed against a wall. Finally, I found the ten seconds of courage to pick up the 10,000-pound phone, to smile and dial. I'm sure I sounded scared and desperate to my prospects. But I pressed on, getting rejected over and over.

Then I got a yes. And another. Each new success was a shot of confidence that I began to build upon, even after I hit my goal.

I could tell you that I now love making cold calls, but that would be a lie. I do not wake up in the morning and say "Yes! I get to make cold calls today." I doubt I ever will. But slowly I am developing the habit of reaching out to at least one new prospect a day. *Ten Seconds of Boldness* has become my muse to help me push through my fears. So far it seems to be working.

I started using this self-motivation technique six months before the pandemic hit. Soon I was working from home full time, alone. Sure, I had weekly sales meetings and one-on-one check ins with my manager to help keep me motivated. But for the most part, I worked alone. Just me, my note, a phone, and a laptop.

Ten Seconds of Boldness Works

Over the past thirty months, my sales have skyrocketed. I found out that by finding this simple principle, my whole attitude shifted and my confidence began to soar.

As a result, the book you are now reading became something far more meaningful than the one I had started in 2017. That Post-it note was the catalyst to clarify what I wanted to say and which personal experiences may best help others like me who struggle with self-confidence.

I am confident that *Ten Seconds of Boldness* will transform your life in a positive way *if* you are willing to do the work. What do I mean? For lasting transformation to occur, we need to learn and apply fundamental principles. You will find them in each of them five essential steps as we progress. These principles will show you *what* to do and *how* to get started. But *what* you choose to do and *why* is entirely up to you.

The five-step process or *Ten Seconds of Boldness* is simple but not easy. It will require honest self-appraisal regarding your belief system and habits, as well as your skills and abilities. For many, these may be the most difficult hurdles to overcome.

As you begin to make bold decisions, ten seconds at a time, you will learn to let go of old unproductive habits and learn to develop new ones which will ultimately improve your self-confidence.

Learning To Adapt

At the beginning of the pandemic, I feared not being able to connect with "my people" because in-person meetings were shut down. And connecting with others is an integral part to maintaining my sobriety.

I began to search online for virtual recovery meetings. I discovered one that felt like my local homegroup. It was safe, helpful, and quickly attracted people seeking recovery from around the globe, including the United Kingdom, Ireland, Australia, Canada, Afghanistan, Pakistan, Israel, and virtually every state in the United States. It was great to hear their stories of a common problem and solution.

Soon I was "sharing" (for those who don't know, many meetings have a period where participants can talk for two to three minutes about what's going on with them in recovery at that moment and how the program is working for them). The next thing I knew, I was getting invited to be the lead speaker one or more times per month.

The Power of Writing Down What We Want

Side note: I actually had set a goal three months earlier and had prayed for a way to get more speaking experience so I could improve, but more importantly so I could reach more people with a message of hope and inspiration.

Since writing that goal on my whiteboard in 2020, I have shared my story over four-dozen times to people all over the world looking for help with addiction. It has not only built my self-confidence as a speaker, but the real-time love and positive feedback I have received from complete strangers about how things I have said literally helped save lives and fills my heart with joy and gratitude.

I share this because a little recognition strengthens and validates my belief in myself and confidence that I truly have something of value to offer others, and I no longer have to be shy about being vulnerable telling my story to strangers.

Success is One Bold Leap Over the Fence of Fear

As a direct result of becoming bolder, more courageous, and self-confident, I have experienced countless blessings: Last year, my ad sales have climbed 22%. In January of 2022 my year-over-year monthly comps (comparative sales) were up a whopping 58%! Many clients have said they appreciate my willingness to learn more about their businesses to discover what problems they are facing and my no-nonsense approach to helping them. That has resulted in annual retention rates of 80% or more. My commissions have also increased by 24% !

Recently, at a quarterly "territory review," our company's EVP and CRO (Executive Vice President and Chief Revenue officer) Michael Turpin said I was one of the top five sales reps he's ever worked with. That compliment made my day. And now it's safely stored in what I call a *confidence bank*, a mental spot where I put things like this for the days when I may feel *less than* or not so confident. When I posted this incredible compliment on Facebook I was blown away by the congratulatory remarks of my friends.: "Not a surprise! Well-deserved accolades." "You are a great salesperson." And this from my manager, Lori Pearce, that went straight to my heart: "Truly deserved. You are a shining star and an example for all."

I will safely store their kind words in the *confidence bank* of my mind for those days when I don't believe enough in myself to press on, or make a tough decision, or do something uncomfortable that may cause me stress and anxiety.

Today, I focus on what *is* working rather than dwelling on what is *not*. Similar to a successful incremental investment plan and strategy, I have built my own self-confidence, one decision and deposit at a time.

All this good fortune is a direct result of my being bold enough and willing to try something new, to do it, and let go of the results.

The Essential Five Steps Work, When You Work Them

For those who feel they need to fully understand *how* these concepts work or some additional quantifiable proof that they will impact your lives in a positive way *before* you try them, I understand. It is normal to approach something new with caution. I just showed you how impactful they have been in my life. It's up to you to use them and experience the benefits yourself. All I ask is that you keep an open mind and become willing to learn and apply a simple five-step solution that can have a positive impact in your life.

I Can't Motivate You. It's Not My Job.

Motivation is an inside job not only tied to *what* you want but *why* you want it. Others can inspire and encourage you, but ultimately motivation is personal.

Prompt: What Problems are You Trying to Solve?

Ask yourself these questions: Why *Ten Seconds of Boldness?* What problem(s) are you trying to solve? I doubt it is because you are already oozing confidence and are successful in all areas of your life. Perhaps you are a CEO, manager, or business owner grappling with recent economic challenges and shifts in the labor pool, if so, *Ten Seconds of Boldness* may provide a much-needed confidence boost to improve employee satisfaction and company sales. Perhaps your job has changed, and you are now required to make more public presentations and you don't have the confidence you may like. This book can help. I also suggest you consider joining Toastmasters.

A Little Bit of Courage Goes a Long Way

There's little that can't be made better with a little courage, confidence, and a process to help resolve your problems. As you will discover, a plan isn't enough. Success must also include finding courage (guts, grit, determination, persistence, or any other power adjective you like), a clear motive (your *why*), and consistent effort on your part. In other words, success takes work.

I know first-hand that the five habits and *Ten Seconds of Boldness* work. They are effective tools for not only solving many common problems, like increasing confidence, but also a process to increase sales, profit, and morale, as I previously mentioned. *Ten Seconds of Boldness* is an essential guide that outlines a process of applying principles and values to five specific steps. It will not define your motives nor outline the specific actions steps necessary to solve your particular problem. Those are questions you get to figure out on your own, as they should be.

The good news is you will have plenty of opportunities to apply these five steps. This book is specifically designed to get you started and build your confidence as we progress. For it to have a positive impact in your life will require mutual respect and trust. I trust that you have a sincere desire to become more confident and want to be successful in many areas of your life. That you are willing to put the effort in to not only learn but to practice what you learn. Your part is that you trust me enough to guide you, that I sincerely have your best interest at heart and will not bullshit you. And more important, that you believe the principles in the book can work for you too, even if you don't have all the answers or quite know what you want yet. We'll get there. Trust me.

It is not necessary to be 100% certain about something *before* you try it. Think of it this way. Do you own a car? Do you know or need to know how exactly it works for it to go from point A to point B? No. A car is a mode of transportation, a means to an end that is relatively easy to operate. After some training, study, and passing two exams, you are issued a license to validate you have the requisite skills required to drive. Once you have your license and a car, all that you need is to put gas in it, turn the key, and go.

Decide Today to Find Your Why

I wrote this book for people like you and me. Those of us who are ambitious but have a tendency to overthink things and to dwell on what we don't have rather than be grateful for what we do have. For those of us with inner critics that constantly nag us about what we should or shouldn't do. Like our moms when we were teenagers, to take out the trash or pick up our clothes. But we are not teenagers, and the voice in our head is not our mom.

Ten Seconds of Boldness is for those of us who have dreams and want to feel more confident to get started and pursue them, but all too often are too "busy" to put together a plan of action to make them a reality. It is for those of us who want to overcome feelings of shame, guilt, or resentment, who replay our own failures over and over again, and who feel like imposters, but don't want our lives to be controlled by our fears.

I cannot convince you to do something you are not ready to. All I can do is share some stories and tools that may inspire you to use them and begin to build the life you want for yourself and your family.

But more importantly, I hope you discover your *why*: Why do you want what you want, and why would you want to become uncomfortable to get it?

Many of the principles, values, and habits I outline in the book are not necessarily new, but when applied, they can change lives, if you use them.

I hope *Ten Seconds of Boldness* inspires you to find the motivation within to break free from those life-sucking habits. They are not helpful. Nor is excessive control or over-analysis or our need to feel we always need to be right. Quite the opposite.

Our need for certainty and control are bad habits. They are part of the problem, not the solution. They represent a mindset that holds us back from becoming confident enough to be great at something. Why, because we tend to be too independent, and don't delegate or ask for help. Instead, if we want something to be done right, we choose to do it ourselves, even when we could afford to hire others who are better than we are. I hope you do, too.

This book is for me as much as it is you. As I mentioned earlier, I've paid a hefty price to earn the right to speak on this topic. I have not yet mastered these skills in all areas of my life. I still make mistakes, and I hope to make lots more because that's how I have learned to improve.

A Grateful Heart is a Joyful Heart

I am grateful for everything that has happened to bring me to this moment. My life is far greater today than it used to be, and it continues to improve a little bit every day. Your life will improve too, if you want it badly enough and are willing to try something new.

Today, I am grateful. I don't take anything for granted and remain curious to keep becoming a better, more loving, and forgiving human.

I forgave my dad years ago. But most importantly, I forgave myself.

If you get nothing else from our time together, I hope you learn to have a little more grace, love, and forgiveness for yourself.

ii
Why This Book, Now?

I wrote this book because I don't want to die with regrets.

Regret for all the things I wish I would have done but never truly believed I could. Regret that I believed the lies of my inner critics, who incessantly questioned my credibility because I don't have three or four letters after my name. That decades of experience overcoming challenges of all kinds did not qualify me to discuss the value of courage and confidence. Regret that I was so afraid of failing that I never found the courage to try.

Somewhere between an unbridled childhood imagination of possibility and the many years in between often fraught with painful life lessons, I allowed circumstances to steal my hopes and dreams. I gave up on me, almost.

I now know and believe that everything I have experienced up to this point has prepared me for what's next. That the good, the bad, and the messiness of my life is exactly why I needed to write this book. Because no matter how much we may want a quick and easy, well-marked path to success, the obstacles—our struggles and strife—are the path.

I wrote *Ten Seconds of Boldness* for you. To inspire you to stop looking for quick-fix solutions to your problems and to find the courage within to make something happen.

To visualize being bold enough to tell your inner critics off. To suit up, show up, and put your game face on. Hands on your hips, shoulders square, confidently staring your inner critics down, and with one deep breath and a mere ten seconds of courage, boldly tell them,

"Enough, already! You don't own me anymore!"

The Birth of My Dreams

For years I have dreamed of fulfilling teenage dreams ignited by motivational and inspirational speakers and authors like: Earl Nightingale, Wayne Dyer, Dennis Waitley, Gerald Jampolsky, Brian Tracy, Zig Ziglar, Shakti Gawain, Dale Carnegie, Napoleon Hill, Tony Robbins, and many, many more. I wanted to become great like them. To help others discover their own greatness within.

I have made a shit-ton of mistakes in my life. We all do. It's how we learn, or never learn if we're too stubborn, or afraid of change.

I wrote *Ten Seconds of Boldness* because it felt like the next right step in my life—to push through my own lack of confidence and share some wisdom and experience that might help a few folks along the way. To put my money, time, and effort where my mouth was. To stop thinking about it and put my butt in a chair and start writing.

"That Won't Work." "You're Doing it All Wrong."

I have had people tell me things couldn't be done or question my process by offering unsolicited advice. Often that criticism stung, sometimes a lot. But if I wanted something bad enough, I usually found a way to get it. I persevered because I believed it was possible and was determined to prove them wrong. And there have been many times where others offered "constructive criticism" that was helpful when I was willing to listen and follow their advice.

Case in point, I wanted to improve my writing. My wife had started taking classes at our local junior college and suggested we take a creative writing class together. So, at fifty-two, I went back to college.

I learned several valuable writing skills in that class.

One was a collaborative evaluation process called "workshopping." Basically, the class was broken up into several groups of four to six. These groups were the reviewers. Their role was to offer critiques of the readers.

The readers consisted of three to five students who would read a section of their story or creative piece of writing they were working to each group of reviewers. They would rotate between the review groups and receive feedback from each participant in that group. To be effective for all, we had guidelines. When evaluating our classmates' work, we were instructed to stick to "what's working and what's not." In other words, provide helpful feedback (critiques) to the student authors that could help improve their work. For example, "The tension you are creating between your main characters is working very well. But the time shifts and flashbacks are confusing."

The flipside of that was receiving feedback as an author. This was hard. Authors were instructed to ask for input in two or three areas before reading. After reading our piece we had to listen to each member's feedback without responding.

First, that is hard to do in any situation. Secondly being vulnerable with people we barely know can cause a lot of anxiety. I thought I was strong enough to take it, but I bristled more than once when classmates told me what "wasn't working."

You may be wondering why I am including this story here. As you will continue to discover through the rest of this book and in life, we all have many critics, most of them are in our own heads. And most of them put the spotlight on what's not working and not on what is. It's up to us to change that internal narrative.

Understanding our propensity to dwell on the negative when receiving feedback or constructive criticism, our teacher suggested we look for consensus, consistency, and agreement. In other words, if more than two or three people say that something *isn't working*, pay attention to their feedback. Otherwise, he stressed, it's just someone's opinion.

The same is true for what *is working*—look for consensus.

The two unexpected but valuable lessons I learned in that class were about the workshopping experience. The first, when it comes to feedback, look for consensus, and choose what we want to keep, change, delete, or improve. The second, is about communications skills. In any relationship, especially when speaking or writing, we need to connect to our audience.

What Happens When Your Own Worst Critic is You?

Why are so many of us the last ones to see and believe that we have something of value to offer others or to believe enough in ourselves to boldly pursue our dreams? I don't know. But I do know that far too many of us suffer from *imposter syndrome:* that uneasy, debilitating feeling that we aren't good enough, or worse, that we don't want to stand out or don't believe we are worthy of the success we have achieved, so we do something stupid to sabotage it.

Confidence Can Help You Attract a Spouse

When I asked my wife, Crissi, what attracted her to me, she said, "confidence." That I had a walk and posture that were confident. I wasn't trying to be. I was just focused, determined, and driven to be a little better at my job, every day. Apparently, that was enough.

Ironically, relatively early in our relationship she was 100% clear on what she wanted but didn't pressure me into marriage.

I was still getting over a recent divorce and was gun shy about committing so soon. In hindsight, I am so glad I did.

Finding Courage to Pop The Question

Long story short, Crissi and I dated for four years. One day after church, our pastor asked when I was planning to put a ring on her finger. "Soon," I said. "We've been talking about it, but I'm not quite ready."

Not long after I finally made the decision. I don't know when or what my exact words were, but I do recall looking into her eyes and declaring that she was right—we should go ahead and get married. I don't know if it was her expression or my own sense of finally making a decision, but all I recall about that moment was one word, "finally!"

I know that doesn't sound very romantic. But that's only part of the story.

I made plans for a weekend getaway at one of our favorite camping spots and, well, Crissi tells the story way better than me; she even wrote a blog about it entitled, "How the Question Was Asked," which you can find at winecountrymom.com.

Here's an excerpt, in her words:

"Not to get ahead of ourselves," I started out, "but wouldn't this be a great place for a honeymoon?" I asked him.

The question wasn't totally out of left field. Mr. W. [Because we both worked at the local paper and wanted to keep our relationship secret, she nicknamed me Mr. Wonderful, or Mr. W. for short.] and

I have been talking marriage for a while, and the only thing holding it up was the ring.

"You need to go pick one out!" he had told me, insisting he wanted me to wear a ring I loved. But I wasn't sure how I felt about that. Did other women pick out their own engagement ring before the question was popped? And honestly, did it really matter that much? I'd once thought I needed a certain type of ring on my finger. But as time went on, it mattered less and less. I knew he was the one I wanted to spend the rest of my life with. Whatever the band was, it would be special because of the meaning behind it.

But a few weeks later, the two of us stood giddily in the jewelry store, the perfect ring resting on my finger. It needed to be ordered in my size, and he shooed me out as the rest of the details were taken care of. All that was left now was the proper proposal.

What better than a kids-free weekend?

"I don't want you to get your hopes up," Mr. W. told me days before we were to leave without the kids. "I'm not proposing this weekend."

I thought it was a joke and grinned. Then I saw the seriousness in his face. I tried to hide the disappointment, but it had fallen in puddles around our feet.

"Why?" I asked him.

"The ring hasn't come back yet from being resized."

"You could, you know, propose without a ring," I told him, but neither of us wanted that.

"We'll find another time to do it, and it will be special," he told me. "But I don't want it to ruin our weekend away."

"It won't," I promised, putting my brave face on. "We need this getaway. Truth is, I'm happy to just get some alone time with you."

And I spent the rest of the week focusing all my energy on not being disappointed. Sure, it only made sense to have it happen in this place. Whenever we needed to escape reality and clear our heads, this was our refuge. But I couldn't let it take away from the fact that we would be enjoying its serenity regardless.

Walking up the path, we came towards a clearing that overlooked the whole grounds. Two girls sat there, listening to the sounds of music below from fellow campers. Mr. W. paused briefly, but then continued walking. All of a sudden, he grabbed my arm.

"Wait," he said, pulling me back. I thought it had to do with the view, even though the girls were sitting where the view was. Or maybe it was to hear the music. But when I looked at him, he was on his knee pulling a silver box from the pocket of the backpack. My hands immediately flew to my mouth, tears springing to my eyes as I realized what was about to happen. The girls in the clearing turned away from the music and were now focused on us, but I didn't even see them. All I saw was Mr. W. holding a ring in his hands.

"We've been talking about this for a while," he said. "I want to spend the rest of my life with you." I could barely breathe. "Will you be my wife?"

In moments like these, when you're so sure the man on bended knee before you is the one you want to be with forever, there's only one thing to say.

"Here? Now????" I exclaimed, my hands shaking. In my surprise, my first answer to his question wasn't YES, but shock. He had to actually ask me later if I had even said YES, to which I assured him that was most emphatically my answer.

Love is the Greatest Motivating Force of All

Being selfish or self-centered doesn't work in any relationship, business or personal. For any relationship to last and be healthy requires a solid foundation built with love. The more important and intimate the relationship, especially with a spouse, partner, or family members, the greater the need to strengthen it with *four basic pillars: humility, honesty, compassion, and trust.* When any of these are missing, the relationship often crumbles faster than a multi-million-dollar home built on a sandstone cliff in California in an earthquake.

As parents, Crissi and I have a shared obligation to teach our kids about personal responsibility—to take risks, make decisions and mistakes, and to live with the consequences of their actions. Kids will be resourceful when we stop trying to do everything for them. As parents, we need to let them be kids.

When we first blended our families, things were tense. Each of us brought our own set of beliefs and values to the relationship and had to learn as we go, to focus on what mattered most—love—for each other and our family.

I won't lie, it took several ultra-tense moments, even shouting matches and ugly cries, but as we chartered the choppy waters of the unknown sea of second marriages and blended family with teenagers, we never gave up. We never lost sight of the safe harbor and sandy shoreline ahead. Regardless of the hurt feelings and tense moments we always reconnected with love.

Love is the Superglue for Life

When all the pieces lay shattered at our feet like an egg named Humpty who fell off a wall, we pick up the shells and glue them back together with love. Over the years, Crissi and I have developed a clearer understanding of our shared roles and goals for raising a healthy family: to be loving, supportive, nurturing leaders for our kids and to each other; to lead by example, as best we can. I learned that from my mom, mostly.

Mom was the cheerleader for me and my three brothers, even when we were flat broke and had to eat Adzuki beans to survive (true story). I used to joke that we were so poor I had to eat dookie as a teenager. No matter how little we had, we never went to bed hungry and always had a roof over our heads. But more than providing the bare necessities, Mom always encouraged us boys to pursue our dreams.

In my case, whether it was deciding to go to college, deciding to raise a family, or helping me buy my first car, Mom did her best not to cast doubt or judgement about my choices and gave me the space to succeed or fail on my own. And she let me know she loved me no matter the outcome.

Besides being honest, kind, compassionate, and loving, two of the greatest lessons my mom gave me was encouragement to dream and the freedom to be me.

I try to model the same for our kids.

My responsibility as a parent is to encourage our kids to become independent, loving, purpose-filled humans, who develop enough courage to believe in themselves so they may pursue their passions with confidence and zeal.

It Really Does Take a Village

Like many relationships, personal or otherwise, effective parenting requires collaboration and teamwork. It is a shared responsibility. One in which the collective value of our individual strengths is greater than the separate roles we each play. When it comes to parenting and life, things are nearly always with others, even for single parents. I know, as I previously mentioned. Among many things, being raised as a teen by a single mom taught me resourcefulness and the need for collaboration, even when we are too proud to say, "Can I get some help."

As we wrap, remember that *love is the greatest motivator of all.* It is the oil for our lamp of joy—especially when it comes to our children.

It's hard to go wrong, as parents or in business, when we "do everything in love."

Lead with Love and Show How Much You Care

"People don't care how much you know, until they know how much you care."

The above quote has been attributed to many successful and influential leaders including Theodore Roosevelt, Zig Ziglar, and Earl Nightingale, and many others. It is one of my personal favorites because of its simplicity and power when incorporated as a value. I love it because it cuts to the heart of leadership, influence, and personal development. It's all about love.

In fact, I wrote this book because of how much I care about others, especially you. Think of it as your personal GPS to lead you from where you are now to where you want to be. As you experiment with its precepts, remember to approach everything with love, because if you believe, according to 1 Cor. 13:8 NIV

> "Love never fails."

In anything I do, whether teaching our kids or working with clients, speaking in recovery, or inspiring audiences and readers around the world, in every one of my relationships I do my very best to *lead with love.* And my ulterior motive in every interaction is to encourage and inspire others to do the same.

Though you and I do not have a familial connection, that doesn't mean I can't love you. I want to help you develop the same confidence I see in each of our kids and which I have personally experienced as a result of principles that have taken me over three decades to master.

The five steps and *Ten Seconds of Boldness* are the condensed version of those principles packaged in a way that I believe will make it much easier for you not only remember, but more importantly put into action. To *practice the steps in all you do, especially when you don't feel like it.*

Success is Whatever You Decide it to Be

Life is far too short to be controlled by fear. As I said earlier, I don't want to die with any regrets.

I have had many successes and failures, some greater than others. Each experience has become a lesson to be learned, a fluid river of perpetual change, making me who I am today. And that's what I love about life—no two days are the same.

I sincerely hope you never give up on yourself or your dreams, no matter how crazy they may seem or what you currently believe. Find what you love and never look back. When you do, success will meet you wherever you go.

How to Get the Most Out of This Book

In order to get the most out of this book you need six things that form the acrostic—HOW TLC:

Honesty: That you are honest with yourself about *where* you are, *what* you would like to change, and *why* it matters to you.

Open Mindedness: That you approach the concepts I share with childlike curiosity, leaving all preconceived ideas and judgment at the door.

Willingness: That you become willing to learn and practice a few principles that may seem counterintuitive at first.

Trust: That you not only learn to trust yourself and your ability to change, but trust in others, and believe that the principles and strategies I outline can work for you if you work for them. Without trust and belief, confidence cannot exist or be further developed.

Love: There are many forms of love, from romantic passionate love to familial and brotherly love to everything in between. Love, in many ways, is what fuels everything in our lives. From motivation, to desire, to our purpose, and *why*.

One aspect of love that may be difficult for some is to learn to love yourself. To remember to be kind to yourself and stop the self-defeating habits that separate you from your maximum potential and joy.

Courage: That you seek to find the grit, guts, bravery, determination, drive, and boldness, that will inspire and motivate you to take the steps forward to become more self-confident. Courage is the rocket fuel that gets you off the couch and into action.

Building Self-Confidence is a Process

Like any new endeavor, you will feel uncomfortable at first. Don't fight it. Instead, accept it, expect it, and embrace it. It's not a race and will take time; therefore, you will need to be patient and kind to yourself as you progress. You will make mistakes; we all do. But the difference between those who exude self-confidence and those who don't is usually a result of three controllable factors: practice, discipline, and repetition.

Those who are more confident keep moving forward despite the negative voices in their own minds, or naysayers who say something can't be done. Some even get fired up when someone says they can't do something. For these people, naysayers, doubters, and critics ignite an inner drive to prove others wrong. To show the world that something is actually possible.

History is replete with determined individuals like this. The story of Walt Disney is a great case in point. He had a vision for what a barren field in Orange County could be and he was determined to make it a reality. Today, that one vision has put smiles on the faces of millions worldwide.

Confidence is a byproduct of vulnerability, courage, and action. You will get the most out of this book if you practice all three. Why these? Because they all require change, and most people don't readily embrace change. We are creatures of habit. We like control and predictability and have a hard time accepting it when things don't work out according to our plans.

Managing Your Expectations

When something doesn't work out the way I expected my confidence is compromised, creating a rift or gap. When that happens, I typically respond in one of the following three ways: First, I get angry at myself or blame others for not getting what I want or doing things the way I thought they should be done. Secondly, I feel disappointed, let down, or outright rejected, and throw a pity party for myself. Lastly, I feel the disappointment, look at what I could do differently, and get back up and try again. There is no rhyme or reason to which way I respond. Sometimes it's all three, but eventually I get to the third response and into a solution mindset.

Practicing the Essential Five Steps of *Ten Seconds of Boldness* is "The Work"

Everything worthwhile that I have ever accomplished was a result of being courageous enough to try doing the work necessary to solve virtually any internal or external problem, or to capitalize on an opportunity. Becoming successful in any endeavor always comes back to courage and effort. Applying what you learn is the best way to become better. To get the most out of this book, use it.

Building a Bridge to a Better Life

Prompt #1: Reflect. What Questions am I Not Asking Myself?

If you are impatient like me and want faster results like me, you need to ask different questions. What do I mean? I highly encourage you to turn each of the five steps—*identify* the problem or opportunity, clearly *decide* what you want, know *why* you want it, write a *clear plan*, and *start* working that plan—into questions personal to you and *write them down*.

Carefully consider each problem you want to resolve, or opportunity you want to pursue with an action-oriented mindset. Note, however, that resolution may not eliminate the problem, but the solution will most likely require a shift in how you think, act, or choose to respond or engage with or respond to whatever it is you want to resolve.

For example, doubt and fear will always exist. Anytime we are faced with something new—the unknown—our normal first response will usually be cautious trepidation. Consider a small child left with a babysitter for the first time. Or any number of first experiences of your life. How do you usually respond? I doubt that you cower or cry like a baby left with a sitter. But you may feel butterflies, anxiety, and your heart may race a little faster. This is normal, especially as you are evaluating whether or not the new thing, situation, or problem, is a serious threat, and whether you need to run for your life. Ever since we were cave men and women, we are hardwired to approach newness with caution. That is fine for life-threatening situations but is completely unnecessary in most others. And yet, far too many of us cower in the face of the great unknown.

How then can we learn to trust our common sense and discover new skills, habits, and tools so we may evaluate our problems with a levelheaded approach instead of one that's habitual or reactionary? This can be difficult when doubt continues to erode our self-confidence. That's why you need boldness and courage, even only just ten seconds' worth to break free from the black hole of negativity that is sucking the life out of you. These steps are designed to help you identify, clarify, and discover not only *what* you want, but *why* you want it. They are the tools for you to develop those new skills and habits.

> Regardless of what you want, without clarity, focus, and a visceral sense of meaning, purpose, or some deep-seated motive greater than the problem or opportunity you want to overcome or capitalize on, nothing will ever change.

When you have the answers to those three—*clarity focus, and why*— all that's missing is *Ten Seconds of Boldness* to get started.

The rest of this book will show you how to discover, develop, and embrace you inner courage, empowering you to quiet your inner critics, minimize your negative self-talk, and help you build self-confidence so you can overcome many of the fears that have been holding you back, especially fear of failure and fear of the unknown. And perhaps like me, fear of abandonment.

Prompt #2: Consider and Respond to the Five Questions Below

Five Important Questions to Ask Yourself:

1. What do I think I really want?
2. What am I good at?
3. What is really holding me back?
4. Why do I want it? / What are my motives?
5. What am I willing to do to get it?

You do not have to answer all of them right now. But I do want you to continue the reflection and writing process you started above. You'll also want to get a notebook, journal, or something to take notes. Start writing by answering the questions above. Jot down your initial thoughts, feelings, experiences, successes, and failures—anything you believe important and will help you succeed.

P.S. Important Reminder: There Are No Right or Wrong Answers

Don't worry about the right or wrong way to do any of these prompts or the five essential steps. What matters is that you find the courage to look at your problems and develop the motivation and discipline to resolve them. Take a page out of Michael Jordan's book with his famous quote, "Don't be afraid to fail. Be afraid not to try."

How you respond today will not likely be the same as a year, two, or five or more years from now. Therefore, as you practice and progress, embrace each new challenge as an opportunity for growth and change. Most importantly build on each success. *Create your own momentum—one small victory at a time. That's how you become more confident.*

The Beginning of a Dream

When I was a teenager I subscribed to the Columbia Record Club, a subscription-based, direct-mail marketing service that at the time offered a great deal on, tapes, or records (LPs). I don't recall the exact offer, but it was too good to pass up, something like "Buy 10 records or tapes for a penny!" The catch, as I recall, was that you had to agree to buy at least one tape or LP a month at the regular retail price for at least a year (then, most were under $10). It was a great way for Columbia House to expand its marketing reach to outlying areas, especially to teenagers. But that's not the full story.

The full story is that when I signed up, I started to get solicitations from other companies marketing "self-help" programs, the first of which was *Lead the Field*, by Earl Nightingale. Immediately, I was captivated not only by his deep resonant voice, but the ease and confidence with which he spoke and his message—the opportunity for hope—to actually make something for myself. He said one thing that I remember to this day:

> "Success is the progressive realization or a worthy goal or ideal."
> -Earl Nightingale

That was 1978. I was sixteen years old. I believed him and have been pursuing and living out his quote ever since. He was right.

A River of Ambitions

You and your dreams are worth the effort it will take to accomplish the change you seek. But you have to invest some time figuring out what that means to you. Without a clear direction and a reason why, all your efforts will be wasted. The temptation to give up before you are halfway there will be too great and you will forever remain where you are.

All greatness requires boldness, bravery, and courage at some point. It's the price of admission. The sooner you understand and accept that fact and start becoming more daring, the faster and sooner you will build the confidence to become the person you want to be and do the things that until now have likely seemed out of reach.

Another way to approach each of the five important questions is to think of them as a river of ambitions and you are in a kayak with a paddle. Somedays your thoughts, dreams, goals, and challenges will be clear, flowing at a steady pace like a river's surface on a calm day; other days may feel like you're in a raging torrent, with white-water rapids, struggling to survive as you twist and turn around huge boulders. This can be exhilarating or frightening or both depending on your experience navigating the ever-changing rivers of life. Whatever your response, don't fight the river. The boulders will always be there. The river never stops. But your course may change depending on the conditions of the day. That is perfectly normal and smart.

Don't fear obstacles or setbacks. Expect them. Be prepared and learn to deal with them. I will admit when it comes to other people's problems it is always easier to offer advice or wisdom. But when the time comes to take an honest look within to thoroughly examine our own thoughts actions, and behaviors we crumble.

For some, the introspection necessary to overcome years of bad habits and negative ways of thinking will seem too painful. It's not.

Like cleaning out our overcrowded garage, we need to start with one cabinet or corner at a time. For the purposes of this book, that one thing is the courage to tackle each problem in turn.

That will build a track record of success and help you become more self-confident.

As you become more adept at practicing these techniques, my hope is that you will realize how they can successfully help you to resolve virtually any problem or take advantage of any opportunity, whether personal, vocational, or relational.

Know that it will not be a smooth process. Life is messy. There will be raging white water rapids as well as eddies and pullouts along the way. Learn from each—the rapids to test your resolve and survival instincts under pressure, and the eddies to pause, reflect and refuel your body, mind, and soul.

Over time you will learn to adapt to the changing conditions, you will learn more about yourself in that kayak on that river than you ever believed possible. There will be times where you go with the flow and others where you have to paddle upstream like crazy to get to where you want to go. So it is with life, worthwhile achievement, and building self-confidence. The river is your guide, your muse, your path. Put on your life vest, step into the kayak, grab a paddle, and go.

It's important to know that your initial answers need not be perfect or set in stone. We all start at the same place: the beginning. And for some, this may be the first time you've given more than a passing thought to these very important questions.

Prompt #3 Brainstorm

Step #1 – Grab whatever you use for notes and find a quiet place to sit for <u>no more than fifteen minutes</u> to *brainstorm*. Start by writing down anything that is important to you right now and what you may want to change. For example: Problems to solve or opportunities that you want.

Don't worry about the *how* or even the *why*. We'll get to that later. For now, just get it all out of your head and onto paper. It's a brain dump not a thesis paper or presentation. If it makes it easier for you, consider organizing your thoughts, ideas, problems, and desires into four general areas:

- Mental
- Physical
- Spiritual
- Emotional

You might also consider using specific headings or none at all. Below are a few examples of what those may include. Incidentally, according to several studies, the first four on the list below are the most common worries.

- Finances/Future
- Work/Job security
- Relationships
- Health
- Beliefs, Attitude, and Worldview
- Family
- Education

Step #2 – Start writing down what you think you would like to be different. Take five more minutes to do this now.

In future chapters I will give you specific steps to take with respect to the problems you want to resolve or goals you want to accomplish. I will also offer prompts in many but not all chapters. These, along with the five steps, are opportunities for you to develop and practice new skills so you can ultimately create new confidence building habits for your success.

Your success is predicated on developing a daily habit of thinking about the changes you want to make and writing down your goals. As you do, you will begin to realign your attention toward your intentions or ambitions. You will begin to make the mental shift from *"I can't"* to *"How can I?"*. But right now, I want you to focus on the problem or opportunity: on what you want to change, get rid of, or accomplish.

Be as general or specific as you wish, but resist the urge to think too deeply about each problem you want to solve or goal you want to achieve. For right now, just write them down.

You'll be amazed at how liberating it feels to actually get started. It's like dropping a hundred-pound sack of rocks off your back and a critical first step to building your self-confidence.

Here are a few examples:

- I want to make more money than month.
- I want to earn $_____ per year.
- I want to get out of debt.
- I want to be more confident in social situations.
- I want to lose _____ pounds and feel better about who I am and how I look.

Step #3 – Consider making your goals personal and meaningful by using your imagination to include as many of the five senses you want to, to bring your dream to life.

Let's take losing ten to twenty pounds for example. How do you think it would make you feel? What would change? Can you feel the new clothes you are trying on because you had to size down instead of size up? What about the way you see yourself in the mirror, the way you walk?

As you play with this image in your mind, are you starting to believe in the possibility of who you *can become*? When you do, do you visualize feeling better about your self-image? More confident? Bolder? More daring? Happier? I hope so.

As your belief and confidence increases through the course of your life, continue to dream even bigger.

Whatever you choose to write down are *your* aspirations and dreams, nobody else's. Protect them like a newborn child. They are yours and nobody can ever take them away from you unless you let them. Remember, you are only a few bold decisions away from manifesting what you want. *Today is a great day to take a chance on you.*

Don't judge them or think them foolish, just write them down. Think of it like the game, "if you had a million dollars what would you do with it?" Or "if you had all the time in the world how would you spend it?"

Another important side note: for those of us who tend to overanalyze things, **stop.** Have fun with this process. Now is the time to release your creativity and imagination.

Also, it's worth repeating, **there are no wrong answers**. This is not the appropriate time to evaluate them as viable or not. Your only homework in this step is to take your list from step #2 then let your imagination roam free as you clarify the vision of what you want to accomplish.

Don't worry, you will have ample time to fine tune them and develop a strategy for resolving each later. When you are done writing, set the paper aside and read on. Committing to this process of reflection and writing is how you will get the greatest value out of this book.

Section I
Identify the Problem / Opportunity

- ◊ Getting Started: Finding Courage to Change.
- ◊ Reality Check: Can You Really Be, Do, or Have *Almost* Anything by Developing Better Habits?
- ◊ Getting Honest with Yourself: Five Truths about Self-Confidence.
- ◊ How Do We Tame our Inner Critics and Become More Self-Confident?
- ◊ Jump!
- ◊ Bridging the Confidence Gap.
- ◊ Increasing Your Self-Awareness by Taking a Personal Inventory.

Chapter One
Getting Started: Finding Courage to Change

"If we fear change, we are blind to the abundance of life."
Mark Nepo, *The Book of Awakening*

For me, life has been one big classroom—a school of hard knocks and perpetual struggle, often a result of my own fears and stubborn resistance to change.

As your guide to help you find the courage to change, here are three things you can expect from me as we continue:

1. **Honesty.** Not only through stories of my own shortcomings and triumphs but what I learned as a result of facing many challenges in my life. *I will not suggest you do anything that I haven't done or wouldn't do to improve my own personal growth or development.*

2. **Empathy.** I don't know about you, but I don't do gloom well. We beat ourselves up enough for our own shortcomings, and the last thing any of us want as we are struggling to get back up again is for someone to bark at us like a drill sergeant in basic training. To protect ourselves we build walls. Some are so thick that it will likely take some tough love and compassion to inspire you to want to begin tearing them down, one brick at a time. In relation to personal advice, I will never suggest anything that has not

been suggested to me or have not personally experienced, with a few exceptions. I will at times refer to or paraphrase the advice or expertise of others if I believe it to be important and helpful to your personal growth and development.

3. **Passion.** I am incredibly passionate about the principles and concepts I will share with you. I know how powerful they have been in my own life, and I hope my enthusiasm is contagious enough to inspire you to be willing to learn, practice, and begin to apply them to the areas of your own life based on your own motives, not mine. I will give you my best, always.

Love and Acceptance

While each of us faces a unique set of circumstances and challenges, I believe that we are more alike that we realize. In a general sense, I believe that every human being on the face of this planet wants two things: love and acceptance.

We want to be supported, heard, encouraged. We want to know we are valued for who we are, as we are. The challenge is that it's unfair to expect that from others without first loving ourselves enough to be honest with who and where we are in life, and to accept the things we can't change but to find the courage to change the things we can.

Self-love and acceptance is an inside job, one that many have not yet mastered. To develop each will require you to become humble and willing to allow others to love you so you can learn to love yourself.

It Takes Courage to Change

Many of us have built a belief system that all too often includes several nagging critics that keep us stuck. They incessantly undermine our personal growth and development and sabotage our success. They are like fingernails on the blackboard of our mind and most of us don't know how to silence them.

Plus, it seems scary and too much effort to look at them. To understand how they have shaped our thoughts, actions, habits, and behaviors. To know where to start before we can decide which we want to improve, and which we need to remove.

It's almost as hard as going through our overstuffed garages and deciding what to toss, donate, or keep. Whenever I take the time to "clean out my garage" and find the courage to let go of that which no longer serves me, I feel like I can breathe again. That begs the question, how do we face our fear of change? I think Nike's slogan, "Just do it," says it best. So does, the title of Susan Jeffers book: *Feel the Fear and Do it Anyway.* I don't recall Dr. Jeffers' key points, but the title remains fixed in my belief system today. I love it's power and simplicity. It says so much with so little. In early recovery I often repeated them as a mantra while battling the parade of feelings and fears that sometimes felt like a three-ring circus in my head.

In short, *Feel the Fear and Do it Anyway* meant learning to do the things I don't want to do so I can become the confident and courageous person I want to be.

Ten Seconds of Boldness is also easy to remember. It, too, focuses on identifying problems, mostly self-imposed and fear-based. In particular, those which impede our ability to thrive because we are operating with an outdated belief system, in desperate need of an upgrade. As previously mentioned, *Ten Seconds of Boldness* is a relatively simple five-step process to reboot your brain. We'll discuss exactly what that looks like later. For now, let's do some mental housekeeping.

CTR/ALT/DEL: Out With the Old to Make Room for the New

To become bold and confident, we have to let go of some of our habits and old ways of thinking. To stop believing the lies that we aren't good enough. That we have "always been this way" and that "we can never change." These statements are lies. Lies we continue to say to ourselves and actually believe, which therefore become self-fulfilling prophecies, a negative feedback loop for our own perpetual doom. How self-destructive!

Fact or Crap?

As brain expert Stephen Campbell points out in his book, *Making your Mind Magnificent,* our brains do not differentiate between fact or fiction. He says, "We behave and act not according to the truth, but the truth as we (i.e., our mind) believe (or perceive) it to be."

The next time we make a mistake, we further reinforce that false narrative by how we talk to ourselves, saying things like, "I'm so stupid," or "I knew that wouldn't work." The challenge with this or other negative input we feed our minds is that it's destructive to our self-image and self-esteem.

Every thought or circumstance that we remember or replay only reinforces the false narrative of our inadequacy. In other words, it forms a neural pathway that, as we keep travelling, becomes a clearly marked trail. One that seems like the right path to take. The problem is, it leads to a dead end or cliff. And if we're not careful, we may slip down that cliff and feel helpless, as if there's no way out, as I did before my first recovery meeting.

To break free of this habit means we will need to replace our old ways of thinking with new productive and helpful thought patterns. I can hear some of you saying, "That's great but you don't know how long I have been this way." You're right, I don't. But I do know that if it was still working, you wouldn't be reading about how to fix it would you? As Dr. Phil says, "How's that working for you?"

Ten Seconds of Boldness **Will Not Solve Your Problems For You.**

That's your job. It will, however, offer you some new tools to help you get off the treadmill of feeling like an imposter, a fraud, or simply never quite good enough.

The practical steps, processes, and suggestions I have included are purposefully designed to help you become more courageous—to take responsibility for your own future, and to help you learn how to break the cycle of negative thinking that continues to keep you from reaching your full potential.

None of the tools, tips, or suggestions I will cover are magic. Tinkerbell isn't going to come along and sprinkle pixie dust on your head so you can step into the unknown and fly. Not gonna happen. That's up to you.

Bottom Line: It Takes Courage to Change

Change is usually messy even ugly, and I love that. Because if our heart doesn't skip a beat or we don't feel a little anxious at the start of anything new, then we either are not fully committed to doing what is necessary to get what we say we want, or our dream isn't big enough.

Some of us may be over cautious or guarded, perhaps because we've been burned before. Haven't we all at some point? Or we are so attached to certainty—only believing what we can actually see, touch, taste, smell, or feel, that we have chosen to sacrifice our imagination and creativity for the practical and tangible? There's a name for that. It's called a comfort zone.

Security vs. Risk: The Battle in Your Brain

Every day, the battle between security vs. risk rages on in our minds. Acknowledging its existence is only part of the solution. Courage is another very important part. But it takes more than courage or even knowledge to find inner peace; to quiet the doubt bombs of our brain.

If you keep doing what you've been doing, you'll keep getting what you've got.

Courage and confidence are built on the battlefield of life. Our greatest battles are fought within. The internal ones we fight everyday between our ears. If you want to break free, it stands to reason you'll have to do a few things differently and a few different things, right? That's awesome, because, even if we won't admit it, don't most of us secretly want to be unique? Well, here's your chance.

When we take a chance on ourselves by finding and practicing *Ten Seconds of Boldness*, our "entire attitude and outlook upon life will change." As we become more confident, we will begin to believe more in ourselves and our abilities, feeling a greater sense of empowerment and joy with each small victory. (Aside—I have Eminem's song "Not Afraid" on a thumping loop in my brain right now. It's just how my mind works, and I love it!). I don't know about you, but I don't want to settle for average. I want to be so confident that I know what I want and to become courageous enough to pursue it despite any trepidation or fear.

Success Requires Commitment

If you are resolute in your quest to become better, you will no longer fear change. As you progress, you will learn to *embrace and accept change as a natural part of your life.* You will learn to *trust your instincts and become bolder*, expanding your sphere of belief not only about who you are, but who and what you can become. In other words, your quest for confidence and courage becomes a cause worth fighting for. One that provides meaning and purpose to an otherwise average life. One which when pursued with passion and persistence can move your life from good to great.

Call in Reinforcements: The Power of Collaboration and Asking for Help

Finding courage and confidence to solve our problems is easier when we don't try to do it all alone. This may seem counterintuitive to those of us who are strong-willed, independent, and have a higher degree of confidence than most.

People who are self-driven tend to resist the need to ask for help even when they are stuck. More often, than I'd like to admit, I am still too proud to ask for help when facing problems, tough decisions, or other obstacles in my path.

I saw a meme recently that said the obstacles are the path. I love that because it means we don't have to "overcome" all of them. We simply acknowledge their existence and move around them. That is the goal. That is success.

Yet when we are in the mess, while battling self-defeating feelings such as pride, shame, or guilt, or some other form of fear, the default response for most of us is denial.

Denial is not a solution.

Unfortunately, we all have blind spots, too. Attitudes, beliefs, and behaviors that have become habits that we are not aware of. This is another area where others who want what's best for us can help. In some leadership and corporate circles, this is part of a 360-degree annual review.

As mentioned earlier, feedback is critical (no pun intended) to our continuous improvement. I don't know of any successful people who do not rely on coaching or input from others to maximize their potential.

Asking for Help is Not a Sign of Weakness

In fact, asking for help is a sign of maturity. Sure, it takes guts to swallow our pride and ego and become vulnerable enough to trust someone else to offer constructive criticism. But as you will experience, the rewards far exceed any risk to our ego.

Prompt #1: Making a List

Step #1:
Take five to ten minutes to make a list of people you respect, trust, and know that may be able to offer you some valuable feedback or coaching in a particular area you need.

Who	What	Contact

Invest five to ten minutes brainstorming names and what they may be able to help you with. Add or organize columns to fit your needs.

Step #2:
Make a decision to call at least one of them in the next thirty days.

Being Willing to Ask for Help May be Harder for "Experts"

I purposely put the word *expert* in quotes because there is a vast difference between someone who has invested the time (at least 10,000 hours of education and hands-on-experience, according to most experts who research this stuff) to learn and practice a particular skill vs. someone who merely has knowledge.

I'll come back to this later. For now, can we agree on the following premise?

Whether you're an expert (as determined by peers, degree, or certification, in your chosen field) or a novice, it is imperative that you keep an open mind and actively seek professional or peer insights if you want to change. It doesn't mean you have to agree with everything others say, but as mentioned earlier, look for consensus and resist the urge to judge, condemn, or discount something or someone you do not fully comprehend as irrelevant or unnecessary.

Consider the following quote by Herbert Spencer, a nineteenth century philosopher, scientist, and theologian, who also coined the phrase "survival of the fittest" seven years before Darwin.

> *"There is a principle which is a bar against all information, which is proof against all arguments, and which cannot fail to keep a man in everlasting ignorance—that principle is contempt prior to investigation."*
> Herbert Spencer

Change is Not as Scary as You May Think

For those who are in the early stages of learning about the power of personal growth and development, know this—**we all struggle with confidence.** And most of us are procrastinators, especially when facing new things. A word of advice, find the courage within to do it anyway. That is how you will become more confident. Don't worry about making a mistake or doing things perfect. **We all make mistakes, and we all fall down.** *Those who become better, even great, are the ones who keep getting back up again.*

For any change to take place, you must have a sincere desire and willingness to become more self-confident. That means facing the truth about what you want and how bad you want it.

It's about courage to try and finding your *why*.

Embrace the Unknown

Variety and spontaneity make life thrilling and interesting. Though most of us like routine, preferring comfort and the status quo, ambitious folks actively seek out new challenges and opportunities. They take calculated risks and, as a result, are usually the ones we see on magazine covers or the big screen. But success is not all about fame and fortune.

Therein lies a big part of why we sometimes feel like imposters, or less than, as if we can never measure up. Success is whatever you decide it to be. With the limited experience we now have, we need to stop comparing ourselves to some inflated ideal of who we *should* be and get busy putting in the work to become the best we *can* be.

One day you may even be on the cover of a magazine, if that's your thing. The point is, you need to be aware of not only what you *can do,* but also clearly identify *what you want to do* or become and *why it's important* to you. Without clear motives and the willingness to courageously do the work to get want you want, success will always elude you and leave you feeling empty. Sometimes the truth hurts, but that's the harsh reality.

It's safe to assume that your fears—of failure, of missing out, of the unknown, of not being in control, of not being good enough, or whatever it is that you struggle with — cause doubt about your own abilities and worth as they continue to haunt you and stand in the way of who you want to become. I have those fears, too. I must also assume that you are ready, willing, and able to overcome, or at the very least, learn to tame the voices in your own head which continue to rob you of the confidence, joy, and feelings of accomplishment you yearn for.

The biggest assumption I must make is that you, like me, have a perpetual curiosity to find meaning and purpose for your life, and have a deep desire to belong. You crave connection and want to feel loved and accepted. And most of all you are ready for a change.

We Are Not Alone

Our struggle with confidence and low self-esteem is real. The tug of war with our inner critics is normal. It's part of being human. According to research by internationally acclaimed self-esteem expert, Joseph S. Rubino, D.M.D., it is estimated that 85% of Americans suffer from low self-esteem. You are not alone if you are dealing with this issue. The good news is we can change when we change our beliefs.

I posed the following question to Neuroscience Expert and author of *Making Your Mind Magnificent*, Steven Campbell, M.S.I.S.

> **Question:** In your professional opinion, can we tame our inner critic and become more self-confident by changing the way we think? If so, how? Where do they come from?

He offered these valuable insights:

> Our inner critics (and there are many of them) are really our self-images, which are innumerable. We have a self-image for every ability, aptitude, habit, skill, capability, capacity, facility, talent, gift, and proficiency we have. Some of them are very high, and some are quite low.
> Where do they come from? THEY ARE LEARNED, AND THEY COME FROM OUR

BELIEFS! In other words, our self-images do not come from how we were raised; they come from what we believe about how we were raised.

And how can we discover our beliefs? By paying attention to our self-talk.

In other words, when a student asks me how he can know what he is believing about himself, I tell him to pay attention to what he is saying about himself.

Now, we cannot remove our self-images because they are hard-wired in our brain. They are also unbelievably difficult to change. However, they can be replaced by choosing to replace the negative messages we say about ourselves with positive ones.

I'll admit, I still struggle with low self-esteem and lack of self-confidence, especially when facing new situations. Over time, I have found ways to overcome my inner fears, doubts, and insecurities so they no longer rule my life. In other words, I now have way more up days than down days. I believe you can too if you are willing to do something new.

What's the Solution?

The solution is to be bold enough to change how we think, and what we say and believe about our self-worth and value to others. To change our self-talk, the dialogue we have with ourselves. Most importantly, it's necessary to *admit our problem, accept it for what it is, and commit to doing a few things differently* so we can create new habits. To do so requires courage, discipline, and effort. Therein lies the rub.

There Are No Shortcuts, So Stop Looking For Them

Mastering the five essential steps: *Identify* the problem or opportunity, clearly *decide* what you want, know *why* you want it, write a *clear plan*, and *start* working that plan, until they become habit will take willingness, time, and patience—lots of patience. I encourage you to be kind with yourself as you progress. You will not change overnight but you will eventually if you become bolder.

What is Boldness?

As mentioned, boldness is a willingness to take risks and act innovatively. For me, boldness is bravery, courage, guts, grit, mental toughness, determination, and an audacious conviction to succeed despite my shortcomings—real or imagined.

Boldness is a temporary moment of fearlessness. It is the catalyst to propel us from where we are to where we would like to be. From who we are now to the person we would like to be. Boldness applied to a specific problem or goal and paired with love as previously mentioned, can literally change or save lives.

One of the keys to your success is finding the courage within to change the self-defeating thought patterns that are preventing you from feeling more confident in certain areas of your life.

The list you started last section may seem like too big of a mountain to climb. But it's not if you *start with what you have*. And trust me, *you have more than you may initially think.*

Look For the Similarities, Not the Differences

Each of us has unique experiences, skills, and belief systems that shape not only who we are but how we think and act. But as humans navigating the journey of life, we are more alike than you may know. How can I say that so confidently? Because I have witnessed it for tens of thousands of hours in the recovery rooms as people come in and pour out their feelings of struggle not only with alcohol, but the greater issues of low confidence, self-worth, and low self-esteem.

When I first got sober, I was so full of fear, shame, and guilt I couldn't look anyone in the eyes at meetings. For the first sixty days, I stared at my shoes, only looking up occasionally to see who was speaking. Soon I began to gain confidence. The lights came on.

As new folks came in—scared, disheveled, lost as I was in the beginning—I began to watch them change. I saw their growth before I could see it in myself. I watched the smile return to their faces as they began to show up and participate in their own recovery. Then, as I progressed and my confidence grew, I began to believe that I could stay sober, one day at a time.

Tough Love

Reminder, there will be times where I am blunt, which may make you feel uncomfortable. That's good. Everything I have written is couched in love, not because I want to be liked, but because I care.

I'm not here to make you feel crappy. We already spend enough time beating ourselves up over what we don't like about ourselves, others, and the world. We invest time in looking for faults, flaws, and what's wrong, but that leads to negativity and is not conducive to building confidence or a positive mindset. As a result, we may become bitter, cynical, and jaded. I do not want to add to that, but like a close friend, we need to be honest if we are to get better. And to get better often requires tough love.

Denial is Not a Rung on the Ladder of Success

All too often, we deny or avoid our problems or worse, believe our own bullshit, which keeps us stuck. To me, that is not how I want to live.

In the pages that follow expect a bit of hope and inspiration so you can find more grace, love, and forgiveness for yourself and others. This will enable you to make more confident decisions about the direction your life. In other words, expect to find the solutions to your problems on the inside, not out.

Lastly, you can expect to change *if* you are willing to develop and practice the five essential habits we mentioned earlier:

1. **Identify** the problem or opportunity
2. Clearly **decide** what you want
3. Know **why** you want it
4. Write a clear **plan**
5. **Start** working that plan

Start With What You Know and Have

Earlier I asked you to take a moment to write down a list of problems and challenges you are facing. Now ask yourself which ones are causing you the most stress right now? What makes them feel so scary?

Prompt #2: Turn Your List of Problems and What You Want into Affirmations

Now take a minute to turn one or two of those challenges into new outcomes you would like as a result of solving your current problems—called an affirmation.

I know we haven't covered affirmations yet, but they are super easy. Consider this a warm-up exercise.

Future sections will offer more specific instructions on how to do each, but for now, it's more important that you start developing some new habits.

Start by <u>making a list</u> of your problems and developing a clear idea of what you want your new situation to be.

For example, if you're in sales or fearful of talking on the phone you may want to try this technique I learned called smile and dial.

Then turn that into an affirmation:

"I am confident with every call I make and it feels great. I ask meaningful questions to my prospects and listen to them. Who knew this could be so fun?"

It doesn't matter if your affirmations are short or long. What's important is that they are positive, as if you already have what you want, and are meaningful to you.

Smile and Dial: How I Use Ten Seconds of Boldness

For example:

Problem: I don't want to be afraid of making cold calls for my job.

Solution: Before I call, I spend a few minutes thinking about what I am going to say and how I may help a new potential client. I sit up straight and close my eyes for a few seconds to imagine myself as prepared and confident. I take a deep breath then say to myself, *I have Ten Seconds of Boldness to do this. There is nothing to be afraid of. What's the worst that can happen? They say no.* To that I say, *'Next!'* then I pick up the phone, smile, and dial.

Here's another example for salespeople:
"I am prepared, clear, direct, and confident before every call. I can hear my own smile as I introduce myself and ask to speak to the appropriate person. Each new prospect I approach responds positively, agreeing to a meeting to see if we can work together. As a result of practicing *Ten Seconds of Boldness* and using these tools to help my clients solve their problems, my sales continue to grow by 15% - 25% year after year.

Or the shortened version: "I am happy. My clients are happy. And referrals are through the roof!"

Cease Fighting. All Life is Suffering.

Don't let your problems and limiting beliefs define you. Instead, let them be a catalyst to motivate you toward positive change. Toward courage and confidence.

Just because I hated my dad for years and my path of suffering led to self-destruction, most of that damage was self-inflicted. It took a long time for me to learn to let go of my anger and resentment toward him. I suffered as a result. But eventually, as I mentioned earlier, I found a path that led to healing, and ultimately forgiveness of him and myself.

Expect to Fail, Frequently

Failure is part of all growth. Complacency and cowardice are not. With each trial you experience, you have a choice: either accept the results, adjust, or move on. That's why *Ten Seconds of Boldness* is so powerful. It's a simple concept that anyone can do. And the more we practice being bold, the more confident we become.

Two things are certain: one, you will never discover what works or what you like until you find the boldness to try; and two, when you find what you like or are good at, you can become great at it by repeating the things that are working and continuing to innovate as you progress.

Now, let's get started.

Chapter Two
Reality Check: You Can Be, Do, or Have Almost Anything By Developing Better Habits

"I can do all things…" Phil. 4:13

For the longest time I have believed that I could do anything if I wanted it badly enough and had the discipline to work hard to get it. I have also heard many famous speakers who inspired millions to be, have, or do, whatever we set our minds to if we have the work ethic necessary to become great.

That's great news if you are mentally and physically healthy and have a big enough motive. A big enough reason *why*. If you choose to outwork everyone, you will likely become great at something.

But before we go further, I want to offer a reality check about this declaration: "…you can be, have, or do whatever you want…" It came from something my friend Cara Wasden expressed during a conversation.

Before I get to that, here's a little bit about Cara:

Cara Wasden has Tourette syndrome and has endured chronic daily headaches for over twenty-five years. Living with struggles has helped her focus on her strengths, one being compassion. She loves making a difference in the lives of others. Until the pandemic, she was a nature guide with third and fourth graders, read to an

Alzheimer's group, conducted impromptu storytelling sessions with seniors citizens, and taught public speaking to youth.

Being a Toastmaster for the past sixteen years has helped Cara recognize some strengths and skills she never realized she had. She has learned how to confidently connect in all her passions through humor, humility, and honesty. Cara is fortunate to be continuing her teaching in public speaking today, something that helps her thrive.

She is one of several people who took me under her wing as a first time Toastmaster, encouraging me to take on roles and give my first speech for the club. I value her input.

Here's what she said:

> I hope you're okay with me expressing my thoughts on one thing you said, which is 'The only thing separating you from where you are and where or who you want to be is you.'
>
> I know a lot of people agree with this and I often hear the saying, 'You can be anything you want to be.'
>
> I disagree.
>
> I believe that everyone has the ability to be much better at just about anything they set out to do if they work really hard at it. But not everyone has the ability to be anything they want to be. I would love to be a professional singer. I could work at this the rest of my life, and I could become maybe good enough for some people to want to listen to me, but there's no way that my voice would allow me to become professional. I don't have the voice for that. If I worked really hard, I could maybe learn a little

bit about medicine, but I don't have the mental capacity or memory to become a doctor. Those are just a couple of examples.

I appreciate that Cara was bold enough to push back. I love that about her. And I'll admit when I first read her reply, I bristled for a minute before calling her for clarification.

We agreed that with few exceptions people can become great at something. But most of us don't know what that something is, yet. And, even if we do or have an idea of what our dreams are or our purpose is, too many of us lack the motivation, courage, and discipline to put in the work necessary for success.

With few exceptions, nearly all great achievement and advancement are the result of many iterations and experiments; trials and errors and making the necessary adjustments to improve.

Bestselling author, coach, and podcaster, Jeff Goins, has a different opinion. In his book entitled, *The Art of Work*, he offers this insight:

> The science of skill acquisition has been the focus of a number of recent studies and books. As it turns out, we are born with very few, if any, natural talents, and skills. Excellence is borne not of any particular innate ability, but of practice. In other words, you can be good at whatever you want.

If you want to be great at anything, you have to practice. Most research studies conclude that success in any endeavor is the result of hard work, not "God given skill, talent or ability." If, as many studies indicate, 97% of our ability to succeed is determined by effort, why do so many of us still struggle with confidence? It's complicated, sort of.

Why Do We Often Give Up Before We Even Get Started?

It's a great question and one we will circle back to time and again throughout the remainder of this book.

I respect both Cara and Jeff, and have worked with each on various projects—Cara on speech development and feedback for Toastmasters; Jeff on writing development in his course, "How to Write a Best Seller." Both are right.

There are some people that have innate skills or conversely have physical or mental limitations that prevent them from being whatever they want to be. That doesn't mean they cannot become excellent, even great, at *something*.

But the key questions we need to ask ourselves are not about our God-given talent or skill or limits. The key questions to ask and explore are: What are we afraid of? Why would we want to overcome our limitations? More directly, what is your motivation, your *why*? Why do you want something, and what would it mean to you if you had it? What are you willing to do to see if you are actually good at it?

Find *Your* Passion and Purpose

Confidence is a product of discipline, motivation, and effort.
History is replete with stories of leaders and professionals from all walks of life who have discovered their hidden talent for something they felt passionate or called to pursue, and found the courage and conviction within to follow their hearts desire.

From movie stars and professional athletes to warriors for peace and those convicted to important causes, like ending world hunger and homelessness, or those who relentlessly continue to fight for social equity and justice and everything in between, we watch and ask ourselves these types of questions:

What do I want?
What matters most to me?
What am I good at?
What brings me joy?

We watch with hope-filled admiration thinking perhaps if we had _____ we could be like _____ too. We idolize and envy those who are living the life of their dreams, but don't yet believe enough in our skills or abilities that we could enjoy success like them. Really? Who said you couldn't? Stop comparing their success to your current station in life. Stop looking at what you don't have and start looking at what you do. Instead ask yourself *why not you?* Who ever said you couldn't? Chances are nobody has. The real critics are in your head. Stop believing them, and tell them where they can go.

Success is a Matter of Belief

All too often, the problem is easier to solve than you think, if you actually *believe* there is a solution. The problem is that most of us, if we are truly honest with ourselves, need to stop believing our excuses and shift our mindset and actions to what we are capable of doing.

We are out of alignment.

Most have not invested the time to align and prioritize what we want and enjoy doing with what we actually do. Instead, we settle for jobs or careers that put food on the table, a roof over our head, and clothes on back. And we stay on the couch content, as long as we have cable and a clicker.

I don't know about you, but I don't want to settle for an average life. One where my dreams stay locked in a musty footlocker in the attic, because I do not yet believe nor have the confidence that I can achieve them. To me, that is not living the American Dream. That's an American tragedy or nightmare.

We Don't Have to Settle For

All of us can be good or great at something, though many of us have not yet found our meaning or purpose. That's okay. If we keep searching and never give up, we will likely find it. The first section of *Ten Seconds of Boldness* is purposely designed to help you find what *it* is that you want.

I already told you in the beginning, I'll be honest with you. I'm not going to sugarcoat it. Building self-confidence is going take effort. Sometimes way more than you may think is necessary. Like me, you will be tested. There will likely be times where you want to cuss me out. Good, I hope you do. Sometimes we need to get fired up before we take action.

Some of you overachievers who love to max out your results may even want to take a few lessons out of Grant Cardone's best-selling book, *The 10X Rule*. His premise is simple: Outwork and outhustle everyone to get massive results, most of them financial, faster.

The cliché "you get out what you put in" is only partially true. I have found that when I consistently put forth my best effort in anything I do and don't half-ass my work habits, the results, over time, are exponentially greater than any input. *And the outcome is not always about money or increased productivity.* Some of the greatest rewards I have enjoyed, such as love, trust, faith, belief, and courage, are not quantifiable.

As you continue, think about what you value and how you would define success. What does success look like to you? Is it more money? Stuff? A better car, home, or job? Or is success something you feel such as courage, confidence, joy, or balance in your life? Maybe it's all of the above. Maybe you don't know yet. That's okay. This book will help you define and clarify what success means to you.

Creativity and Pragmatism: Life is All About Balance

I first heard that phrase, "Life is all about balance" from my stepfather, David O'Connor, during one of our many conversations about life, relationships, and career choices. I'll share more on those later. For now, let's look at building confidence as a balance between art and pragmatism, fueled by imagination, creativity, and passion.

If we as creative, dynamic, intelligent humans, only believed the facts of what we know, and limited our forward progress by what we think we can do, or what others say we can or cannot do, without ever exploring other possibilities of what *could be*, what kind of life would that be? A boring one. An empty one. One filled with a whole lot of regret, and I wish I couldas. There would be no innovation. No intellectual progress. No technological or medical advancements. I cannot imagine a life without electricity, computers, internet, cars, or air travel, Disneyland, or for me, a higher power I have found through recovery. To me, a life lived without creativity, imagination, and enthusiastic pursuit of innovation is not a life I want to live.

While I agree that there are some things we cannot do, I also believe that we are all capable of expanding our perceived mental and physical boundaries beyond facts and what we currently believe is possible. That we can harness our creative energy and ignite our imaginations to accomplish great things. That if our dreams are great enough and we are bold enough with few exceptions, anything is possible.

What Do Dick Tracy and Steve Jobs Have in Common?

When I was a kid, I read Dick Tracy comics and thought how cool it would be to have a watch that was also a video phone. Steve Jobs made the video phone a reality. Three years after Steve's death, Chief Designer at Apple, Jony Ive, invented the Apple Watch. The "Dick Tracy Watch" had become a reality. One never knows the power of a dream and imagination until we step into the vast unknown and discover for ourselves what it's like to cross the divide between possibility and reality.

The point is, why put self-imposed limits on our own creativity before we even try something? I am a firm believer that when inspiration strikes and doesn't evaporate as quickly as it comes, that it's worth exploring.

What hidden talents have you yet to discover or embrace? Or which do you have that you don't use?

To me, missing opportunities because we lack belief and courage to take a chance on ourselves is one of the greatest tragedies of life. *I would rather take a few calculated risks and stumble a few times than not try at all.*

> Sometimes you have to ignore the facts and critics and do it anyway.

Ignore the Facts and Succeed Anyway

While in a twenty-eight-day rehab program, someone told me that only 3% of people succeed at staying sober. I wondered, *Were they trying to scare me? Test me? Pull a "Scared Straight" move?* I don't know.

Regardless, it pissed me off. There I was, finally broken and willing to seek help, and somebody tried to sabotage my hope before I even got started. I could have given up right then and there and said *what's the point?* I didn't know if what they said was true or not. I couldn't check Google or a cell phone because neither were invented yet.

I'll show you, I thought. My arrogance and self-will worked for a bit. But eventually I listened and committed to following a twelve-step program of recovery. I found a sponsor to guide me and eventually came to believe that some power greater than myself could help me stay sober.

Even with a higher power, I had to "do the work" (practice the twelve steps) before I could fully heal and find the peace within.

Chapter Three
Getting Honest With Yourself: Five Truths About Self-Confidence

"Each one has to find his peace from within. And peace to be real must be unaffected by outside circumstances."
Mahatma Gandhi

I agree with many neuroscientists and psychologists that the biggest obstacle to us having more self-confidence exists in our minds. That's where the lies we believe about our abilities or lack thereof, live. Whether or not we are honest enough to admit it, how we think and what we believe, is the problem. What we do or don't do with our thoughts determines how we feel about ourselves, which directly impacts our self-esteem and therefore our self-confidence. In other words, do we accept what we can't change or have the courage to change what we can? More importantly, are we wise enough to know the difference?

Fact: 85% of Us Suffer From Low Self-Esteem

Several studies indicate that 85% of Americans suffer from low self-esteem. That's a huge problem. Unless you are part of the top 15% of self-actualized individuals living in a perpetual state of bliss, enlightenment, or Nirvana, there is a high probability that you, like me, suffer from occasional bouts of low self-worth or have your confidence shaken from time to time. Our confidence and self-esteem problems will not go away on their own. To successfully combat our low self-esteem, we have to not only get honest about what our problems are, but may need counsel to guide us through the gnarled mess in our minds.

Before we get too far ahead of ourselves (something I still do way too often), let's take a moment to explore the differences between low self-confidence and low self-esteem. They are very similar, but still different.

Low self-esteem is when we lack confidence about who we are, (our self-worth or perceived value). Those with low self-esteem often feel unloved, incompetent, and inadequate. Simply put, those of us with low self-esteem do not feel worthy or good enough. Some call it "Imposter Syndrome."

Self-confidence, on the other hand, is what we believe about ourselves and our abilities. It's about trusting ourselves to accomplish our goals or a task.

Self-esteem is more about how we feel about ourselves and is more inward facing.

Self-Confidence is more about what we can do and is generally outward facing. It is also easier to develop than self-esteem.

The two are mutually exclusive and yet it's common to attach our identity (worth) to what we do or have—our careers, income, status, looks, etc. As a result, the lines between the two become blurred. Those external measures are superficial and not part of our core character unless we place a higher value on how much money we make versus how well we treat others.

This is a challenge because our culture promotes and perpetuates a false narrative of our individual worth and value by attaching it to external things like career, status, beauty, image, homes, cars, and achievement. Don't get me wrong. These "things" are nice, but they are temporary, not lasting values.

A problem arises when we never feel we're good enough, rich enough, or when we attach our *identity* to something external, believing that these things to be indicators of success. That's not true. It's no wonder so many suffer from low self-esteem and self-confidence.

This success gap is further exacerbated by many in the personal development field which predominantly still promotes externally based measures especially those about increasing financial wealth.

I am, however, noticing a business and cultural shift away from money and status-based object-driven rewards to more subjective, value-driven, and intrinsic-based rewards like a sense of accomplishment based on effort.

I like what my friend Joe Millar mentioned in a recent conversation on success, "there is a common misnomer with success that it is construed an arrival." I agree, success is not transactional. As others have pointed out, it is about who we become in the pursuit of a goal. Of doing our best, of setting goals, and knowing that we did all we could to accomplish them.

Several employee satisfaction studies show a greater emphasis being placed on internal measures of success, especially with regard to a sense of belonging and recognition.

Akin to climbing Maslow's Hierarchy, there is a clear trend toward personal growth, spiritual enlightenment and awakening. In addition, issues-based goals to increase cultural awareness and affect change especially with issues or equity and justice are fast becoming new barometers of success, especially for the next generation of leaders.

The yin and yang of what success means is best interpreted by those who seek it. I know that my self-esteem and self-confidence are strongest when I am doing the things I believe will help me solve a problem or accomplish a goal.

A Simple Science-Based and Empirically-Tested Solution for Improving our Self-Esteem

While there are many solutions for overcoming low self-esteem, one is closer that you think. Both the problem and solution can be found in one word—belief. According to Stephen Campbell and other neuroscientists, the inner critics in our head lack discernment between fact or fiction. The brain, according to Campbell, "...believes EVERYTHING we tell it, without question, no arguments."

This is important to understand because it validates the tired cliché, "Garbage in. Garbage out."

I am not going to get on a soapbox and preach to you about *what* you should or should not feed your brain. But I am going to encourage you to be mindful (pun intended) of how your brain processes input. It's important to understand that these voices or critics are reflections of thoughts about ourselves, our abilities, and our worth in the world.

Unfortunately, many of our beliefs are false. They are lies we've held for years, perhaps initiated by criticism from parents, bosses, teachers, or other influences in our lives. Because, as mentioned, our brains don't know what to believe, the critical voices are reinforced by our own negative self-talk, especially in areas related to our self-esteem and self-confidence.

This is not healthy. *To the extent that we give them power over our lives, the critics in our minds are toxic.*

I will explore this further in the chapter about belief. But for now, we can celebrate because *identifying the problem and admitting it is the first step to solving it.*

The great news is that we can change if we somehow find enough courage to do so.

You may be thinking, *That's great. Tell me something I don't already know.*

How do I find courage? Good question, but a better question we must ask ourselves is *why?*

What does that mean and how is it related to self-confidence? It means everything.

It's no secret that when we not only change the way we think but what we choose to believe, our world changes. Our perspective shifts as we replace outdated beliefs about ourselves with new ones.

And, according to neuroscience, everything we believe is tied to patterns we have created in our minds, to what we chose to believe.

Neuroscience expert Steven Campbell explains further:

> One of the most exciting discoveries in the neurosciences is how our brain is continually creating patterns, based on what we learn during the day. It creates these patterns at night when we are asleep. And the number of patterns it creates is beyond imagination.
>
> The latest research estimates that our brain has about eighty-three billion neurons, and each of these neurons are connected to an average of 10,000 neurons. That's not a multiple; that's a power! In other words, the connections, which determine the number of patterns the human brain can carry is eighty-three billion times eighty-three million, 10,000 times. It is no wonder that the scientific community agrees that the human brain is the most complex organism in the universe.

And while the brain is incredibly complex, when it comes to learning new things, simple is always better. The problem, as Stephen points out, is that our brain never sleeps. And as he will explain in greater detail later, it doesn't know what is helpful or detrimental to your self-esteem. As a result, the thoughts and feelings we have throughout the day, good or bad, are on a perpetual quest to connect to similar thoughts, beliefs, or feelings in our brain. This further reinforces existing beliefs, good or bad, thereby creating patterns that will continue until challenged.

In my case, low self-esteem and self-confidence have manifested themselves in a myriad of negative thought patterns, beliefs, or emotions in my life. Here are a few examples, which are variations of thinking and behavior rooted in fear.

- Jealousy
- Resentment
- Anger
- Pride
- Ego
- Blame
- Guilt
- Shame
- Micro-Management
- Control
- Fear of Failure
- Fear of Making a Mistake
- Fear of Being Wrong
- Fear of the Unknown
- Fear of Rejection
- Fear of Abandonment
- Fear of Public Speaking

- Fear of Confrontation
- Fear of Success
- Fear of Death
- Fear of Missing Out (FOMO)

I'm not going to elaborate on my struggles in each of these areas, but trust me, I have a lot. Still do.

For me, life has been a series of endless battles with my own inner critics, with one major difference. Today I am far more aware of them and am not so quick to deny their existence nor act out in some unhealthy ways as I have in the past. I am more aware of my actions and reactions in stressful situations and more mindful to consciously replace them with more positive beliefs about who I am and who I want to be. As a result, my self-confidence continues to improve a little bit every day. So can yours if you want it to.

For me it always comes back to being willing to want to change and creating new habits. Out with the old to make room for the new. We'll talk more about building habits and changing mindset and belief systems in subsequent chapters. But for now, as you review the list, think about which beliefs may be causing you stress and sit with your feelings for a moment.

Step #1: Identify and Admit There is a Problem

You can't find a solution if you don't know what the problem is and how it makes you feel. In other words, we need both emotion and logic to understand and solve problems. According to Daniel Goleman, best-selling author of *Emotional Intelligence*, and many other researchers, our emotions are controlled by the amygdala and prefrontal cortex of our brains. Both are responsible for our decisions and beliefs about how we feel. All this to say you can't find a solution until you identify and admit that there is a problem (think fight, flight, or freeze; courage over fear).

I know it's painful to get honest with ourselves, but the rewards are priceless. According to Goleman, increasing our understanding of how we think and how our brains process emotions is a key to increasing our emotional intelligence, which will have "immediate benefits to our health, relationships, and work."

It's normal to want to avoid our problems or pretend they don't exist. There's a word for that, it's called denial. I've been there too, more times than I'd like to admit. But as I learned many years ago, admission is the first step to recovery.

Step #2 Reflect: What Do *You* Think is Holding You Back?

Next, consider what things continue to cause you stress, anxiety, and apprehension, possibly paralyzing you from forward progress. My natural tendency in a stressful situation is to hold on tighter. To muster all my will power, to "white knuckle it" and push through. This can be especially challenging when facing situations beyond my control.

Sometimes the best thing I can do is let go.

When stressed or anxious, it's easy to retreat and not face your problems. To go back to your old ways of coping. Those are no longer a viable option. Don't feel that you must go a hundred-miles-per-hour to outrun them. Running or being busy never really addresses the problem. Learn to slow down. Pause, and allow yourself to sit with your feelings, as uncomfortable as that may be.

Stop Fighting Fear

To grow and not allow your life to be ruled by fear does not mean you fight fear. Rather it means you accept and understand it. That diminishes its power over you. Then you can summon the courage to look behind the green curtain at causes and conditions, and your habitual patterns of responding to stressful situations or problems. That means letting go of your attachment to them and the fear or what might happen if you fail.

Letting go of your fear of failure or rejection requires courage. *Ten Seconds of Boldness* is often all it takes to disrupt your negative thought patterns and refocus your efforts on solutions and outcomes. In other words, ask yourself, *what can I do not necessarily to eliminate the problem, but to change my attitude?*

The real problem is not what you usually think it is. That is a symptom. You may need to look deeper into root causes and conditions with a trained professional such as a psychologist, therapist, or coach.

The real problem is how you choose to respond when something causes you stress or doesn't go your way. How do most of us respond? By blaming others? Playing the victim? Beating ourselves up by saying to ourselves, "there's no such thing as good enough. I can always do better?" Or calling ourselves stupid?

The key is to pay attention to how you *react* (a function of patterns and habits, and your old belief system) and learn to *respond* differently. This shift will not happen immediately. No change ever does. But if you really want to move past your fears and are willing to be unconformable as you learn new skills, the peace of mind you gain in the process will be well worth the effort.

Learning to Accept Our Shortcomings

Stop focusing on the negative. Instead, let that shit go and make a commitment to do better next time. Replaying our failures is a sure-fire way to stay where we are. Acceptance of things as they are is one of the most liberating and empowering things we can do. **Shit happens. We cannot control or change all of it. The only thing we can change is our attitude and begin to develop new ways to respond to people and situations that are and always will be out of our control.**

This is what I mean by letting go. We need to let go of our own crap and stop trying to fix others. Own it if it's ours. Let it go if it's not. Simple, right?

Yet how often do we try to "fix" others' problems or somehow attempt to change a situation that we have little or no control over? To best suit *our* needs and expectations? Unless you are a wizard or have a magic wand, that type of thinking is ludicrous. What's more, it's a complete waste of our time, energy, and resources. We need to "stay in our own lanes." Sweep our own side of the street first. Otherwise, we are just another hypocrite.

This may sound a bit harsh but it's the truth.

> The sooner we learn to accept personal responsibility for how we think and act about things that happen "to" us and instead find the courage to change those things we can, the sooner we will break free from the anchors that have been holding us back. If you want to sail across the open sea of life, you must weigh anchor first.

Prompt #1, Part 1: Moving Past Our Excuses

This is one of a few "tough love" moments I alluded to earlier. It may make you want to curse and throw *Ten Seconds of Boldness* against the wall or pull the blankets over your head curling up in a ball, hoping if you pretend it doesn't exist that you will be magically better tomorrow.

Do as you must, but I urge you to invest the time to start this next exercise. *Answer the following questions as honestly as you can without any shame or guilt.* Just write down every answer you can think of in twenty minutes or less.

Question #1: What excuses do you keep making for where you are in your life?
Question #2: Why do you think you continue to make them?
Question #3: What continues to cause you stress?
Question #4: What would you like to change or eliminate?
Question #5: What have you done to change?

Do not miss this very important opportunity. Sit alone and have a serious heart-to-heart internal chat about how you have allowed excuses or other negative self-talk to invade your past, present, and future. And consider the bigger question, the one you will need courage to do: **what are you going to do about it?**

When you feel like you have exhausted everything within the allotted time, put down your pen and paper and be still for a minute. Pay attention to your feelings. Do not fight them. Guys, you too, especially if you're type A or hyper analytical at times, like me. Acknowledging and sitting with your feelings makes you strong, not weak. Park your ego at the door for a few minutes and be still and vulnerable. You're not gonna die.

Prompt #1, Part 2: Reflect and Relax

How did it feel to do this exercise? What do you find? These are rhetorical questions, write them down if you wish, I just want you to start paying attention to the decisions you make and how they make you feel. That's it. We will talk more about ways to make this process easier in the future. But for now, congratulate yourself for some heavy lifting.

Now take a break and go do something fun.

Prompt #2: The Breakup Note

When you return from your break, take five to ten more minutes to read everything you just wrote about yourself.
 Next, grab a pen and a piece of paper and *hand write* the following breakup note to your excuses:

> I am more than the excuses I make and limitations I have believed about myself. I am enough. As I look over my list of excuses and how I feel when I keep making them, I realize it's time to end this unhealthy toxic relationship that's lasted way too long. Goodbye excuses, I don't need you anymore!

If you're feeling extra empowered and courageous after writing down all your excuses, you may want to burn them. Up to you. Either way, this can be a very cathartic exercise with a lasting positive impact on your life if you give it a try.

The Miracle of Letting Go

One of the most important and life changing steps in my recovery was the third step. It's premise is all about turning my will over to a power greater than myself and trusting in that unseen power as a spiritual means to overcoming my addiction. I'll never forget the day I did the third step with my sponsor.

"Shawn," he started, "you have been carrying around a lot of crap. It's like a sack full rocks—all your guilt, shame, doubt, worry, anxiety, and fear. And it's weighing you down. Everything that stands in the way of you being able to get over the mental obsession and compulsion to drink."

I stared at the dirt. He was right.

"Here's what we're going to do," he continued. "See that garbage can over there near the church? We're going to kneel in front of it and hold hands and say the third step prayer. That is the third step. But before we do, I want you to close your eyes, and feel how heavy all those rocks are. Then I want you to imagine walking over to that garbage can, lifting the lid, and dumping that entre sack of rocks in the trash."

I did as he instructed.

"You got it?" he asked. Again, I nodded, "Great. Now I want you to slam the lid shut and let that shit go."

I laughed and followed his instructions explicitly. We then said the third step prayer out loud. As we were reciting it—two guys holding hands in broad daylight, kneeling on a dusty hillside beside a church near a garbage can—I experienced a miracle. In that moment, all the fear and worry and anxiety and compulsion to drink was lifted. A wave of chills rippled across my arms, and I wept. In that moment I experienced freedom for the first time in my young adult life.

I will never forget that pivotal miracle and the impact it has had on my life. I often go back to that dusty hillside and that garbage can when the weight of other burdens seems insurmountable. I do the same thing as I did then—I lift the lid, dump the rocks, then slam the lid shut.

Honesty Equals Peace of Mind

Getting honest with yourself is the best thing you could possibly do for your happiness, confidence, and peace of mind. Without a willingness to take an honest, non-judgmental look at who we are and who we want to be and address the real or perceived obstacles in our path, we will never get better. We will forever remain stuck in the prison of our own minds and become bitter or angry at ourselves, and those closest to us. Worse, our stubborn resistance to change may cause us to spiral into the dark pit of hopelessness and despair resigning ourselves to the belief that it all is just a waste of time.

I've been there. And it flat out sucks. I hope and pray you become brave enough to face your own personal critics and teach them a new language. One of hope and possibility. Of confidence and success.

Five Truths About Self-Confidence:

1. Research and thinking alone will not increase your confidence. Confidence comes from action, while you are in pursuit of a worthy dream or goal—while you are actively practicing the five essential habits.
2. Nobody else can motivate you or make you feel more confident. You can become inspired by others, but

motivation is an inside job; it is unique to you and what you want. Your level of motivation depends on your why—your dream (or nightmare), and how badly you want a different outcome.
3. Nothing will ever change until *you*
    a. decide to change
    b. find the courage to change, and
    c. do something different
4. Failing is a prerequisite to confidence and success.
5. Nearly everything becomes easier with honesty and courage to face our fears. Equally important are becoming willing to ask for help and doing the work necessary to accomplish what we want.

Upgrading Our Belief System

There are many ways to move through our mental blocks, whatever they are. And I say mental because, for most of us, that's really all they are—lies we continue to believe about our self-worth and perceived value to others, whether real or not.

As mentioned earlier, many neuroscience experts agree that the brain is like an unlimited hard drive, unable to discern whether something is fact or fiction. The process of creating connections and how we attach value to something is complex, and beyond the scope of this book.

Neuroscientist, Steven Campbell, was kind enough to offer additional insight into this process. He explains:

Another exciting discovery about our brain is how it believes EVERYTHING we tell it, without question, no arguments. That's scary, and it's wonderful!

The scary part is when we exclaim to ourselves, 'I simply cannot do this,' our brains say, 'Okay! If you say so!' And then it makes sure you can't!

In addition, when we keep giving ourselves those negative messages, our brains not only believe them, but they also rewire themselves to make those messages a mindset. Over time those messages become who we are! The wonderful part is when we CHOOSE to replace those messages with, 'I CAN do this!' our brains immediately say, 'Okay! If you say so!'

They then become obsessed with finding a way to do it!

For a more thorough study on neuroscience, I encourage you to read Steven Campbell's book, *Making Your Mind Magnificent* and to research Neurolinguistic Programming (NLP). Personally, I can geek out on anything that explores the power of our mind. It's a fascinating topic to study and apply.

Now, let's focus on a simple premise, *garbage in, garbage out*.

I am sure most of you have heard of this concept. Basically, it means we become what we think about. If we continue to think of ourselves as inadequate and unworthy and do nothing to change what we think or say about ourselves to the contrary, we reinforce the pre-existing connections and patterns that continue to keep us where we are—feeling inadequate. Imposters.

But here's great news—we can change.

Most neuroscientists agree that we can reprogram our minds. We can change how we think and who we are by changing what we choose to believe.

This is not a new concept. It's been around for thousands of years or more. It's even biblical: "As a man thinketh in his heart, so is he." Proverbs 23:7 KJV.

Zig Ziglar also talked about it many years ago, "You are what you are and you are where you are because of what has gone into your mind. You change what you are and you change where you are by changing what goes into your mind."

If lying to ourselves is the problem, then it makes logical sense to get honest with ourselves, right? So how do we do that? It involves taking a "fearless and personal" inventory which we'll explore in detail in chapter seven.

For years, the solution has been lying dormant between our ears. Ironically, both the problem and the solution are in our minds—our beliefs. The solution rests in willingness to change; to make adjustments to our attitude, perspective, and belief system.

Attitude is a Choice Controlled by Patterns and Habits

Whether you believe it or not, attitude really does make a difference. And our attitudes are connected to our belief system which is a product of choices we have made that, when repeated, become patterns and habits. Are you beginning to see why 85% of us suffer from low self-esteem? So, if we want to change our attitude, it makes sense that changing our thinking and actions is a good spot to start and to create new habits.

Sounds simple and easy enough. But it's not. Why? Because if you're like me, we refuse to loosen our white-knuckled grip on our current belief system even though it's not producing the results we want. Our attitudes and beliefs probably have been the same since we became young adults, perhaps longer. And yet we wonder why we are where we are and why the same problems continue to crop up in our lives. At some point, we need to let go and learn something new.

> If we want to change what we believe about ourselves, we need to update our belief system.

Self-Care: Do Something Good Everyday

Whether you want more confidence, courage, inner peace, joy, or something else that you equate to a sense of accomplishment, achievement, or success, the simplest way to change your attitude is to do something good for yourself every day.

It can be eating better, getting more rest, or taking a vacation day, as I do frequently when I'm beginning to feel burned out, to refresh and recharge. I use that time for some form of self-care—exercise, a walk, a massage, reading in the sun, or making sure I get plenty of rest.

Refreshed, I almost always feel better the next day. Being good to ourselves is a first step toward not only a better attitude but shifting our beliefs about everything. Everything just seems to be easier when we feel good about ourselves, doesn't it?

Here are a few more basic suggestions I have used which I encourage you to try. I usually do these throughout the day when I feel myself becoming impatient, negative, frustrated, or angry with myself or others:

- Smile more. Frown less.
- Help someone. Expect less.
- Listen more. Talk less.
- Love more. Hate less.

Prompt #3: Introspection Time

Start by asking yourself what you really want. I know we already addressed this earlier. But it's worth doing again because most of us have no clue what we want. Or, if we do, are not clear about where to start.

Here are some questions to help you accomplish both: If you are not happy with how you have been thinking and what you have been saying or doing, I've got to ask, *how badly do you want to feel better?* Are you willing to do some more hard work to begin to change? How would your life be different if you had ____ (fill in the blank)? What's preventing you from having it now? Are you paralyzed by fear? Would a little inspiration and motivation help? How about a shot of courage? What would you do if you had less fear? What would be a great first step toward what you want?

Spend as much time as you need contemplating these questions. Let your imagination run free. Journal about them if you like.

When you feel done for now, take a deep breath, exhale, and boldly step forward into the fear, determined to make new decisions about who you are and what you want to become.

Pay Attention: Become a Keen Observer

Pay attention to everything around you. How you think, act, feel, and what you believe. Look at how people do things and what they do that's innovative. Every advancement in human evolution has been in response to a problem: first identifying it, then turning it into an opportunity by seeking a solution.

As humans, we are hardwired to solve problems. Our bodies are incredible self-healing machines for many things. Unfortunately, our autonomic, sympathetic, and parasympathetic systems cannot solve every problem or heal every ailment we face. Similarly, most of us lack the intellectual resources and knowledge to self-diagnose or treat our own mental and physical ailments without professional help. That is why we pay doctors, psychologists, coaches, trainers, teachers, etc. These are experts, professionals, and people who have invested countless hours to study and practice because they have a passion for serving and healing. And yet how stubborn we remain. Even after seeking and paying for expert advice, all too often we tend to regress back to old habits, our comfort zone. Most of us are reluctant to change. But nothing will ever change until we do.

Case in point, I have been on a see-food diet for most of my life. I see food and I eat it. I love bacon and cheeseburgers and crispy French fries. While it all tasted good at the time, my cholesterol is high which increases my risk of heart disease and could shorten my life. If I want to live longer, I need to make changes to reduce my cholesterol to a healthy range. Like most people, I don't like change. But my desire to live is greater than the inconvenience. So, I am following my doctor's suggestions to take daily supplements of, red rice yeast, flaxseed oil or fish oil, and a multivitamin. She also suggested I eliminate or reduce fast food and limit the amount of red meat I eat. I asked her for a prescription for a Statin, but she recommend I first try these dietary changes, along with adopting a Mediterranean diet of fresh veggies, seafood, and low-fat proteins. Then we can reevaluate after three months.

I'll admit at first all this sucked. I wanted what I couldn't have. I'd drool every time I saw a commercial for a greasy cheeseburger.

I love the smell of bacon in the morning, and soon I was obsessing about what I couldn't have. I started to think about wanting bacon and eggs for breakfast every morning when I woke up, the same way I used to jones for a cigarette and a cup of coffee as soon as I opened my eyes. I quit smoking ten years ago, but I doubt I'll ever give up the morning cup of joe.

Perhaps that's how it is for others who want to lose weight. I don't know. But I was determined to not let my desires control how I felt and am slowly getting used to it. It doesn't mean I have to eliminate red meat, bacon, or French fries altogether. It means I need to pay closer attention to diet, develop new eating habits, and get more exercise if I want to increase my lifespan. To be honest, I still struggle with all of the above.

More Tough Love

We all have degrees of guilt, shame, and low self-esteem. Many are deeply embedded into our belief system, primarily because we keep playing the same broken records over and over again, expecting different results. That, according to Albert Einstein, is the definition of insanity. The secret is to change the record and stop feeding the inner critics.

Read anything by Brené Brown. She not only understands this but has done extensive research and written several bestsellers which address the inner voices as they relate to our feelings of guilt and shame on a deeper level. While many of us have the capacity and ability to change how we think. Some "issues" may be deeper than we can manage alone. Like any serious condition, medical or physical, it's wise to seek outside professional help. I did, at the advice of my sponsor.

My abandonment and relationship issues were beyond the scope of his experience with recovery. He referred me to a therapist who I saw one to two times per week for five years. In the process, therapy coupled with my work in recovery, I learned new skills and patterns of behavior that literally saved my life.

Therefore, any advice I give from here on is based on personal experience of time-tested principles that have made my life better. The benefits of implementing these tools for the past three plus decades have given me more than I ever could imagine. Not just materially, but emotionally, physically, relationally, and spiritually.

In some cases, they helped me make more money. Others taught me how to not be a dick. *Still others taught me that* **everything starts with a dream.** *And that what we do or don't do is most often what separates those who "succeed" from those who don't.* In other words, what we think and do are key influential factors of our individual success or failure. I also learned about the three A's which taught me how not to overthink things.

Admit, Accept, and Adapt

Admit:

Unless it will hurt someone else more, admit it when you are wrong. Some cultures believe it is more important to save face than admit shortcomings. I respect the norms of other culture, but for me, admitting when I'm wrong reduces stress because I don't have the burden of guilt or shame weighing me down.

Accept:

"It is what it is." One of my former co-workers, often said this whenever she was faced with situations that were challenging or didn't go as planned. She didn't dwell in self-pity. Instead, she learned from the situation and took responsibility for what she could do better next time, then moved on. The key to acceptance is to develop the habit of having grace with yourself and understanding that mistakes are a normal part of life.

Adapt:
This is where our mettle is tested. If it's important enough, we will find a way to accomplish what we want. We will adapt out of necessity and because we have a big enough reason to want to. **If we don't have a big enough want, need, or desire, we won't change. Period.**

One of the greatest obstacles to our own success is our tendency to take simple solutions and complicate them. We think too much and act too little. It's not rocket science! If you are anything like me, you may overthink and overcomplicate things. Many believe that research and knowledge will change your life.

News flash—it won't. Change requires action. Sure, planning, research, and study are important parts of that. But planning alone will not guarantee your success. Why? Because the best plans are flexible and adaptable.

We'll explore these ideas further in subsequent chapters. For now, can we agree that change is inevitable and that you have the power to control some of it?

> We will never rise above our fear and doubt until we muster enough courage to change and take the first step in a new direction.

The Barren Desert of Doubt and Indecision

As previously mentioned, most of us struggle with low self-esteem and confidence in some area of our lives. We allow fear to block us from achieving our dreams and fully experiencing a life filled with meaning and purpose. We become stuck in the land of doubt and indecision. Stuck in a barren desert, under the blazing sun, where all we want is a drink of water. But, surrounded by sandy dunes, we feel lost, trapped with no guideposts to show us which way to go.

Though we are not lost in a desert at all, we still wander aimlessly, listening to the inner voices that say *we can't* rather than search for the ones that say *we can*. We believe the voices that tell us that we aren't smart enough, skilled enough, or lack the necessary courage to break free from whatever is holding us back.

Rather than risk our pride or ego to face our fears, or perhaps because our need to be perfect is greater that our want, need, or desire for change, we choose to give up before we are even halfway there. Wherever *there* is. Instead, we listen to and believe the voices in our head that screams, "You could never do that." We play it safe, the voice wins, we settle for average, and then we die. Full of regret and a whole lot of "I wish I wouldas" and "if only's."

To me, that is not a life. That's a prison sentence in a jail built from self-imposed fear. One where we have consciously or unconsciously shackled ourselves to a wall in a dark, cold cell of lost opportunity, or addiction, or self-doubt, effectively slamming the door on our hopes and dreams. *The worst part is that we hold the key to escape whenever we want but all too often, we choose not to use it.*

Freedom is in our grasp, but like a circus elephant, we stay tethered to a stake by a thin line because we believe we can't break free. How crazy is that? Not really, because it happens all the time. In fact, it's normal because we either haven't learned the requisite tools to flip the script in our minds or developed the habit and discipline to apply incremental changes to how we think and what we do.

The Answers Are Inside

The fact is, we can change the way we think and how we respond to our inner critics. It's not easy. It takes courage, diligence, and time, but the rewards of following a process to develop a healthier mindset are immeasurable. I can say this with confidence because I've done it. I've lived through the ups and downs that are a normal part of this journey we call life and will continue to ride the proverbial rollercoaster until I die. For me, life is a series of struggles, challenges, and opportunities—valuable lessons to be learned and repeated less frequently.

Every struggle I have faced—every fear, disappointment, and unmet expectation—all have been learning experiences that presented me with a choice: *Accept what I can't change or find the courage to change what I can.*

Discovering new solutions has been and will continue to be a lifelong process. Thus far, for the past forty years, I have learned how to not panic, and stay centered in the midst of any sandstorm, self-imposed or otherwise. I understand the value of building a positive, forward-thinking mindset, and continually do things to build my own self-confidence by practicing *Ten Seconds of Boldness*. I pay attention to how I feel and continue to battle the negative self-talk that still tries to hold me captive. I doubt my inner critics will ever completely go away. But I feel more confident in knowing what to do when they try to hijack my progress.

Preview: Tips for Taming Our Inner Critics

Today, when things don't go as I would like, I am rarely surprised. I don't wallow self-pity and feel like a reject or utter failure nearly as often as I used to. I do my best to try to look at a situation objectively and not make it more than it is. I practice the five habits, (*Identify* the problem or opportunity, clearly *decide* what you want, know *why* you want it, write a *clear plan*, and *start* working that plan, consistently over time your life will change), accepting things I cannot control, cutting myself some slack when I fall short, and committing to do better next time. Now, instead of blaming others or myself or playing the victim, I accept that situation as one more opportunity to learn and grow.

When situations arise like traffic or long lines or things that happen which I can't control, I don't fight them. I may pound the steering wheel and bark a few expletives, but when something doesn't turn out the way I want it to, I am more accepting today than I was ten years ago. Plus, I am much happier when I don't get pissed off over little things. When I take a page out of Richard Carlson's book *Don't Sweat the Small Stuff.*

I have learned that **my peace of mind is inversely related to my level of expectations about a desired outcome.** And my attitude is directly related to my level of acceptance. Instead of getting angry about something I can't control, I look within and try to see what it is that I can do differently. I ask myself or pray, "What is this trying to teach me? And how can I master my response to it."

Some days this comes easy for me. Others make me want to break glass in the recycling bin. And that's just the way it is.

Repeating this process of reflection and change has not only made me more self-aware (able to catch myself before I say or do something I'll later regret), but over time it has enabled me to shift my mindset about problems and inconveniences, at least most of the time.

As a result, I am happier, healthier, and more confident. In many ways, I've matured and become more responsible, especially when it comes to admitting my own shortcomings and finding the courage and discipline necessary to change my old ways of thinking. Plus, I sleep better at night.

Prompt #4: Self-Awareness Reflection

Consider and write a response to these two questions:

1. What three things continue to cause you stress?
2. How do you respond to them? In other words, what are your coping mechanisms?

Take five to ten minutes to do this now.

Check in: How Are You Feeling Right Now?

I know there was a lot of heavy stuff in this chapter, but it's incredibly important. I hope that you are beginning to see how some of the limits you've been living with can be removed or replaced.

In the next chapter I'll share a few tips on how I developed a healthier attitude around confidence, success, and failure by learning to quiet some of the many negative voices in my head. And as we continue and move from the heavy lifting of introspection into the process of making decisions, putting together plans, and setting those plans into motion, it will get easier.

Prompt #5: Break Time

Take some time to chill. Reward yourself for the hard work you've done thus far and go do something fun.

Chapter Four
How Do We Tame Our Inner Critics and Become More Self-Confident?

"As man thinketh in his heart so is he."
Proverbs 23:7

My inner critics love to wear t-shirts, especially brightly colored ones with negative messages like: "Who do you think you are?" "You? Really? Ha!" "That will never work," "What's the use?" "I'll never get out of debt!" Or my personal favorite, a grey t-shirt with a picture of Eeyore on the front, stuck in mud, looking defeated, and a big cartoon bubble that says, "Why me?"

What t-shirts do your inner critics wear? Can people notice what they say? If you could change the message, what would it say? "No Fear." "Be a kind human." "Love is the answer." "You are enough." Or Nike's famous slogan: "Just Do It!"

The good news is we get to choose the message we'll wear. Nobody else has the power to dictate how you feel on any given day. Those messages are outward manifestations or affirmations of our desired level of self-esteem—how we feel or want to feel about ourselves, and our self-confidence—how much trust we have or want to have in our skills and abilities.

What's interesting is that we don't need to wear a t shirt to reveal how we feel or our levels of confidence. Our behavior and what we say or don't say communicate our internal state of esteem and confidence more than any t-shirt ever will. What's more, for the most part, we are in control. It's a feedback loop controlled by our thoughts, decisions, choices, and actions. As such, we do become what we think about most.

I have battled my inner critics in all areas of my life and probably always will. That's part of life. I accept it for what it is. Now I take responsibility for how I react when something doesn't go as planned. I no longer kick and scream like a hangry two-year old.

There is No One-Size-Fits-All Solution or Magic Formula

I've spent countless hours and thousands of dollars trying to find some magic formula or panacea that would take away all my doubts, worries, fears, and insecurities. As empowering as external motivation, will power and self-help, or spiritual enlightenment can be, by themselves, they are not enough to sustain lasting transformation. To overcome my shortcomings, real or perceived, and to feel more confident, I needed something more. But what?

First, I needed to become more self-aware and to know what motivates me to become willing to change. Second, to face my fears and insecurities, I needed courage. Third, I needed a plan. Last, I needed to work that plan.

If I was to break free, especially from my addiction, it was necessary for me to take personal responsibility for my own growth but not rely completely on self-will. It was highly recommended that I find someone to guide me (a sponsor). *I had to humble myself enough to not only admit that I had a problem but also be vulnerable enough to ask for help.* I followed the suggestions which ultimately led me to a mental, physical, and spiritual awakening and long-term sobriety.

In recovery, I found a spiritual solution to my mental and physical problem— I learned and practiced a twelve-step program that taught me about surrender. That explained a spiritual solution found in a power greater than myself, which I call God or Higher Power (HP), to develop the courage to humbly look deep within and find the inner strength necessary to break free from the negative voices in my head.

It was also recommended that I don't try and do it all alone. That I get a sponsor, someone with experience, who could counsel me on the steps necessary to overcome my addiction.

The suggestions I learned in recovery have helped me believe in myself again, rebuilding my self-confidence and self-esteem. I could not have done it without a sponsor, a support group, and finding a higher power I could rely on. As I alluded to earlier, I tried. Believing, "I got this," without guidance and reliance on a higher power or others, for me, is a recipe for failure.

Asking for help is a not a sign of weakness. Whether in recovery, work, relationships, or business, many seek expert guidance from professionals such as mentors, coaches, counselors, and therapists.

The benefits of seeking professional help far outweigh the risks to our ego and pride.

Here are seven highlights (tips) of my ongoing transformation journey toward healing and spiritual awakening which have not only helped improve my self-image but have literally saved my life.

Seven Tips for Improving Our Self-Image:

1. There are no shortcuts to self-confidence or success. All worthwhile achievement in life is a direct result of having a dream or a vision that requires learning, practicing, and

developing the habits necessary to be, have, or do that which you desire.

At its core, confidence and success must start with you. Nobody else can determine your dreams or goals. No amount of external motivation will fire you up long enough to develop the confidence necessary to feel a meaningful sense of belonging, purpose, and accomplishment.

All you need to succeed is willingness to face the unknown and apply the principles of *Ten Seconds of Boldness,* and enough courage to make a decision and take the first step.

> **The only thing separating you from where you are and where or who you want to be is you.**

2. It's normal to suffer occasional blows to our confidence. We all do—even star athletes or celebrities. So why then is confidence so hard to build, develop, and maintain? Can it be that we feel the need always to be at the top of our game? That we are so afraid of failing that we don't ever really try. Or is it more like the song, "Looking for love in all the wrong places"? Are we trying too hard to find confidence in things outside ourselves?

3. Confidence is not some magic potion. It is built and developed over time, through countless hours of practice and repetition.

4. Confidence is an experience of being fully present, and at peace with who you are, where you are, now.

5. Confidence is acceptance of things as they are—"It is what it is"—while also believing that if you don't like who you are or where you think you should be, that you have the power to respond and react differently. You have the power to change.

6. Building self-confidence is a perpetual quest; it is found in the process of discovering who you really are and who you want to become.

7. Life is a lot more fun with confidence. When I think of confidence, I think of Stephen Curry. He is, in my opinion, a quintessential superstar. Because of hard work, lots of practice, mental and physical conditioning, creativity, and his willingness to take risks, he dazzles fans around the world with his ball handling and shooting mastery playing the game he loves—basketball. He exudes fun, joy, humility, and a sense of teamwork that, to me, is the epitome of confidence.

Prompt #1: Pause and Reflect

Before we continue, please give some serious thought to the areas of your life that you may want or need a confidence boost and what more courage and confidence would mean to you.

As you mull that over, let's shift our focus from problems to solutions. Specifically, how to tame your inner critics and help you become more confident, productive, and prosperous. We'll start with a conversation I had with a friend and successful CEO and Coach, Aaron Locks.

A Once Scared Man Who's Helped More than 300,000 Kids Become Confident

Aaron Locks is the founder and CEO of National Academy of Athletics and has worked with over 300,000 kids in 131 cities across four states. He has an extensive sports background spanning four decades, working with many Hall-of-Famers including Rick Barry, Al Attles, Magic Johnson, and legendary UCLA coach John Wooden. He has run programs for Don Nelson, Pat Riley, Dusty Baker, and many others.

I asked him to share his perspective and insights on confidence as an expert, business owner, father, and coach. Specifically, about what it takes to develop and help kids grow and evolve into more confident individuals. Not just in sports and athletics, but in all areas of our lives.

To kick off our conversation, I asked Aaron this question: Where did your inspiration come from?

He immediately related the story about finding his passion.

His dad left when he was three years old. So, he says, "I was raised by a pot-smoking hippie mom." He had three older sisters and a younger brother and, in his words, "was probably Marin County's biggest sissy in late '60s and '70s." He wanted to play but was too scared to try out. One day, as he put it, his mom got "fed up and drove me to the baseball field and dropped me off and said, 'That's your coach. I'll be back in an hour.' And she left."

At seven years old, that was his introduction to sports. He grabbed a bat and kept swinging at every pitch. No matter how many times he swung the bat, he couldn't get a hit. In frustration, he threw his helmet down and started bawling. *He was ready to give up before he even got started.* Suddenly, he heard a loud voice, "Are you kidding me? That's unacceptable." It was his coach, Marty Islas.

Coach sat Aaron down in the dugout and asked him who his favorite baseball player was. "Willie Mays," replied Aaron, looking at the ground.

"Well, don't you realize that Willie gets out seven out of ten times? So why do you, your first time at bat, think you're going to be better than Willie Mays?"

Aaron had no reply. But that exchange left an indelible impression on him that became the proverbial mustard seed for building his confidence. In Aaron's opinion, "there is no better life-skill, teaching-tool than sports. Because playing sports is really about failure."

He went on to talk about being afraid of the ball, so coach Islas made him the catcher. And to help him get over his fear, Coach used to chuck tennis balls at him over and over again until Aaron learned to block or catch them. It worked. As a seven-year-old on that dusty field, Aaron found the inner courage to overcome adversity. For the next four plus decades, he kept pushing himself and finally realized, as he says, "Failure was not my enemy."

He's right. Failure is really a matter of perspective. Of belief.

Belief is a Matter of Perspective

Perspective is determined by what you currently believe and what motivates you. Anyone can change their perspective at any time. It's a matter of choice. A decision. All it takes is studying and practicing these concepts and finding *Ten Seconds of Boldness* to tell your critic off and to take the first or next step toward fulfilling your dreams. Confidence starts when you say to yourself, **"enough!"**

Finding the Courage to Act

After decades of practice, I have discovered that in any uncomfortable situation it is my responsibility to find courage and act. Those are two things I can control. However, I cannot control the outcome and I need to stop believing I can.

Years ago, I learned that my inner peace and serenity are, as I said before, inversely proportional to my level of acceptance and expectation. When my expectations for a particular outcome are not met, I become frustrated, irritable, and tend to "try harder." It's still not easy to be humble too admit my shortcomings nor recognize where I need to improve. To reflect and be introspective enough to look at how I respond when things don't go my way: How do I feel and act when I don't get what I want? Do I sulk? Blame others? Give up? Am I so driven that I impose my will into a situation trying to make it work out the way I want? Or do I let go and look inside?

These are questions I often ask myself to become more self-aware; so I can do better next time.

Prompt #2: Consider and Reflect

How do you respond when something doesn't work out as you planned? Do you accept it? Are you honest with yourself about the level of effort you put in? Or do you expect a grand result without effort? Do you give up too soon? Do you doubt or second-guess your ability to succeed?

These are some of the greatest obstacles to building self-confidence. Unaddressed, they impede our productivity, feed our inner critics, and further reinforce any negative thoughts or beliefs we already hold. Most of us, if we are honest, can relate to Aaron. We want to throw our helmet down and give up too soon, not fully committed to putting in the effort to get what we think we want. Instead, we fool ourselves into believing we tried hard enough. But our attitudes, actions, calendars, checkbooks, and scales say otherwise. We create excuses, and justifications, or worse, compare our present state to that of someone who has invested the time to become "successful."

Success is relative. All too often we assume someone we don't know is happy or successful or has it all together. We base our opinion on the public side of what we perceive success to be. On their image or highlight reels on social media.

But we don't really know them, do we? They may appear to be successful by our measures, or they may be perfectionists and feel as if they still aren't good enough. So why waste time comparing ourselves to the polished images of others which may not represent their true character?

Stop. Just be you. *And if you don't like who you are, find the courage to change.*

We Are More Than What We Produce

While many of us struggle with perfectionism, we will never be perfect. We all can always do better. Many of us also attach our sense of worth to what or how much we produce. Being right and producing a lot are not inherently wrong. But attaching our self-image to what we produce or how few mistakes we make is a double-edged sword. When we fall short of our expected ideals many sink into negative thoughts about who they are.

That shit needs to stop if you want to build your self-confidence. You need to *separate who you are from what you do*. You are a human *being* not a human *doing*. And, because you are human, you will make mistakes.

Even righteous folks with great faith fall short.

At the risk of pissing a few believers off, I have to say this: **"It is done."** That debt was paid. Stop beating yourself up for falling short of perfection and accept a little grace. *If you truly believe, this should not be an issue.*

Love and Acceptance

Whether we admit it or not, all of us have a deep longing to be loved and accepted. What that looks like is a matter of personal preference.

It's understandable why. We are conditioned to focus on outcomes; to believe that our worth is defined by our level of productivity and status/income, the amount of money we make, our zip code, the toys we have, the cars we drive, our looks, our home, our standing in the community, our likes and followers, and platforms, etc. The list never ends.

These are supposedly objective measures—personal KPI's (key performance indicators)—of our value and worth to an organization and society. But in reality, most are subjective measures. Ones we believe and have bought into and which, in the big picture, are grossly inaccurate if not completely false. Who said that you have to be rich or the best to be happy?

I love Abraham Lincoln's perspective, "Folks are about as happy as they make up their minds to be." Over one hundred and fifty years later, those wise words are never truer than today.

Beware of Comparison and Judgment Traps

How many of us constantly compare our stature and worth to others often with little or no regard to their back story, their work ethic, and what it took for them to be considered successful. Do you really know what it took for them to get to where they are?

For example: If I live in the 90210 zip code (Beverly Hills) and have a multimillion-dollar mansion, millions in the bank, and all my kids are going to the best schools, and I have a gardener, housekeeper, nutritionist and personal chef, therapist, and get massages every other day, and so on... does that make me better than you? On the surface I may appear to have my shit together, but I might also have scores of other problems you don't even know about. But all you see is my highlight reel on Entertainment Tonight or the global highlight reel, Facebook. All you see are the masks I want you to see.

Most of the external rewards I have experienced in my life, while nice to have, do not make me better. Yet for most of my youth and early adulthood, I chased a mirage of who I thought I should be and attached my identity to being a good student because the recognition—honor role, valedictorian, praise from parents, teachers, and peers—validated my sense of worth and purpose in the world. But there was something that always bothered me. Most of those straight A report cards from grammar school had a comment from the teacher. *"Working below potential."*

Things came easy for me, and I didn't have to try too hard to do well in school. That ease carried over into work as well. And on several occasions in work, I became cocky, lazy, and complacent and it cost me dearly.

In fact, it wasn't until decades later that I began to understand what my teachers meant. That it wasn't all about me. That I could help someone else and learn even more if I put in more effort and applied myself.

Change of Perspective

The intrinsic reward was to shift my focus from an external results-based orientation toward problems, opportunities, goals, and dreams, to one which develops an attitude and approach that is inward focused. The first is a transactional orientation. The second is a transformational orientation.

I believe the reason so many suffer from low self-confidence is because we have been looking for confidence, like love, in all the wrong places. If you want to have more confidence and control, you need to focus on those things you can control. Namely, your attitude, belief, effort, and motivation.

Stop comparing yourself to others and start working on making yourself great.

Prompt #3: Overcoming the Comparison Trap
Reflect and Write

Question #1: Who do you envy? What about them makes you feel jealous?

Question #2: What ways can you think of to avoid the comparison trap? To stop looking at the success of others with jealousy and envy and start looking at what you can do to get what you want?

Get into action: Spend fifteen minutes to reflect and respond to the above questions, *in writing.*

Chapter Five
Jump!

"What's important is that you make the leap. Jump high and hard with intention and heart."
Cheryl Strayed

Did you know that the African impala can jump ten feet high and cover ten yards? Yet this magnificent animal can be confined within walls only three feet high. Why? Because unless it first sees where it's going to land, it's too afraid to jump.

We aren't much different.

Many have said the only way to face challenges is head on. To go through them. Avoiding them or denying they exist is not a viable solution. In fact, avoidance is part of the problem. To build self-confidence and become more productive, we must not only identify the mental blocks and fears that we let prevent us from the lives we want, but we must also find something greater than fear—fear that tethers us to mediocrity and feeling less than. That one thing is courage.

Where do you find courage?

The simple answer is *Ten Seconds of Boldness*. This is the key to unlock the door to solving problems and building self-confidence. It is where we discover our true value to ourselves and the world. It is how grit, guts, and determination to persevere are established, developed, and mastered. How you find it is a personal matter. But without boldness or courage, you will never advance beyond where you are now.

Boldness is the catalyst to move one step closer to our dreams despite our fears; where the willingness to take a chance on ourselves is borne. And *it is by doing, not just thinking, that we move closer to success.* As a result of courageous action, we become more productive, happy, and prosperous.

> The only thing between who you are now and who you want to be or what you want to have or do is finding the guts to practice *Ten Seconds of Boldness.*

Keep it Simple

My goal is to help you get to know yourself so well that personal growth and confidence become a habitual response to your life experience. Living a bold and courageous life becomes an end unto itself. That is the goal: the process of becoming.

I am a firm believer in simplicity. Simple doesn't mean easy. But therein lies the challenge; we are complex individuals who tend to overthink things and spend way more time thinking than doing. Worse, most of what we think about is negative. Negativity will not help you gain confidence, but finding courage within to step forward into the unknown while simultaneously letting go of any preconceived fears will.

The moment you stop holding back the right doors will open. The people and resources to help you will serendipitously appear.

Be Strong and Courageous

"Have I not commanded you? Be strong and courageous. Do not be frightened, and do not be dismayed, for the Lord your God is with you wherever you go." – Joshua 1:9

I don't know where you find your inspiration or if you believe in a power greater than yourself. But for me, it is an inner voice that says it loves me and wants the very best for me. It is an assuring muse to counter the inner critics that say I am not good enough, smart enough, or don't have the courage to face uncomfortable situations.

Whenever I am facing a challenge, I have found a principle that works for me virtually every time: Do the work and leave the results up to God, the universe, or whatever power greater than me and my self-will that I choose to believe in.

Self-Will is a Double-Edged Sword

Before I go further, I want to clarify what I mean by self-will. Self-will is a double-edged sword. It is the engine that fuels our drive and ambition. But it can become a liability when we lack humility or the willingness to be coachable. I'm sure any coach, teacher, or manager will agree that those with too much self-will tend to become selfish, self-centered, and overconfident in their abilities, which, especially in any team-based environment, can be counterproductive. Side note: Read Patrick Lencioni's, *The Five Dysfunctions of a Team.*

Some of the most painful lessons I have learned in my life came when I thought I had all the answers and didn't. When I told myself, "I got this."

"I got this" may appear to be an empowering phrase, full of strength and courage. It is if someone has the experience and confidence from having paid their dues, or says and believes it as an affirmation to overcome the fact that deep down inside they know they really don't "got this."

"You got this" is often used by coaches, parents, teachers, and trainers to encourage others. In the right context, "you got this" is good. But when used as a sense of self-importance (not as an affirmation), that phrase can be hazardous to your health, leading to false confidence, denial, self-will, or even arrogance. I know because, as I mentioned earlier, those three words nearly cost me my life.

Even after I got sober, I made many stupid mistakes because I thought I knew what I was doing and was too proud to ask for help. For me, those two phrases, *"I got this" and "I'm fine,"* are warning signs that I am operating under the illusion that I can control everything. In most cases, whenever I say, "I'm fine" or "I got this," I am being dishonest with myself in not allowing others an opportunity to help me. In recovery, that can be deadly. In work or relationships, those words can build walls that isolate and prevent you from fully experiencing the joys of connection, collaboration, and community.

It may seem counterintuitive to many, but you can actually expedite your confidence building process if you are humble enough to ask for help.

Nothing Will Keep You in Everlasting Mediocrity More Than Ego and Pride.

For me, the key to a world of infinite possibilities is found in quiet moments when I'm humble enough to ask for help and pray. When I realize and accept that everything does not, nor will it ever, solely depend on me. There's a freedom in such surrender that I find liberating.

In nearly every instance when I let my ego get in the way of making smart decisions, it ultimately costs me more time and money than if I had asked for help in the first place. That has been a very painful lesson. One I am still learning.

Circling back to the beginning—in every worthwhile endeavor, we need to *identify* the problem or opportunity, *decide* what we want, know why we want it, make a *plan*, and *implement* that plan. Ultimately, our task is to gain the knowledge, seek the advice, and find the courage to take the next step in each phase of our development. **Our progress is more effective and efficient when we don't try to do it all by ourselves.**

As we will discuss later, humility and remaining teachable and coachable are also critical for our personal development. **We can't learn if we think we know it all.**

Prompt: Self-Awareness: Beyond Ego and Pride

Part 1: Getting into action: Make a list of areas you might want or need to ask someone for help.
Part 2: Make a list of areas you are aware of that you struggle with ego and pride.
Part 3: Review both lists. Are there any similarities? If so, make those a priority to solve first. Then consider who you will ask for help.

Chapter Six
Bridging the Confidence Gap

"It's not what you think you are that holds you back, it's what you think you are not."
Dennis Waitley

For Father's Day in 2021, my son treated me to a zipline tour. For two and a half hours we traversed the treetops across seven ziplines and two skybridges. The only things that separated us from the forest floor two hundred and fifty feet below were a harness with pulleys, a 3/8" cable, and **the courage to let go.**

It was the most exhilarating and memorable Father's Day ever!

Though I was anxious on the first two zips, I relaxed by the third. I found my legs, so to speak. Until we approached a hundred foot long, wobbly skybridge made of ropes and planks. I stared at it, then the ground. My knees began to shake. Unlike the ziplines which meant harnessing up and letting go to enjoy the ride, to continue our adventure meant I had to put one foot in front of the other and cross that rickety bridge seventy-five feet above the hard ground below. I watched as others crossed first and realized it wasn't impossible. I grabbed the rope rails, and after finding my balance, found it was not as scary as I thought. I took a few steps then skipped the rest of the way across. When I got to the other side, My son asked, "What was that all about Dad?"

"I decided to have fun cause I knew it was safe."

Your Confidence Gap is Not as Big as You May Think

The bridge between where you are and where you want to be is shorter than you think. In fact, for most people, it's only six to seven inches: the average space between your two ears.

This chapter will look closer at ways we can gain the knowledge, seek the advice, and find the courage to take the next step in each phase of our development. Each of these steps is critical for building the bridge between where we are and where we want to be. To inspire boldness to conquer your fear of falling and keep putting one foot in front of the other. The goal of this chapter is to inspire you to take the next step forward. To help you bridge your confidence gap.

When I have too many projects, goals, and to-dos going on at the same time and can easily get scattered and lose focus. They all seem important, but whenever I look at them all at once, I get overwhelmed. It's like an overstuffed garage or closet, or a home office with disorganized drawers, boxes of notes, and yes, even file drawers bursting with old utility bills, notebooks, etc.

Eventually the clutter of my environment and my mind becomes so great that I feel ineffective. To regain focus, I take time to organize and declutter.

When I finally decide to tackle big projects, organizing or otherwise, I do it *one drawer, one closet, one room at a time*. I focus on making progress in one area before moving on to the next.

I feel much better when I am productive and creative, but I don't obsess over results. I strive to maintain a healthy balance between work and relaxation, remembering to also take time out to celebrate my accomplishments, small or large. To chill or go for a walk or have a date night with my wife or coffee with a friend.

This process also works for my goals, such as writing this book, or any other area I want to work on. When I keep things simple and don't try to do too much at once, or worry about what might happen, like the harness breaking or falling off a bridge, my productivity skyrockets and I feel better about myself. As I do, I become more confident.

This process has become a set routine or habit. Just like making my bed in the morning.

Prompt #1: Make Your Bed and Take Out the Trash

It's important to pay attention to unresolved problems or unfulfilled ambitions you have and how you typically respond to them. Watch for:

- Procrastination
- Denial
- Blame
- Avoidance
- Shame
- Guilt
- Fear
-

Choose one area, one skill, attitude, belief, that's been bugging you or that you've been procrastinating over and make a decision to do something about it as soon as you finish this chapter.

It can be anything. Making your bed. Taking out the trash. Starting a load of laundry. Anything. The key is not to just *think* about it, but to actually *do it*. Decide what it is, then make a plan, write it down, set a date, and get started. That's how it's done.

As you apply the skills you learn in the book, it will become readily apparent how easy it is to transfer them to other areas essentially building your confidence one closet or room at a time. The cure to overcoming any and all of the above: Be bold. Practice the five steps. Decide, commit, and let it go, now.

Let it Go

In my conversation with Aaron Locks, I asked him what, in his whole career, he would consider to be his biggest failure and how did he overcome it.

"11/11/11," he said without any hesitation. "It's a day I'll never forget." That was the day that his partner walked away with over $680,000 of the business's money. That his wife, as Aaron recalled, "decided another's man's company was better than mine—we parted ways."

He lost everything. He had to reinvent himself. In three and a half months, he did.

"In a weird way, I knew there was nothing that would stop me from being able to do it."

But he added, " I had no fucking idea what to do next."

He got really clear and "found ways to sit really still." There were times when it was all so new. He recalled staring in the mirror for thirty minutes, like Robert De Niro in *Taxi Driver,* talking to himself, "Are you a man or are you a chump. What you got?"

He continued, "I started reading John Maxwell, and [Stephen] Covey." Eventually he realized it was time for him to start walking the walk. He put together his personal mission statement: "I am put on planet earth to enhance the lives of the people I come in contact with by being an inspiration and a role model. I'll do everything I can to make those lives around me better."

He recalled the three powerful words from coach Islas: "Let it go." He also added that when "holding [onto] anything negative, the only one who gets hurt is you."

That mission helped him build his relationship with his own kids. The rest is history. At last count he has helped over 300,000 kids in his programs in 131 cities across four states. And he's living out his mission on a regular basis. His "worst day" turned out to be one of the best, because he made a decision. He drew upon all his years of playing sports and being a coach and business owner and did it anyway. Then, as in the beginning, he *let it go*.

Professional Advice for Bridging Your Confidence Gap

I also asked Aaron what advice he would you give to kids, parents, or adults who struggle with self-confidence. What could help others bridge the confidence gap of where they are, and where or who they want to be?

"There's no magic wand," Aaron said. "First, visualize what you want. What does your life look like when you're happy?" He added, "When we are younger, we tend to want *things*. As we get older, we want *feelings, adventure, and journeys*." Clarify what that looks like for you.

In summary, he said there are three steps.
1. Look at where you want to go.
2. Let go of your failures. Instead embrace them and look how far you've come.
3. Ask yourself how you overcame them and do that.

He added, "There are lots of pieces in us already and that's where the confidence comes from. It's like kids learning to walk. As parents, we don't need to say, 'Okay, it's time to practice.' Kids are going to want to learn how to walk. They fall down and keep getting back up again, and again. We all have that in us. **What we have to do is let go of the fear of falling down. And focus on the fact that we want to walk."**

Humble Beginnings to Fulfilling a Dream

In March of 2020, I hit the wall with this book. Something was missing but I didn't know what exactly. One day, out of the blue, a voice said, reach out to Coach Steve Lavin.

Steve and I were high school classmates and share a love for the game of basketball. We often guarded each other in practice and basketball summer camps.

As a professional coach and broadcaster for the past three decades I felt Coach Lavin could offer some valuable insight and perspective that I felt I was missing. I followed my gut and reached out to him on Facebook.

In September of 2020 we had a chance to catch up. What transpired over the next hour and forty-five minutes, was an incredible conversation that went beyond surface-level strategies about the importance of visualization, practice, and work habits as they relate to coaching basketball.

What struck me most was Steve's candor and vulnerability. He talked about his humble beginnings: how at age twenty, he knew he wanted to be a coach but didn't know what it would take. He found a mentor in Kevin Wilson at Chapman University. He then began asking other coaches for advice—what books to read, what clinics he should attend. He asked them, "What steps I should take, because

I someday aspired to walk in their shoes." He figured reaching out and establishing rapport with experts on the field of coaching and teaching "was a good place to start."

Then he went back and visited those coaches in action. He spent a month in Indiana watching Bob Knight's program. Later he spent time at Purdue, UNLV, and other schools to "watch these masters in their element." He took notes, watched film, and started picking it up. It began to add color to the vision he had of becoming a college coach.

On many levels, Steve understood the importance of being present—in the locker room, on the bench, and in practices to see and hear all the nuance of what it takes to be a great coach; the correction, the empathy, all the skills necessary to lead and encourage young men to be their very best, on and off the court. But he also shared something I had no idea about until our interview—that as a kid he struggled academically and was diagnosed with dyslexia and dysgraphia.

For him to fully grasp the things he needed to learn required immersion, repetition, taking notes, seeing, and hearing, and experiencing all he could. In essence, he became a sponge. He had an unquenchable thirst for knowledge and the courage as well as humility to seek it out.

Those early beginnings of his own journey would come full circle when he finally did get his big break and, as he told me, coupled with his own learning disabilities gave him a "degree of empathy, compassion, and understanding with his players." He was able to view coaching through a different lens.

In terms of ingenuity, it gave him a new skill set and enabled him to connect on a personal and deeper level with his players. He became a voice of encouragement. He passed on the "generous spirit" of coaches, counselors, and mentors who paved the way for his own success. He admitted, "Those early years were lean." He didn't have the resources and racked up huge debt to pursue his dream. He couch-surfed and paid his dues, and eventually got his break.

Finding Your Big Break, By Cultivating Relationships.

In the summer of 1988, the door opened when Purdue Coach, Gene Keady hired Steve as an assistant. That led to him meeting John Wooden, which would later play a part in his move to UCLA where he spent twelve years as a coach—first for five years as an assistant under Jim Harrick, then as a head coach for seven. Steve mentioned that getting the nod to become the head coach really "would not have happened without the relationship I had built with John Wooden."

None of this would have happened if he didn't seek out and follow the advice of others or trust his gut to reach out to Keady two years earlier.

At thirty-two, Steve became the youngest head coach in UCLA history and, including his stint at St. John University, led teams he coached to ten postseason appearances, including eight NCAA Tournament berths and nine seasons of twenty or more wins. Lavin's cumulative record is 226-131.

But he readily admits, it wasn't the win-loss record that mattered most. It was the impact and influence of others on him and how he paid that forward to have a positive impact on the loves of many young men who became successful NBA players, coaches, broadcasters, businessmen, and just good people.

Stop Striving and Follow What Brings You Joy

When I asked Coach Lavin about where his dream started, he said, "Joy plays a big part." He mentioned picking up a basketball for the first time. "For others," he said, "it could be soccer, or baseball. But basketball stood out." I could relate. That's what we share, a love for the game of basketball. And how sport, in particular basketball, is a wonderful unifying metaphor for life.

He talked about basketball summer camps in high school where Sir Francis Drake High, Cal State Champion Coach, Pete Hayward began "inculcating what it takes to win in terms of fundamentals." Those camps were really the foundation of belief. Later as Lavin began to coach the kids at summer camps and win championships, he **"began to believe that, hey, maybe I can do this." And so, he did.**

Fatherly Advice From Kevin Miller

For those who don't know Kevin Miller, here's a portion of his official bio: A former pro cyclist and lifetime entrepreneur founding fourteen businesses, Kevin has devoted himself to unearthing the root issues of positive, personal change, and motivating people to discover and commit to their unique contribution to the world. He hosts three podcasts which have eclipsed 52 million downloads and held the ranking of #2 in All-Time Career podcasts in Apple Podcasts for all of 2020.

When I asked Kevin Miller what advice he would give to kids, he recalled a recent situation with his twenty-year-old daughter. I explore this in greater detail in the chapter on belief. But there are two things he said that stuck with me which are worth saying twice. First, he told her, "You've been brainwashed by me. Now it's your job to go re-brainwash yourself." He also said, "One of the best things I can do as a parent is to say I don't know."

Not knowing is 100% okay. Anything new is a process of discovery. Of trial and error. Of making mistakes and being humble enough to ask for help. You will bridge your confidence gap once you decide to keep moving forward.

Prompt #2: Pause For a Moment of Gratitude—Here. Now.

Take five minutes to write down everything you can think of that you are grateful for. And everything that brings you joy. Read your list, close your eyes, and let the feelings settle in.

After a few minutes, open your eyes and continue reading, knowing *you can come back to this place of gratitude anywhere, anytime you want to.* All you have to do is **stop. Pause.** And **be grateful.** Yes, it is that easy.

My Own Moment of Gratitude

As I edit this section, I am struck by an immense level of gratitude I have for those who have helped me bring *Ten Seconds of Boldness* to life. Especially the open conversations I had with Steve Lavin, Cara Wasden, Kevin Miller, Aaron Locks, and Jon Diamond.

One of the greatest take aways I got from my interviews is that regardless of their present stature or levels of accomplishment, none of them are that different from you or me.

They faced many of the same challenges we all do. But in the process, each found the inner strength and courage to persist. And as a result of their determination to never give up on their dreams, have paid it forward. From sharing their wisdom here, to all who they have encouraged in their roles as coaches, instructors, and leaders, inspiring hundreds, thousands, if not millions, to become more confident. I will forever be grateful for their selfless generosity and contributions.

Neither *Ten Seconds of Boldness* nor any individual has the power to control what you do or do not become. That's for you to figure out. But what I can promise you is that with focused effort over time and a dream larger than your excuses, you will become, have, or do what you want with very few exceptions.

The only exceptions, of course, are for those who may not have the mental, physical, or spiritual ability or willingness to take a chance on themselves.

As Cara Wasden pointed out earlier, she wanted to be a singer. But she wasn't born with a great singing voice. That doesn't mean that she can't sing, it just means that it's not a good fit for her dream of becoming a professional singer.

Instead, she found her calling to inspire others to become confident by overcoming her own lack of confidence.

Life is like that sometimes; *our biggest obstacles can become our greatest blessings, which shape our life's purpose.*

You'll Never Know Until You Try

The most confident people I know have a desire and willingness to continue to push themselves and get in the game. They are willing to try. They do not sit idly by. They take risks. They take the hits and get knocked down, like Rocky. But, unless the towel is thrown, they pull themselves up by the ropes, and live to fight another round.

> One thing is certain—if you never try, you will never know. **Don't believe the lies in your head.** Until you invest the time to seriously pursue something of interest to you, you will remain where you are. **Don't quit before the miracle.**

I have been knocked down so many times in my life, but I don't stay down. Blow after blow, no matter what, I don't give up.

Your biggest obstacle will likely be to your resistance to self-reflection. To seriously make a list of your assets and liabilities. To become introspective enough to fully grasp, embrace, and accept your strengths and weaknesses. This is no different than what businesses do when deciding to open their doors.

"Know thyself," means more than who you are and what you have done. There are two deeper questions you need to ask as you make your way through the rest of the book: First, *what* **do you want?** Second, *why* **do you want it?** And, perhaps even more importantly, is to accept that *you don't need to have all the answers before you get started.*

A Lesson from Vilfredo Pareto: Get the 80% First!

Have you heard of Pareto's law or principle? To paraphrase, it means 80% of your results and outcomes are the result of 20% of your actions or activities. In other words, invest your time, energy, or resources, in activities which have the highest potential return on your investment.

The question is, do you want to waste 80% of your time, energy, and resources on the missing 20% or invest wisely in those things with a greater potential value? A greater return on your investment?

To me it's a no brainer. I'll invest twenty for a return of eighty all day long. That's a 4x return on my investment of time.

That strategy has helped me meet my goals time and time again. It's effective, efficient, and fun!

80% is Enough

When it comes to bridging a confidence gap, 80% is more than enough in most cases. The remaining 10-20% of what you think is missing almost always falls into place as you advance toward your goals. If it doesn't, don't worry, you probably didn't need it anyway.

The point is **your confidence will build while you are in pursuit of a dream or goal.** The key word is *pursuit.* That means *action.*

Your confidence will also be shaken, tested. Expect to stumble. To make mistakes. It's part of learning. As you shift your attitude about the inevitable setbacks and mistakes you will face from *"I'm a failure"* to *"That didn't work, I'll try this instead,"* you will begin to change how you approach any task or goal and become more confident and successful in the process. You will begin to *build a solution mindset* and will reap the appropriate benefits.

*Side note: Out of respect for professions that require specific skills and accuracy, as with airplane pilots, surgeons, etc., 80% won't cut it. But for most others, 80% confidence is plenty to be effective. Those who are wise will not waste time for the extra 20% if the return is not worth it.

Prompt #3: Reflect and Answer

Question #1: What are the 20% most impactful things you can do right now to advance?
Question #2: Is 80% confidence enough for you? If not, why?

Chapter Seven
Increasing Your Self-Awareness by Taking a Personal Inventory

"To know thyself is the beginning of wisdom."
Socrates

Most of us don't want to look in the mirror or take a look at where we may be coming up short. At work. In relationships. Of our perceptions of success. But until we have the courage to take an honest look at ourselves and become willing to do some things different, we will remain where we are, stuck.

This chapter will expand on some of the problems we discussed in chapter three. Specifically, to stop perpetuating the lies we believe about ourselves and abilities, or lack thereof.

Here we will focus on the importance of getting honest with ourselves and/or our business by becoming more self-aware. We will explore several underlying issues which frequently inhibit our productivity, confidence, and success, and briefly review a business evaluation tool you may be familiar with called a SWOT analysis (Strengths, Weaknesses, Opportunities, and Threats). This is one of many effective personal or business assessment tools to help identify problems and opportunities for growth and improvement.

Finally, to offer you some encouragement to look at your own mess and inspire you to clean it up, we will discuss common traits of successful individuals and companies.

Ask *What* not *Why*

When we make a mistake, rather than asking *why* it happened, ask *what* can I do differently? To paraphrase extensive research by Dr. Tasha Eurich in her book, *Insight*, asking *why* can often lead to us filling in the blanks with negative thought patterns that are counterproductive to increasing confidence and self-awareness. In other words, our judgment is clouded. Asking *what* focuses on solutions rather than more subjective causes and conditions.

This may seem contradictory to what I said earlier—that we need to know why we want something in order to have the motivation to persist. But in many respects, they are the same.

Let me explain.

Our *why* (motivation) is really a question of *what*. What drives us? What will it mean to us if we do or don't find the courage to face our fears, take a chance on ourselves, etc.? In other words, our motives (our why) are best answered by the question "what's in it for me?" (WIIFM).

What An Expert Has to Say about Self-Awareness

If you are interested in the psychology of motivation, you may want to research more on your own. I encourage you to do so, starting with the results of a recent study about self-awareness led by Dr. Tasha Eurich which can be found in her latest book entitled, *Insight*.

Dr. Eurich is an organizational psychologist, researcher, and *New York Times* bestselling author. In ten investigations of nearly 5,000 participants, Dr. Eurich and her team explored internal and external self-awareness—what each is, how they relate to our motives, and what we can do to increase them.

To paraphrase, Dr. Eurich says that to advance, we need to know what our motives are so we can determine if our current belief system is helping or prohibiting our ability to get what we want. She mentions how introspection alone is not enough because most are not doing it correctly.

In her Harvard Business Review article entitled, "What Self-Awareness is (And How to Cultivate it)" Dr. Eurich says, "As it turns out, *why* is a surprisingly ineffective self-awareness question." Her research shows that most do not have access to the deep-seated unconscious thought, feelings, or motives we are searching for.

The problem, as neuroscientist Stephen Campbell pointed out earlier, and Dr. Eurich's research validates, is the mind believes what we want it to.

Regarding our motives and trying to understand *why*, Dr. Eurich adds, "we tend to invent answers that feel true." Even if they are wrong. That's a problem because it creates a false sense of confidence based on faulty beliefs.

This is important to understand because introspection and self-awareness are integral, not only to understanding our motives, responses, thoughts, and actions, but vital to improving our self-esteem and self-confidence.

What's more, most people are not as self-aware as they believe they are. The data from Dr. Eurich's research showed that only 10-15% of the people they studied fit the criteria for being self-aware. However, most rated themselves more self-aware than their peers did. Once again, research validates the premise that our minds are not as reliable as we think they are.

Now that we have a little more insight from a self-awareness expert, can we agree that advancing toward our goals and ambitions will require deeper analysis, assessment, and action? We don't need to ask more *why* questions, which can quickly lead us down a path of negativity further exacerbating the problems we are trying to solve. Instead, to become more self-confident and aware, we should be asking ourselves more *what* questions. Doing so gets to the heart of what drives us and will provide us with the greatest opportunity for improvement.

Carefully consider these five questions, some of which we have already talked about earlier.

1. What do you think you want and why?
2. What are you good at?
3. What do you like or not like?
4. What is really holding you back?
5. What are you grateful for?

Prompt #1: Self-Assessment Exercise

Take twenty minutes total to answer each of the above questions. Put your answers on five separate pages, one question per page. If your page is full, stop and move on to the next question. Once you've answered all five questions, take a ten-minute break.

When you return, compare these answers to any you have previously written. What do you see? If there are similarities, circle them. These are the big issues for you to resolve. They fall under your "what" category.

Continuing to ask these five questions will help you increase your self-awareness. You may also want to add more specific personal questions that help you clarify what you want or feel you need to work on.

For example:

- What do I do well?
- What do I like and what would I like to be different?
- What would I like to do better or have more of?
- What kind of person would I like to be, etc.?

Again, notice that all of these are *what* questions, not *how* or *why*.

It's easy to fall into the how to or why to trap before we have clearly identified what we want. Don't get me wrong. *Why* questions are important, but more as they relate to what motivates you, and even then, as I mentioned earlier and Dr. Eurich validated, *what* is a better question to ask than *why*.

My apologies, if you feel like you have just been put through the Abbott and Costello routine, "Who's on first?" It is not my intention to create more confusion. We'll explore this further in the section, Find Your Why.

For now, in terms of becoming more self-aware, I urge you to avoid the temptation to self-diagnose and go down the rabbit hole of trying to figure out *why* things are as they are. Instead focus on *what you want and what you can do about it*. This is one reason why I think "self-help" as a non-fiction genre is a misnomer. We cannot do everything on our own. None of us is "self-made."

There is nothing wrong with research. It's part of learning. Most of us are curious and love to solve problems. But unless we are experts, we should stop pretending we are.

Besides, that's why there are coaches, counselors, and therapists. They are experts whose job is to help you peel back the onion layers and expose causes and conditions that will enable you to not only understand how they came to be, but, more importantly, help guide you to healthy solutions.

Forward

To help me stay focused after I've identified a problem and made a decision to start working on a goal or some behavior I want to improve or remove, and to help alleviate my tendency to procrastinate, I frequently ask myself these questions: "Will this move me closer to where I want to be? Is it in alignment with my purpose? Am I avoiding something uncomfortable? What moves me? What do I get excited about?"

As you find clarity about who you are and who you want to become, as well as what you want to do, you will likely become energized. Keep searching and trusting that you are moving forward.

Do small things repeatedly until they become habits that will eventually lead you to success; to becoming the person you want to be. Building healthy habits requires discipline and repetition. That is why I have included simple but challenging prompts throughout the book. They are specifically designed to help you eliminate old habits and develop new ones. Do not expect any earth shattering results, without effort.

I encourage you to do them.

Incrementalism

Steve Lavin referred to this positive habit building process as "incrementalism." But he also added that over time we tend to amplify the values and virtues, "the fundamentals of achievement" to where we eventually find "joy in practice. Joy in refinement. Joy in rehearsal."

To Steve's point, self-awareness is about character and mindset. It's about developing traits and virtues that build up rather than tear down our self-esteem. We develop healthy self-esteem with practice and repetition until we form a new habit.

This process never ends.

As you peel back one more layer of the onion, you discover more about what you value and where you need to improve. To refine your character, your belief systems, and your conduct so you reduce and minimize your negative traits and expand those which serve your greater vision of who you want to be.

The Twelve Values

Below are twelve values I discovered from a friend a while ago. While similar the twelve steps of various recovery programs, they are not directly part of nor sanctioned by them. I am including them because I believe they are fundamental pillars to building our self-esteem.

When I practice them on a regular basis, I am happier, have less stress, and don't worry as much about things I can't control. In short, as another friend frequently says, these twelve values are integral to "doing the next right thing." Here they are:

1. **Honesty** – Fairness and straight forwardness of conduct: adherence to the facts
2. **Hope** – To expect with desire; something on which hopes are centered
3. **Faith** – Complete confidence; belief and trust
4. **Courage** – Firmness of mind and will in the face of extreme difficulty; mental or moral strength to withstand fear
5. **Integrity** – The quality or state of being complete or undivided; soundness

6. **Willingness** – Prompt to act or respond; accepted and done of choice or without reluctance
7. **Humility** – Not proud or haughty; not arrogant or assertive; a clear and concise understanding of what we are, followed by a sincere desire to become what we can be
8. **Love** – Unselfish concern that freely accepts another in loyalty and seeks his good to hold dear
9. **Discipline** – Training that corrects, molds, or perfects the mental faculties or moral character; to bring under control; to train or develop by instruction
10. **Patience/Perseverance** – Steadfast despite opposition or adversity; able or willing to bear; to persist in an understanding in spite of counter influences
11. **Awareness** – Alive and alert; vigilance in observing
12. **Service** – A helpful act; contribution to the welfare of others; useful labor that does not produce a tangible commodity

By Unknown Author

Law of Reciprocity: Eyes Off Self and Onto Others

Being aware of and doing my best to live by these principles has been crucial to improving my own self-confidence and reshaping my worldview. Their power really lies in how we use and apply them in our relationships with others. It's a paradox. When we take our eyes off ourselves and focus on others, we actually gain so much more. It's a law of reciprocity. Of giving to receive.

If you want to be seen as trustworthy, be trustworthy. If you want to be seen as courageous, be bold. If you want to be perceived as dependable, be accountable to yourself and others. In other words, be a person of conviction and integrity. To do so requires discernment and personal responsibility. Let your own moral compass guide you. Be mindful of areas where you may be selfish, self-centered, or afraid.

Also, remember the golden rule. Grandma was right, "You catch more flies with honey than vinegar." Before you say something you may later regret, pause for a few seconds, channel your inner Rumi and ask, "Is it true? Is it necessary? Is it kind?" If what you are about to say doesn't pass muster, it is probably best to keep your trap shut. Trust me. It's not worth the potential backlash. Words can hurt. Choose yours carefully.

When you think about it, honesty is really at the core of becoming more self-aware and therefore more self-confident. For true transformation to occur, as I said in the beginning, you'll need to start by being honest with yourself.

A Lesson in Honesty and Humility

In Shakespeare's *Hamlet*, Polonius offers one last piece of advice to his son Laertes: "This above all: to thine own self be true, And it must follow, as the night the day, Thou canst not then be false to any man."

If you are not honest with yourself about *what* you want or *why* you want it and are not humble enough to ask for help or learn something new, then your chance of success is greatly diminished.

Again, this may sound counterintuitive to many, but as I mentioned earlier, the biggest threat to my own success has been overreliance on my own willpower. This notion of individuality and self-reliance that has been pounded into our heads—that we must have all the answers and do the work ourselves in order to feel worthy—is not entirely true. In fact, as mentioned earlier, self-help can be a liability not an asset.

After we invest thousands of hours studying, learning, and mastering our craft, we can become experts. But claiming to be an expert after attending a seminar or reading a book or two, without application, effort, or continuous learning, is not only pompous, it's foolish. And yet…

Even expert surgeons, scientists, and leaders or elite athletes, actors, or performers, are always learning, always being honest with themselves about what they did well and where they could improve. Experts stay on the cutting edge of their chosen field of interest or vocation. They seek honest feedback so they can be better.

True greatness demands continuous, honest self-assessment, as well as feedback from others. The Beatles became great because they practiced and performed as a group as much as they could. Steph Curry has an intensive workout regimen and warmup routine. He and many others who are "great" put in the work necessary to become great. They don't settle for average.

> **You will not be an expert overnight. Stop thinking you can.** There is always room for improvement. That's what I love about life: being a perpetual student, always learning something new, and continuously improving, a little bit, every day.

Prompt #2: Bridging Your Gap

Referring back to your "What I want" lists, consider what's missing. For example: Suppose you have written down "I want to make $100,000 per year." Ask yourself, "What's missing?" What do you think you need to do to bridge the gap between present reality (your current income in this instance) and future success (your goal of wanting to earn $100,000 per year)?

Start with this fill-in-the-blank exercise: To get _____ I think I need to (do, change, ask, etc.) _____. That's it, for now. Think of this exercise like conditioning camp for athletes, to get in good mental shape before you work on fundamental drills.

When you're done, take a break. Have a milkshake. Listen to the wind. Call a friend or relative. Take some time to let this sink in.

Congratulations, you have made great strides forward.

Success and Greatness is Learned and Earned

Most people we would consider successful or great have at least five things in common: They are *bold, passionate* about life and their goals, *humble* and never stop learning, *confident*, and *have great communication skills.* In a nutshell, they have everything we are talking about. Success and greatness always circle back to personal effort, experiences, values, and beliefs.

Those who are successful invest the time to learn, prepare, and rehearse what they need to in order to feel successful. They understand that risk and making mistakes is part of the process. In fact, their process is what makes them successful.

They are really no different than you or me. They had a dream and vision of who they could be and were bold enough to try something new and humble enough to ask for help to get what they want. It's a winning formula, a habit, if you will, that begets more success.

I don't know what your dreams are or what motivates you, but as I mentioned earlier, 85% of us suffer from some form of low self-esteem at various times in our lives. If you sometimes feel like you are part of the 85%, keep reading.

Are You Brave Enough to Try Something New?

Those who want to become more confident are usually the ones **brave enough to do something different so they can succeed.** They are highly self-aware individuals who have developed the wisdom to know what they need to work on individually (putting their own masks on first, so to speak), so they can improve their own character traits—confidence, courage, belief, etc. (internal) so they can be more effective, productive, and prosperous (external and internal).

Embrace the Gray

I don't do gray well, but I'm trying to learn to like it.

I prefer things that are black or white. Linear patterns of cause and effect. If this, then that. To me, it's easier. Predictable. But it can also be boring.

Life is far more than either/or. In fact, it's often the gray areas of life that make it so interesting. *Creativity and resourcefulness are found in the gray spaces between black and white.* **The unknown is where you harness the limitless power of your imagination** to make sense of the one hundred and fifty shades of gray in your mind. *It is in the gray that you discover yourself, your strength, your mettle, and your capacity for innovation.*

A Fork in the Road

In early recovery, my mom gave me another greeting card. On the front, was a kid on a dirt road staring up at a wooden signpost with a puzzled look on his face. On the post were two whitewashed, crisscrossed boards in the shape of arrows. One pointed to the left and read, "Don't look back." The other, pointing the opposite direction read, "This way." Inside my mom said, "Son, you've come too far to go back now. Keep putting one foot in front of the other. I'm so proud of you. Love, Mom."

You have a decision to make with respect to what you want to do about your problems. You already hold the keys to unlock the door to greater self-confidence and much more. The question is *do you choose to stay where you are, safe but wanting more? Retreat to what is familiar and comfortable? Or do you chose to use the key, unlock the door, and be bold enough to step through it to see what's on the other side?*

Nobody else can make the decision for you.

If you are willing to keep following a few more simple suggestions and apply them to the problems and goals you have already identified in the preceding chapters, your life will be transformed.

How you think about yourself and your goals will change if you do the introspection necessary to find your inner strength and motivation. You will develop more self-confidence by becoming bold enough to take the first step. And then another. And another. Even when you fall down, keep getting back up again. Just like a toddler learning to walk, with each step your confidence will grow. You may even get that wide-eyed smile of joy—like the one we see in kids' faces when they finally realize they did something big like take their first steps or pass their drivers test. They know because hopefully Mom or Dad or someone important in their life was there to say, "Good job." I say hopefully because a little praise and recognition go a long way toward building confidence and self-esteem in all of us, especially our kids.

Patience and Delayed Gratification

Patience is paramount. Practice delayed gratification, knowing that each step you take is moving you closer to who you want to be, or what you want to have or do. Put in the quality time and effort and leave the results up to the universe. **Don't fixate on the outcome. Focus on the present. Here. Now.** Ask what you can do now to move you closer to the goal you have established. Then do something. Every time you do is like a deposit on your confidence bank. That is worth more than anything else. Why? Because nobody can ever take it away. It is not subject to business cycles. It is yours. Don't let anyone or anything steal it from you.

Expect setbacks, mistakes, and problems. Like change, they are inevitable. Learn from them and adapt. Don't expect perfection, at least immediately. Instead, strive for progress.

It is well known that many high achievers are control freaks and perfectionists, including me at times. We are never satisfied. We over-think and over-analyze things to death because our fear of failure is so great, we rarely ever start. Somewhere we developed the belief system that we must be certain of success in order to pursue a given endeavor. That's not true.

Besides where's the fun in that? Nearly every major breakthrough in my life was not planned. Expecting perfection is playing God. We are not that powerful. For my faith-filled friends, I offer this—pray and do your part to minimize risk (follow the five steps), and get started, even if you are only 80% confident of success. Don't rob yourself of the unknown power of the universe to fill in the gaps. If you truly have faith and belief, this should not be a problem.

That's tough because, if you are like me, you are impatient. You want what you want when you want it. And that is usually right now. Again, that's not how life works.

The sooner we learn the art and habit of patience and delayed gratification, the happier and more successful we will be. Why? Because we won't be wasting precious mental energy on worry, doubt, and insecurity. We will develop trust in our process and stop trying to control things we cannot. That enables us to invest more time and energy into planning and doing the things that we can control, such as attitude and effort.

Patience is a Learned Skill

Just like confidence, patience is an acquired skill and habit. As you gain more knowledge and experience from *doing, not thinking*, your confidence increases as does your patience. That's true for just about anything—your commute, the amount of time it takes to bake cookies, or how long it takes you to mow your lawn. After you do something enough times you know about how much time it takes to accomplish it.

When it comes to doing new things, give yourself more time to learn, to adapt, to master. It's called a learning curve for a reason. Stop placing unrealistic expectations on your outcome because you see how easy it is for someone else. Find your own rhythm, your own pace, and own it.

Prompt #3: Next Steps, Now

List two to three areas of struggle you would like to resolve, or two or three areas of opportunity you would like to explore further. Ask yourself, *what are the next few steps I can immediately take to progress?*

Minimize Expectations and Disappointment: Do the Work and Let Go of the Results

It doesn't mean you put in half-assed effort and expect miracles. Nor does it mean you pray and hope for the best, yet do nothing. *Building confidence takes effort.* Everything in life requires showing up and *doing something.*

Stop expecting immediate results without getting knocked down a few times. Get in the game, take your hits, but keep getting up. Eventually, if you never give up, you will develop the confidence you need to succeed at virtually anything you wish.

These are very simple steps. But it begs the question: if they are so simple, *why are there not more people who are successful?* I don't know, exactly. I believe it's because most of us think too much. We analyze, study, worry, and tell ourselves a hundred and one reasons why we can't do something or why something won't work. And guess what? As Stephen Campbell mentioned earlier, "We're right" most of the time. This is not a new phenomenon. People have battled with worry, fear, doubt, insecurity, and perfectionism forever. Probably always will. Every one of these responses are anchors. Anchors set deep in the mud of the ocean floor, which hold us back from becoming more self-confident, productive, and prosperous at home or work. You probably will never be fully rid of them, but you can learn to minimize the negative effects they have on your life, as you weigh anchor.

Look Inside First

As I mentioned earlier, start by taking a thorough and honest inventory of your strengths and weaknesses, likes and dislikes, habits ("good" and "bad", and everything in between) and attitudes about yourself, others, and the world around you. There are many free tools available online to help guide you to greater self-awareness. One is a SWOT analysis.

SWOT Analysis

In college, I learned a concept called a SWOT analysis. SWOT is an acronym for Strengths, Opportunities, Weaknesses, and Threats. For those not familiar, it is basically a rubric for businesses to evaluate their company's health in relation to its competition and/or the market. But a SWOT analysis is an evaluation tool, not a strategy. As such, it's an effective tool to address our first step: Identify the problem or opportunity.

Simply put, a business must know why it exists in the first place. In other words, what problem does it solve? Who does it help? Is the company's vision and mission clear? Are the company expectations and benefits clearly communicated to all stakeholders—leadership, staff, customers, vendors, and, if a publicly held corporation, shareholders? Are they embraced by and reflected in the company culture? In other words, does the brand have significant value?

What's Your Brand? What Do You Want to be Known For?

Before you can answer that, you need to know *what you want*. Do you know your strengths and weaknesses? Are there threats to your health, ability to earn a living, or relationships that you have been avoiding? Have you admitted that you are not good at certain things but really good at others? If so, what are they? Are there things you think you'd like to do or be or have but lack the confidence or tools necessary to take the first step? If so, *write them down*.

If you are anything like me, looking inside at how we think and what makes us tick is a daunting task, one we tend to put off until the first rainy day in November. Well guess what? Like a sliver under your fingernail, avoiding reality is a problem which only leads to more pain and possible infection. Eventually you'll need to grab a pair of tweezers and yank that sucker out. Then and only then will the infection go away, and the wound begin to heal. Once you identify the problem or what you want, and are honest about your current reality, then and only then is it appropriate for you to begin to exploring solutions.

Stop Worrying About What You Don't Have and Start Working With What You Do.

Questioning your values, dreams, and purpose in life is normal. The relentless pursuit of improvement is part of who you are. To the extent that you allow it, your past shapes our future. What you think about, dream about, worry about is both an asset and a liability. It can be an asset for clarity and conviction if you rely heavily on logic to solve your problems. But while analysis, data, and application of scientific methods are integral to discovering solutions to many problems, when it comes to building confidence or any personal development needs, they are missing a key variable: Emotion and the human experience. The internal web of thoughts, beliefs, biases, and socially programmed or learned ideals, are as unique as your fingerprints. You already have what you need to solve most of your problems.

You cannot logic your way into self-confidence. Take a risk and **stop analyzing and start experiencing.** In other words, you need to fail so you can feel what it's like to fully experience success.

Obsessed with More

There is another pandemic: more. A major problem for most of us, is we are never content. We attach our happiness to things outside of us: people and things beyond our control. We have become a culture obsessed with more. As a result, we are never satisfied. We want more money, bigger homes, and fancier cars.

We've accepted this as normal in our marketing and ad-driven culture and it's driving us mad. I've heard this mindset referred to as "scarcity" thinking. That we never feel like we have enough.

The corollary is abundance thinking. A mindset of possibility and resource and a belief system that is solution oriented, rather than problem based. A belief system that understands the natural ebb and flow and cycles of the universe. A mindset that understands there is plenty to share and that we don't need scramble to fill our plates, like a hungry teenagers at dinner time, or our shopping carts with sixty rolls of toilet paper during a pandemic because we're afraid we will run out!

Life's Not Fair. It is What it is.

The brutal fact is this: **You are where you are as a direct result of the decisions you've made to get there.** As my mom used to say, "Life's unfair." Bad things happen to good people. And vice versa. It's all out of our control. To rise above or move closer to where we want to be, we must take responsibility for our own response to life's rotten tomatoes that hit us in the face. And it starts with an honest self-assessment. The good news is, that you've already started. Each of the previous prompts are part of the self-assessment process.

Prompt #4: Complete a SWOT analysis

Grab a fresh sheet of paper or a word doc and create four columns. Label each with the appropriate headers: Strengths, Weakness, Opportunities, and Threats. Choose one or more of the wants, needs, problems, or opportunities you have already written thus far, then in the appropriate columns, list your skills, abilities, and obstacles to you accomplishing what you want. When you are done, you should have a clearer picture of what you already have, what you need to eliminate, and where you need to improve. This exercise is your frame for improvement and positive change.

Note: Use the opportunity column of the SWOT analysis to list the benefits/outcomes you expect once you solve or accomplish that which you are seeking.

Strengths:
_____
_____
_____
_____
_____
_____

Weaknesses:
_____
_____
_____
_____
_____
_____

Opportunities:
_____
_____
_____
_____
_____
_____

Threats:
_____
_____
_____
_____
_____
_____

Chapter Eight
Ten Seconds of Boldness: Finding Courage Within to Start

"Courage starts with showing up and letting ourselves be seen."
Brené Brown

Are You a Cowardly Lion or a King/Queen of the Forest?

I remember when my son, Andrew, was in third grade, he played the role of the Cowardly Lion in the Wizard of Oz. Like me at a young age, my son was shy. I knew this part was causing him major anxiety, but he did it anyway.

When the time came, he took centerstage, in his tan lion costume, puffed out his chest, and in as big of a voice as he could muster, delivered the powerful line, "If I were king of the forrrrrest!"

I lost it. I was so proud of him. He did it! In my book, Andrew was the king of the forest.

Once you've spent some quality time soul-searching and completing a thorough self-assessment, you'll need a little courage to put it into action. *Ten Seconds of Boldness* should be enough to get started. In theory this works fine, until you start overthinking the decisions you need to make.

Putting *Ten Seconds of Boldness* into Action

Sometimes it may feel as like you need to psych yourself up to make the decision to act or not. For me, my confidence seems to rise and fall based on my level of fear. To counteract that, I use this concept of *Ten Seconds of Boldness* and a few other tools to muster the courage I need to face whatever is blocking me from moving forward.

More specifically, I pray. One of my favorites to use is the serenity prayer which we have already discussed. Another prayer I say frequently is this: "God guide me and give me the courage I need to be confident and decisive in all of my affairs throughout the day so I can be of maximum service to you and others."

I use *Ten Seconds of Boldness*. I say a prayer in my head, breathe, visualize what I would like the outcome of my efforts to be, and take whatever action is necessary in that moment. For example, anything that I am avoiding—a decision, a phone call, a conversation, a task— the point is, I don't overthink or procrastinate my decision as often as I used to. I find the courage I need and act immediately.

Sometimes if I feel myself getting too uptight, wound up, or like I am spinning my wheels, I just stop whatever I am doing. Rather than continue to try to force my effort, I stop and go for a walk or do something for someone else. Anything to get out of my own head for a moment.

Stopping when you need to regroup is a bold move, especially if for those who have difficulty delegating, or asking for help, or letting go. Or if you feel like your whole world will fall apart if you are not there to do it all. Guess what? It won't.

The work will be there when you get back. When you return, you will likely have more clarity and get more done in a shorter time than if you keep trying push through whatever obstacles are in your path. In fact, studies have proven we are more productive when we take breaks. *So, stop trying to "figure it all out" and take some time to chill.*

If you struggle with control and letting go, I recommend you read *Don't Sweat the Small Stuff, and it's all Small Stuff,* by bestselling author, Richard Carlson. He reminds us, when facing a problem, to ask ourselves if it will matter a year from now. Almost always it won't. When I would go to my stepfather, David, with a problem, he'd listen. When he felt I was done, inevitably he'd grin, then ask me, "Do you think this will matter five years from now?" I always said no.

I can't remember what I had for dinner two weeks ago, so why should I get worked up over something that's not really going to matter in the grand scheme of things? I know, it's easy to talk about, but much harder to actually do.

The better you get at knowing what you want and why you want it, as well as what you *are* or *are not* willing to do, the easier it will become to find the courage to go get it. As previously discussed, discernment is developed through a combination of self-awareness, clarity, conviction, and courage. Put another way, *the road to greatness and self-confidence starts with a bit of courage, vision, motivation, planning, and action.*

Building a Brick House, One Brick at a Time

Like a mason, confidence is built *brick by brick.* One layer at a time, held together with mortar. The choices you make in life are the bricks. The mortar is your confidence, the cement that holds it all together. Without it, your structure will crumble and fall.

Every choice, every decision, every dream, every plan, goal, or problem is yet another opportunity to place a brick, secure it with mortar, and build a structure that will last a lifetime or longer. The structure is you, your life, ambitions, who you are and what you want to be.

Finding Courage

None of the anxious moments I've experienced over the past few decades—from my first date, first job, first speech, first book, to making cold calls for work—were threatening enough to cause my adrenal glands to flood my body with courage-inducing chemicals that initiate a fight, flight, or freeze response. But I longed for that adrenaline rush or dopamine hit of immense pleasure as after a good meal or sex. Instead, I turned to drugs and alcohol. That worked for a while. Then the fear of death set in. Once sober, I had to find a new way.

It always came back to taking a breath and having ten seconds of courage and jumping in. This concept is not new. Look around at people you would consider successful. Learn about those you admire or want to emulate. I guarantee you they all have one thing in common, **courage**.

Prompt: Quick Brainstorm

Take a sheet and create two columns. Above the columns write: What is most important to me

At Work	In Relationships

Then start listing all the things that you value. For example, at work, praise, recognition, respect, and money. Under "Relationships" you may include trust, love, people who are good listeners, kind, or good with kids. It's your list, make it personal. Take five minutes to do this now.

Note: All the reflection and introspection you have done with each of the prompts will make the rest of the action steps so much easier. Hopefully you are beginning to have a clearer idea of the work you need to do to get to where you want to be.

The next section will smooth the rough edges of your ideas thus far and help you formulate the next key steps of planning and action in sections IV and V. Now let's dive into section II, on decision making.

Section II
Clearly Decide What You Want

- ◊ Five Key Questions to Become More Decisive
- ◊ Make a Decision and Don't Overthink or Second Guess it
- ◊ The Five Decisions
- ◊ The Not-So-Secret Power of Prayer, Meditation, and Creative Visualization
- ◊ Finding Ten Seconds of Boldness to Become More Decisive
- ◊ Building Clarity, Vision, Mission, and Purpose

Chapter Nine
Five Key Questions to Become More Decisive

"Indecision is the greatest thief of opportunity."
Jim Rohn

It took me ten years to earn my college degree. There are several reasons why. One was that I didn't believe I had strong enough math skills to pass calculus and statistics, prerequisites for me to finish my upper division courses.

I only needed a few more classes before I could graduate but statistics and calculus stood in my way. I had already dropped them three times and was ready to throw in the towel. After nine years of school, I called my mom to say I was thinking about quitting.

She reminded me that it was my decision to go in the first place. She didn't try to convince me otherwise. She knew my ambitions and supported me regardless of the path I chose. In essence, she told me to be true to myself.

I thought about it and realized that my dream to earn a degree was greater than my fear of failing, and the only way for me to matriculate was to pass these classes and the handful of others afterward.

As I mentioned earlier, I made a decision and did what I had to in order to earn a bachelor's degree in Business Administration from San Francisco State University. Ultimately, it took me four times before I passed statistics and calculus. Ironically, I earned an A in each of them.

In the my semester, reality started to set in. Now that I had come this far, I worried that it would all be for nothing because I didn't know exactly what career path to take. I had invested thousands of dollars and hours to earn a piece of paper that said I earned a college degree. That I was worthy. And yet, I was lost. I had no real-world experience in marketing or advertising, nor did I know what area to pursue.

Sure, I had a general idea of the types of jobs available, but I was unsure whether I would like them or even be good at them. *I didn't know what I didn't know and had no clue where to start.* So, I asked my mom what I should do. She suggested I talk to my stepfather, David O'Connor who, at the time, had over four decades of experience in marketing and advertising. It turned out to be one of the smartest decisions I made in my young adult life.

Be Brave Enough to Ask For Help, Again and Again

It was a cool spring day, in April. My stepfather David and I sat outside on the deck of his hillside home in West Marin beneath old oaks and towering pines, talking about my future.

I don't recall how the conversation started, but I do remember feeling my heart thump in my chest because at that point, I felt as if I should know what career to pursue but had no real clue. I had never even written a resume.

I was lost.

"Congratulations!" he started. "You're graduating and you're going to get married. That's terrific! Now what do you think you want to be when you grow up? What kind of job do you want?" Immediately I felt my gut tighten and stammered a feeble reply. "I don't know, that's why I am here." He continued trying to get me to open up, to say what I wanted. I grew frustrated because he wasn't telling me what I should do. Instead, he was trying to guide me to figure it out for myself.

David, perhaps sensing my trepidation, told me something I will never forget. He said, "You are one of the most courageous people I know."

Surprised, I leaned back in my chair. "What do you mean?" I asked.

"You not only found the courage to stop drinking at a young age, but you have the grit and determination to finish school and start a family at the same time. That takes guts." For the next hour or so, I asked him more relevant questions to zero in on what I might or might not like in a career. He also assured me that no career decisions are final. That it is perfectly normal and acceptable, even advantageous, for people to change jobs. He added, "Most people work for six or seven different employers in their lifetimes." With his coaching, I decided to pursue a career in media sales. Next, he helped me come up with a game plan.

That meeting took place nearly thirty years ago. I have used those lessons numerous times since. In fact, I can hear David's deep powerful encouraging voice in my head as I continue to grapple with my own lack of confidence as an author: "It sounds to me like you already know what you want to write about. I say, go for it!"

It took a while for me to get used to his direct coaching style. Like a curious five-year-old, he would keep asking me *why* over and over and over again until I got pissed off.

Maybe that was part of his plan. I never asked. But it worked. I will always remain grateful for all the times he mentored me before his passing.

In hindsight, the love and wisdom he shared with me have become some of the most valuable lessons I've learned in life.

Without a solid reason why or a benefit to me or others, I am prone to wander aimlessly, chasing dreams and goals, and what I think I should be, rather than looking inside or asking for advice.

As David challenged me, I hope you not only discover the power of bold decision making, but in the process, become more confident as you continue to ask yourself *why*.

Confidence Changes Everything

Why is being confident so important to us? For me, confidence is like money—life is generally easier when I have more. That begs the obvious question, how do we get more?

Those critical questions could be asked and applied to virtually any quality, skill, goal, opportunity, or plan, we want to develop, or any obstacle, challenge, or problem, we want to overcome or resolve. What can we do to become more confident, perhaps even "unstoppable," or a "Bad Ass." Where do we look? What do we have to do?

Make a Decision

You may be asking, "What if I can't?" Then start with what you think you want and commit to making it happen. Ask for advice. You don't have to do it all alone.

You will never know what you are capable of until you find the courage to start. And the best part is the rewards will likely be greater than you could even imagine.

Unexpected Rewards From Fatherly Advice

Here are some unexpected insights and rewards of that conversation with David O'Connor thirty years ago:

1. It launched me on a successful career path that continues to this day, even though after the first two weeks on the job, I wanted to quit.
2. It led to me getting married, having a wonderful handsome son, and buying a house.
3. It helped me navigate other tough decisions I've had to make in the years since and be bold enough to start over in jobs, relationships, and attitudes.
4. It helped me accept and embrace change. As the publisher at my job frequently says, "The only thing constant in life is change."
5. But one of the most impactful rewards for me was having an opportunity to share that story with my son when he came to me for advice about changing his educational path. He, too, asked questions, then made his own decisions. Two years later, he earned a Bachelor of Computer Science at Sonoma State University and is currently employed by a well-known company in the sports gaming industry. I am so proud of who he is and what he's done so far in his young life. What more could a parent want?

Which Way Do I Go?

As a kid I loved Looney Tunes. *Bugs Bunny*, *The Road Runner*, and the Merrie Melodies Cartoon *Of Fox and Hounds*. For those who may recall, George was a smart aleck fox who loved to mess with a dumb hound, Willoughby. George disguised himself as a hound and when Willoughby asked George, "Which way did he go?" Referring to the fox. George would point over a fence across a field, and pokerfaced would say, "He went that-a-way." That-a-way was off a cliff. Sick and twisted as it was, it was hilarious.

Cartoons are supposed to be funny. But for us, deciding which way to go is no laughing matter, especially if we feel like we are headed for a cliff.

Indecision doesn't have to feel like a crisis. Sure, making tough decisions and asking for help takes guts. Because it means trusting that those who give you guidance aren't like George the fox. That they aren't going to lead you down a crumbly sandstone path and off a dangerous cliff to be impaled by the jagged rocks in the pounding surf below.

Find a guide you can trust and the courage to follow some suggestions then take the first steps. The path is not so dangerous if you know where to step.

You become more confident you we make clear decisions and see them through. Ultimately, the choices you make and paths you are fully your responsibility. You get to accept the results of those decisions or make new ones. That's it. *The decisions you make only have power over you to the extent that you allow them to.*

Building self-confidence comes from the experience and wisdom of making thousands and thousands of decisions and mistakes. You learn to make better decisions after you've made a few poor ones. Or at least that's what you can hope for.

Referring back to chapter seven about self-awareness and self-assessment, here are five questions for your consideration:

1. What are you good at or like to do?
2. What do you think you want?
3. Why do you want it?
4. What is holding you back?
5. What are you willing to do to get it?

Prompt: Answer the Five Questions Above

Before you read on, I urge you to spend five minutes writing down your answers to the five questions above. If you already wrote them down in chapter seven, do it again. Then compare your answers to your original thoughts. Look for similarities and focus on those things that you feel are most important now, ones that you feel passionate about.

Stay focused on your objectives and motives—*what* you want and *why* you want it. Understand too, that it's perfectly normal for your motivation, goals, and problems to change over time. Roll with your passion, but don't be like chaff in the wind. Stay focused long enough to resolve. Long enough to understand success.

This iterative process will help you develop the habits of perpetual self-evaluation and assessment as you continue to keep asking yourself, *why* and *what drives me?*

Again, with practice you will become more courageous, confident, and decisive to take the next step forward.

The next chapter will cover tools you may use for effective decision-making and how you can become more resolute.

Chapter Ten
Make a Decision and Don't Overthink or Second Guess It

"Don't let process get in the way of productivity. That's a form of procrastination."
Crissi Langwell

This chapter expands upon what we discussed in chapter four, "How to Tame Our Inner Critics" We will briefly discuss common decision-making roadblocks before completing a simple self-assessment exercise.

Ever Been Stuck at the Corner of Walk and Don't Walk?

We've all been there before, at the corner of walk and don't walk. We're stuck because, we are not sure exactly where we want to go. Or, if we do know where we want to go, we are not sure about the best way to get there. So, *we loiter in doubt and indecision, stuck.*

It's no surprise we feel stuck, or perhaps even stressed and overwhelmed with the multitude of choices we must make daily. According to various studies, we make more than 30,000 decisions every day. That's a lot of decisions to process. And not all are easy or routine, such as brushing our teeth, or getting the kids ready for school. When weighing our options for bigger things such as goals, purpose, and direction for our life, we are like someone at a street corner, staring at the traffic signal in a trance, lost.

We press the button hoping that will make the light change quicker. We may step off the curb then the red warning light flashes, "Don't Walk." So, we wait. Perhaps we consider crossing the other direction. The one where the icon flashes a white cartoon character walking. Or maybe we follow the voice from a hidden speaker above, that barks, "Walk. Walk. Walk."

Whatever intersection we are at the simple fact is this: **We can't just stand there.**

As Crissi's quote at the start of this chapter suggests, don't get hung up on the process. Instead, keep an open mind and have fun with it.

The self-awareness exercise in the prompt below is specifically designed to help you identify and clarify your skills and strengths as they relate to achieving your goals. And it will allow you an opportunity to see where you need to improve.

Clarity is critical in making decisions. Writing down what you have and don't have or can and can't do is a major step to becoming more decisive.

Beware of Poor Planning, Laziness, and Fear

I'll rat myself out. As often as I have preached about writing things down, I am often too impatient to take the time to think things through enough to establish a clear plan. I keep pushing the button faster, hoping the light will change sooner. It never does.

I'm pretty good about writing down goals about money and income and to-do lists. And most of that stuff gets done. But when it comes to bigger deeper issues, I waffle. I procrastinate, just like most of us. My struggle is real.

When faced with new problems or opportunities, it's easier for me to rely on old habits and outdated decision-making criteria. But old thinking is not always the best thinking. It can often lead to greater problems or keep us stuck in a pattern of thinking and behavior that feels like we are in a pit. I once heard someone say that the best way to get out of a hole is to stop digging.

The problem lies in my false belief system that says if I ask for help, I may be perceived as weak or not confident. So, I forge forward with what I think is best and completely miss the opportunity to learn a new or better way of doing something.

I've done this all my life. Still do in many areas. Inevitably I lose creativity and an opportunity to be innovative. I avoid bigger decisions because I don't want to risk failure. Instead, I keep *doing things the same way expecting a different outcome* which, according to Albert Einstein, is the *definition of insanity*.

My decision-making becomes a habit, like brushing my teeth or washing my hair. No new thought needs to be put into it. When I apply old thinking to new and bigger decisions, I become complacent. Eventually, like companies that stop innovating, I risk withering away into obscurity and obsolescence.

Clearly deciding what you want is one of the most important action steps you can take. Now is the time to put into practice the concept of self-awareness discussed in the last section. Doing so will help you better evaluate and clarify what you have to work with and what motivates you. In addition, you will uncover things you don't have and things you need to get rid of to become more confident in the decisions you want or need to make.

Prompt #1: Self-Awareness Exercise

Start by making a two-column list of pros and cons for a decision you need to make in some area of your life—something you want to be, do, or have. To make this exercise easier, I have a created a "Self-Assessment Tool" which you can find in Appendix I. Copy and use as you wish. Find a free PDF at bit.ly/ShawnLangwellMotivation (case sensitive). It's important to invest the time to complete a fearless and thorough self-assessment. Don't just make a list in your head. *Write it down.* The act of writing it out will help clarify and cement your decisions into your subconscious mind and increase the likelihood of your success. Several studies support this claim. Self-assessment is the most rudimentary and, I would argue, effective evaluation tool in the world. Sadly, even though it's free, it is one of the least used.

I encourage you to use the self-assessment sheets in the appendix, but it's not required. If you don't want to use them, a pen and paper will work just as well.

Instructions:

Grab a sheet of paper and draw a line down the middle. On the left side write, "What I like about myself" Next to that write down, "What I'd like to change about myself."

Don't think too hard. Just write.

What I like about myself	What I'd like to change about myself

Grab another sheet: Draw another line vertically down the middle of the page. At the top of the left column write these words: "My Strengths." At the top of the right column label, it "My Weaknesses."

My Strengths	My Weaknesses

Continue this process for anything else you can think of, for example:
- What do I enjoy? Don't enjoy?
- What I am grateful for? What I am ashamed of?
- What makes me feel proud? What do I feel guilty about?
- Wins. Losses.
- What do I say to myself? What do others say about me?

We will build on this list later to address specific areas of *what* you want, and *why* you want it as well as creating a gratitude list. But for now, just write down your thoughts and let them simmer, then read on.

I've Done This Before. What's the Point?

The point of this exercise is to become comfortable looking inside and facing some of the things easily dismissed or swept away. The time you invest in *honestly completing a rigorous self-assessment without judgment or criticism will do two things:*

1. It will help you feel good about the things you do well or like about yourself.

2. By honestly looking at all the things you don't like or would like to change, it will diminish their power over you. And as long as you don't face them, they will continue to own you and therefore keep you where you are, stuck at the corner of Walk and Don't Walk.

That is why you need *Ten Seconds of Boldness*. Admitting your faults or shortcomings to yourself, let alone anyone else, is scary at first. But once you've done it a few times, it is easier. And the benefits are immeasurable. Not only will you gain confidence, but you will also create new habits that keep you moving away from *I can't* toward *I can*.

The last thing I want is for you to feel more shame or guilt about what you do or don't do, like or don't like about yourself. That is not helpful. But neither is living in denial. That shit will eat you alive. Yet we all deal with guilt, shame, denial, procrastination, etc. The trick is to stop. *Stop doing the things that perpetuate these feelings because they are not helping you become more confident.*

We All Do Stupid Shit, Sometimes

Because we are human, we're gonna do stupid shit. It reminds me of the time I stole firecrackers from my dad's dresser. I was four years old. I knew it wasn't right, but I wanted to blow up a beer can. I'd seen my cousin do it on the Fourth of July and also had watched my dad do it, too, in the vacant lot next to our house in Daly City. I loved the bang!

Nobody found out because I couldn't get the match to light. But I still felt guilty and told Mom. When she told Dad, I got the belt.

But that didn't stop me from trying something else. Sometime later, I took some newspaper down to a fort my dad had built in the backyard. The fort was just a few pieces of plywood painted white and nailed to our fence. It looked more like a three-sided doghouse than a fort. Anyway, I took the paper and matches and went outside to make a "bonfire." My plan was to make one just like Grandpa used to at the cabin in Yosemite. "Keeps the skeeters away," he'd say tossing another log into the outdoor fire pit, while sipping a glass of wine, watching the hot flames rise into the starry night.

Only in Daly City, where we lived, there weren't any skeeters. Just cold, damp, heavy fog. So, I crumpled up some newspaper and set a match to it. Then a breeze caught the flaming "green section" (sports pages) of the San Francisco Chronicle and sent it airborne. Fascinated, I watched the glowing edges float into the fog. I watched them drift toward our neighbor's house and panicked. Those neighbors were super strict with their kids, all prim and proper. The ones whose kids thought playing Cowboys and Indians was super cool, but my mom and dad didn't, even though that's what kids played back then.

I digress. The point is that thankfully, no houses burned down, and nobody got hurt. But, unlike the firecracker incident, I couldn't hide this one. As soon I walked into the house, my mom asked, "Why do you smell like smoke?"

This time though, even after she told my dad, I didn't get the belt. Instead, my punishment was hearing about the time he caught his parents' house on fire. I wonder if that's why he became a fireman? I never had a chance to ask.

The point is, we all have done or will do stupid things that we are not proud of. Or we keep putting off things for a multitude of reasons (mostly fear-based) which are only more excuses to procrastinate. Some we keep repeating, as I did four years later, when a friend and I got caught by the Woodacre Fire Department for lighting a small grass fire in a drainage culvert.

Again, one healthy thing we can do to feel better is *admit when we make a mistake,* to ourselves or another, if our mistake affects others and it won't make a bigger mess when we do.

After that, *let it go* and strive to do better next time and not make the same mistakes over and over again. This last part is the best prevention to circumvent guilt and shame. And when we repeat the cycle, because we will, repeat the forgiveness steps of admitting our mistakes and vow to do better next time. *Then let it go until you stop doing the same stupid shit over and over again expecting different results.*

Now this stuff may seem obvious, but I forget that it took me a long time to learn some of it. Maybe Grandpa was right when he used to jokingly call me a "knucklehead." I may not be the sharpest tool in the shed in other areas, but when it comes to turning the compost heap of my mistakes into a beautiful yard, I'm a Master Gardener.

If you want to keep moving forward confidently in the direction you wish, then you need to minimize mistakes and setbacks and get back up when you fall.

Too often, we develop coping skills like justification, denial, and avoidance and pretend that we really don't need to change. Or worse, we compare ourselves to others and say, "I'm not that bad." Or "everyone else is doing it." Yeah, if you want to be like everyone else, then keep doing the same things, expecting different results. *If you want to be bold and confident, you're going to have to do something new. Something different.*

My Dysfunctional Relationship With Money and Debt

Let's talk about money and debt, because, for better or worse, both yield power and influence in our lives. I have had my own tumultuous relationship with money and debt, living paycheck to paycheck for more years than I'd like. Being broke but never hungry. Being in debt up to my eyeballs.

Today, I count my blessings that I have always been able to find work when I had to make ends meet. There are many who are not so fortunate, who have lost jobs, homes, and go to bed hungry. On the flip side, there are millions who have plenty, some way more than they could possibly spend in a lifetime. Any anxiety and stress related to financial concerns, especially debt, sucks. And when it comes to money, *I believe it is better to have more than you need and no debt than to have too little and mountains of debt.*

Fortunately, the tables have turned for our family in the past several years, but I never take our good fortune for granted.

Did you know that as of April 2022, the average personal savings rate in the United States is 4.4%? Yet in the middle of the pandemic in March of 2021, it was 26.6%. and in March of 2020 it peaked at 33.8%, the highest it's been in decades. Granted, travel and entertainment, as well as many other non-essential services were shut down so consumers had little to spend their money on.

But despite that, recent studies show that over *54% of people live paycheck to paycheck.*

Perhaps more surprising is that *40% of those earning over $100,000 per year are barely making ends meet.* Still other studies show that on average, *59% of Americans are a paycheck away from being homeless.* These stats are frightening.

Part of the problem is the cost of living, especially high relative housing costs as a proportion of income. The other, bigger problem is the amount of personal debt we carry. From credit cards to car and home loans, to student loans, millions barely earn enough money to cover all their monthly expenses.

According to finance guru, Dave Ramsey, the average household credit card debt in America is $14,241. The average car loan debt is $31,142. Combined, the average household debt is $14.96 trillion despite a collective net worth of $141 trillion. That may not seem like high leverage (a little more than 10%) for a business. But this is personal consumer debt. Given the precariousness of cash flow, job security, and high risk as already mentioned, money issues are crippling individuals and families.

Ten Seconds of Boldness will Improve Your Relationship with Money

If you want more money than month—enough to cover your expenses and have money left over for savings and entertainment—you need a financial plan. The five habits for solving any problem can help you develop better habits with money. So can taking a financial planning course like Dave Ramsey's *Financial Peace University* (Dave is not paying me for the plug), or many others.

My wife and I took Ramsey's *Financial Peace University* (*FPU*) Course four years ago and applied the principles Dave teaches to create an emergency savings account. I also set aside six months of income and paid off my car and all my credit card debt. We are still working on paying off the mortgage and a small personal loan. But we are well on our way to being debt free. It feels terrific. I don't like being broke or in debt. It's like trying to run a marathon while dragging a bag of rocks. It makes it very difficult to finish the race.

As of this writing, my wife and I are in Kauai celebrating an early ten-year anniversary. It has been one of the most relaxing and spectacular vacations ever, capped by a zodiac tour along the Na

Pali coast where we saw spinner dolphins, explored sea caves, snorkeled, and had a traditional kalua pork lunch, then toured an ancient Hawaiian Village. The sea was calm and weather perfect. An added bonus, no debt. The entire trip was prepaid with money we had saved.

Earlier, I mentioned that when my dad left, we were broke. We could never afford a trip like the one my wife and I just took. But we did what was necessary to survive. Sometimes that meant eating rice and beans because that's all we had. But it bothered me, a lot. And it also fired me up enough to make a decision to go make something of myself.

Soon I had a job and as a teenager made really good money in the restaurant business. While my mom taught me a lot about budgeting and stretching what we had to keep a roof over our head and food on the table, I had nobody to teach me about saving or building wealth.

I did what far too many people do without a plan. I pissed it all away, literally. I wasted thousands of dollars on beer and drugs. Later, it was gambling or racking up credit card debt or refinancing our home to buy another, only to have the market crash and nearly have to declare bankruptcy.

There is Nothing Wrong With Wanting to be Wealthy

Ever since reading *Richie Rich* comic books as a kid, I have wanted to be wealthy. Not only for me and my family, but for others I could bless with my abundance.

Which leads me to something I was going to leave out, but it's been nagging at me for over twenty years ever since I first started going to church and reading the Bible.

Even though I don't attend church anymore, I feel that the topics of money, ambition, and personal achievement need to be addressed because there's no clear-cut answer among believers. There doesn't have to be, with one exception, in my opinion: **greed and the love of money is not healthy for anyone.**

To add clarity to this loaded topic, I asked my friend Jason Lam, owner of a successful budget and financial coaching business called *Sentinel Coaching*, to share his opinion about material wealth from a biblical perspective.

My question to him was this:

Are Financial Goals Selfish and Therefore 'Sinful'?

Here's his thoughtful reply:

> I'm not a Bible scholar or theologian, but I do understand how life works and what I believe God wants for us here on this earth as His children. Many Christians will take scripture verses and break them apart bit by bit to understand what God is trying to say to us. There are many scriptures that talk about money, in fact, there are more than 2,300 verses that talk about money, but I'd like to take a different approach regarding this topic.
>
> If we take three key principles from what we know about God, I believe we will come to understand that not only is having financial goals not sinful, but it's also actually pleasing to God.
>
> **Principle #1:** God is our Father. If you have children, most likely you love them and want them to be happy. God has given us this analogy to help us

understand that He put us on this planet to enjoy it, be happy, and be fulfilled in all areas of life, including our finances.

Principle #2: He wants us to serve His other children (humans). It is important to know everything we do here on earth should be focused on us becoming our best and sharing those gifts with God's other creation. This includes being financially stable so we can help others.

Principle #3: Most importantly, it **comes down to the condition of our heart.** We can make good or bad decisions in any area of life. We can turn wonderful and holy things into abominations based on our heart and motives. Finances and money are no different. We can use it for our own personal gain in a corrupt and greedy way, or we can use it to become our best selves and in turn help others.

Ultimately, if our hearts are for God and for others, it is imperative we set financial goals to create a solid foundation so we can in turn help others. This is what I believe God put us on the planet for.

I love that last part because it has become a foundation in my recovery and life. I get it. I believe that we are not put on this planet merely to exist or consume. Nor to drown in debt or be too reckless or frugal with what we have.

I believe that I have a responsibility to love God, myself, and others, (Matthew 22:37-39). I believe so firmly in that purpose, that I have it tattooed on my calf. It is the core of my personal purpose statement: **To love and empower people to believe in themselves.**

In my heart, I know and believe I have been put on this planet to love and help others. And that's what I've been doing for the past three and a half decades and will continue to do until my last breath. I am living my purpose. And every day to the best of my ability, I am true to myself.

Prompt #2: Encouraging Reminders

Here are some reminders to help you feel better about the decisions you make and not second guess them:

- Be true to yourself.
- Don't be afraid to try something new.
- Find the courage to do what it takes.
- Know why you are doing something. And go do it.
- Then, let go of the results.

Prompt #3: Listen and Sing

Listen to the Rolling Stones song, "You Can't Always Get What You Want." And sing the chorus out loud!

Chapter Eleven
The Five Decisions

"A peacefulness follows any decision, even the wrong one."
Rita Mae Brown

I heard someone say something at an event a while ago, originally coined by author Evelyn Waugh, that is harsh but true, **"When we argue for our limitations, we get to keep them."**

Stop arguing with yourself. Find ten seconds and make a bold decision without overthinking or second guessing it. If you spill some milk, cry if you like, then grab a paper towel and wipe it up.

Continuous Refinement

In the last section, you were introduced to taking personal inventory and increasing your self-awareness. This section will expand upon those first steps and focus on refining your decision-making process starting with this chapter.

For many, this may be one of the more challenging chapters in the whole book. Why? Because we fight an internal battle between what we want and what our inner voices of fear, doubt, and insecurity have to say about it. We struggle because we want to look good and make the "right" decisions and are afraid of not being good enough. We worry that if we make a mistake or make the wrong decisions, people will think less of us or worse, we will feel inadequate, unworthy.

To that I say, so what? Admit your mistake or fear. And decide to do better next time.

I can hear some of you now: "But you don't understand…"

Uh—yeah, I do. I've been in that neighborhood before, and I don't like it. I try to avoid it as much as I can. It's dangerous, unhealthy, and will suck the life out of your dreams and ambitions if you stay there too long.

91% of Your Fears Are Lies You Believe

According to recent studies, 91% of our fears will not come true. They are worries and lies—figments of our imagination—which serve no good purpose to building our self-image. Most of our fears are not real, but when we believe them, they are.

As Stephen Campbell points out, "another exciting discovery about our brain is how it believes EVERYTHING we tell it, without question, no arguments. When we exclaim to ourselves, 'I simply cannot do this,' our brains say, 'Okay! If you say so! ' And then it makes sure you can't!"

The Illusion of Control and Certainty

One of our biggest and most common problems of decision-making is our desire for certainty. We want to be right. We want to be in control. Most of us also want to be accepted and thought of as smart, or at least not stupid. And we personalize what we think others think about us, whether they tell us or not. Everything isn't about us.

Guess what? Most people are too busy thinking about themselves to worry about whether you messed up unless it affects them. Then you'll probably hear about it. When that happens, as already mentioned, admit it, then fix it if you can.

In a work situation, demand clarification. Don't assume you know what others' expect of you. There's nothing worse than working to achieve a moving target. Been there. Done that. Won't ever work for a company without clear expectations again.

Fortunately, right now I have pretty awesome bosses who trust and treat me like a professional. I've earned their respect by achieving results.

If you are a manager, CEO, boss, or owner, do yourself and staff a favor, make your expectations and job description crystal clear *before* you hire. *Then train your employees and give them clear rails for making responsible adult decisions.*

This is not easy. I never said it would be. I've had to learn to stop personalizing my own mistakes or worse, absorbing other people's problems and making them about me. My loving wife points this out to me more often than I would like to admit. There's a word for my behavior. It's called *co-dependency*. If I didn't "cause it, I can't change it or control it." I can only take responsibility for my own attitudes and actions.

As I've said several times, we all make mistakes. We all do stupid shit from time to time. Our bigger challenge is not taking ourselves and what we do so seriously. The question we need to ask ourselves is, *how do I lighten up, and not attach my worth to what I do or don't do?*

When I make a mistake, it doesn't mean I am a failure. It only means that way didn't work.

It requires personal responsibility and humility to admit it when you mess up and to vow to do better next time. *But for the ambitious folks like you,* **choosing to play it safe is not a solution, unless you want to stay where you are**. Developing a humble mindset takes patience and time, but the rewards are worth every bit of temporary discomfort you will surely feel. All worthy endeavors begin with making a decision, or five.

So, let's rip the Band-Aids off and look at some of the common decisions we face and how to break them down into what James Cleary refers to as "micro habits" or "habit stacking" in his best-selling book, *Atomic Habits*.

Prompt #1: Decision Making Practice

Let's take our five essential habits for problem solving and turn them into five decisions:

1. Decide to *identify and admit* there's a problem
2. Decide *what you want* and what you're *going to do* about it.
3. Decide to *find out why* you want it.
4. Decide *what* you're *willing to do* to get it.
5. Decide to *get into action* and to *never give up*.

Review the self-assessment list you started earlier and turn your answers into decisions. *Write down what you decide.* This is the next step forward to *turn your wants, needs, and desires into agreements.* As you make a decision something magical happens. You advance from the *I wish zone* into the *solution zone*. Making a decision and writing down your intentions is a giant leap forward to accomplishing that which you want. **Invest the time to do this very important step, now.**

Here's an example:

Want: I want to replace the funky, 1980s style kitchen cabinets that are missing doors and look like crap.

Decision: Today, I will research the options for replacing our cabinets, including styles and costs.

I have found this process to be relatively simple and effective.

Whether increasing my sales at work, planning a kitchen remodel or a vacation, or working on some defect of character that continues to crop up, like impatience or procrastination, whenever I diligently follow these steps, my confidence, productivity, and confidence increase dramatically.

Regardless of the problem I am trying to solve, or the opportunity I want to achieve, the five essentials, *Ten Seconds of Boldness*, "habit stacking," "one-day-at-a-time," or any other strategies we choose to employ to shift our mindset and solve problems, **one thing is certain: spaced repetition over time with a solution mindset is how beliefs shift, confidence is built, and positive change occurs.**

A Conversation with Kevin Miller, Host of the *Ziglar Show* Podcast

Again, you may wonder, "If it's so simple, then why aren't more people successful?" That's a good question, but let's turn it inward and return to my conversation with Kevin Miller for his thoughts. I asked Kevin this direct question: "Do you think people have a hard time believing in themselves?"

> Kevin: I, uh, you nailed it! When we get past, 'Okay, here's something I want,' whether it's an expectation—a should, in essence, and they say, 'No, I really do believe in that want.' And often times they say , 'I would like that— I have a desire there.' But do they really believe they are capable of achieving

> it? Can they see themselves doing it? And that's when a lot of times they'll say, 'No. I don't.' And I've started labeling that—**they don't really want it. They want to want it**—They're not making progress toward it because when it comes down to it or they're yo-yoing—they don't really see themselves being able to [achieve what they want]— and then we've gotta dig into why they do not believe in themselves.

Why don't we believe? That is the billion-dollar question.

> **"We don't want it bad enough. We want to want it."**
> **- Kevin Miller**

Kevin then addressed our tendency to compare ourselves to others and our limiting self-beliefs. He continued:

> In particular those who had less going for them. And they achieved it. And we think, 'why do I think that I can't?' I mean they had less ability, and they did it. [It] kind of takes away my excuse. Then I just have to look at my own belief in myself. Or get real. [They say], **'I just don't want it enough. It's not important enough to me'** or 'I've just got a self-image issue.' But either way we're getting to the root of where we need to turn. And so many times we're out here it the personal development world, we say **'You just gotta want it more. Grit your teeth and go after it.' No—we need to go back to the root and just get to where you can honestly see where you're at. When we do that, you don't need so**

much motivation and inspiration. Once you can see yourself there.

I find it interesting how a personal development conversation inevitably comes back to belief. To our motives—our why. To visualization. To awareness. And to making bold decisions then putting in the effort to see them through.

> Whatever *it* is, when it comes to decision-making, **I don't think we have an idea problem. We have a confidence problem.**

We are so afraid of either making a mistake or worrying what others will think of us, that we freeze or procrastinate. We overanalyze. Our prudence, disguised as "due diligence," which I agree is important for many areas, can be one more excuse, like procrastination, to *not make a decision*.

Indecision is riddled with doubt. *With too much doubt, you cannot have confidence.* For those of you whose dominant personality trait is logic-based, I have a couple questions: What's the worst thing that could happen if you took a chance and made a mistake? What in life is certain, really?

I like this litmus test which I mentioned earlier. When we make a mistake, rather than agonize over the *potential* repercussions, ask ourselves instead, *Will this matter five years from now?* Most of the time it won't, for two reasons: one, we won't remember it. And two, even if we do, the problem isn't the mistake we made, it's how we feel about ourselves for making it in the first place. *Unless it impacts someone else, let it go.* It's not worth losing sleep over the embarrassment of making a mistake or being wrong.

> If you want to move closer to 100% confidence, then eventually you're going to have to be willing to make mistakes and learn from them.

Mistakes are rarely fatal. So, stop worrying that the world will think less of you if you make a mistake and go make more of them. **If you're in sales, get more nos. If you're an author** and want to be traditionally published, write better and more often, hire a great editor, and send out more query letters. **Get more rejections.** If you're an athlete, run more, shoot more, ride more, swing more. **If you are shy, ask more questions.** You won't have to talk as much. You get the point.

Don't Let Perfectionism Prevent You From Becoming Great

You will accelerate your learning curve and find all the ways that don't work far faster by taking a risk and getting started than if you hypothesize and research and theorize about the best potential outcomes.

It reminds me of Jia Jing. Jing is the best-selling author of *Rejection Proof*, winner of the Toastmasters Golden Gavel Award, and a highly sought-after keynote speaker who commands a minimum speakers fee of $20,000 per virtual event. His Ted Talk, *100 days of Rejection*, is one of the most viewed of all time.

Jia was terrified of rejection. His idea was to have someone follow and videotape him for a hundred days making outlandish requests to get "Nos." He wanted to be rejected. Some of his off-the-wall requests are hilarious. Like day two where he went to a burger joint, ate his lunch then went back to the counter to ask for a "burger refill." But the turning point came when he went to a donut shop and asked for "Olympic donuts." Yes, he wanted donuts connected and in the colors of the Olympic rings. You have to go look it up because no amount of explanation here will do it justice. Spoiler alert, the store employee and manager went out of their way to meet his outrageous request. The video of the incident got over five million views on YouTube, which led to interviews for newspapers and talk shows and he basically became famous.

The point is, he is no longer afraid of rejection. And because he was bold enough to make silly requests his confidence grew each time people said yes.

Jia Jing has since gone on to become highly paid speaker focusing on overcoming rejection. He took his biggest fear and turned it into his greatest strength.

> I guarantee when you clearly decide what you want and commit to courageous pursuit of it, you will feel happier because fear of rejection or failure will no longer control you.

Commit and Don't Second Guess Your Decisions

Then there's the other side of the coin. The one where we finally muster up the courage to start, then second guess our decision at the first obstacle. Learn from it. Consider any obstacle to be yet one more challenge. One more problem to solve, finding out what isn't working so you can get closer to what will. Stay the course. The intel you gain from this iterative process is no different than a scientist using the scientific method. The process is the same: form a hypothesis, test, trial, and error. Record and repeat, until you find a solution. Then continue to innovate and improve results. But unlike a typical science experiment in a lab, the subject of study is you and your problems. Your obstacles and motives for accomplishing your dreams, goals, and aspirations. And because we are emotionally vested in the outcome, our objectivity is not always clear. Quite the opposite. In fact, our judgment is clouded by our belief system.

So, I'll ask again, "Why don't more people believe in themselves or have greater self-confidence when it comes to accomplishing goal or solving problems?"

My working hypothesis is because too few people actually stick to anything long enough to reap the rewards. Some studies indicate that as many as 70% of those who actually set goals don't achieve them. Concurrently, **other researchers agree that the number one reason people don't achieve their goals is a lack of self-confidence.** That is often followed by not wanting to get out of our comfort zone, lacking perseverance, not believing in ourselves, listening to the wrong advice (critics, not experts), lack of desire, or lacking motivation to work hard.

I agree with and have experienced all of these at various times in my life. I'm sure you have, too. I'd also add impatience to that list.

In our instant gratification culture, we want instant results but for the reasons above, we don't do the work and give up too soon.

Another problem, as discussed earlier, is that people place too much value on external measures of success and hollow rewards like *things* and *status*. Most people are too full of fear, guilt, shame, pride, ego, etc., and are not willing to change to overcome these impediments to success. Because, like me, most people are too lazy, scared, and stubborn to learn what to do to develop new habits and skills or actually believe the effort is worth it—that they can actually have a lasting impact in all areas of their lives: financially, physically, emotionally, spiritually, and relationally.

Or we are convinced that we must know it all before we can start anything. Don't believe me? Haven't you ever suffered from analysis paralysis? Scared and unsure about the outcome you bang your head against the wall like an overstuffed washing machine.

If that's you, you may want to rebalance the load and trust that the clothes will be clean when the machine beeps. Times up. Put them in the dryer and do something else.

Imposter Syndrome: The Arch Enemy of Success

Kevin Miller even admitted to me and to himself his own shortcomings in these areas, "I am blown away by the imposter syndrome in my head." And that comes from a guy who is devoted to uncovering our motives, our drive. Who discusses this and many other topics on his podcasts to more than fifty thousand listeners every week.

Kevin elaborated further, "You know, I have regrets. Regrets about a lot of wasted time. I'm a very impatient person. I don't like inefficiency and yet I'm not ever really stepping back in my own life and questioning, 'Do I really want that?' And again, 'why?'" He talked about dissecting his own drive and lack of patience, even compared it to his own kids who "are further along in that regard." Then looking at what and why, Kevin hypothetically asked, "Why do we not want that much? And when we do, where do we go awry?"

It's a great introspective question. He talked about self-sabotage, even going so far as mentioning that he had others who "Brought that to light for me. To help uncover 'what are these consistent patterns of sabotage in me?' They looked at the swings of ups and downs and found the pattern—we are all driven. We are just often not aware of what's driving us." He elaborated that our *why* may be sabotaging our ability to succeed. He offered a couple examples: "I am blown away by the reality of 'imposter syndrome' in my head. It's there, I know it now. I can look at it. Recognize it. And wave and know that it doesn't have any value... I'm good at what I do. Yet I feel like [an imposter]. I have not irradicated that... I know how to manage it. And go past it anyways." He referenced a guest, author Ruth Soukop, and her book titled, *Do It Scared*®. "That's a great title," Kevin said, "But I'm not a 'no fear' guy. I'm not gonna have the 'No Fear' shirt on because I don't believe it."

I commented that I sincerely felt that he and I are two different people rowing the same direction with different oars. That we all struggle with "imposter syndrome and procrastination."

He jumped right in without hesitation and said, "I'm a professional procrastinator."

After he said this, we wrapped up. I mentioned how grateful I was for his time and congratulated him again on his upcoming book and all his success; for being flexible to have an unscripted conversation.

In that moment it hit me. I had just walked through an instance of major fear and imposter syndrome of my own by interviewing someone recognized by millions of people worldwide as a leading podcaster in personal development, and he was open and honest and vulnerable with me. What a gift. We did it. And he made it easy because of who he is.

His final words to me were, "I am humbled and honored."

I felt the same.

Our "Need" For Certainty is Just Another Smokescreen for Fear

Why do so many of us feel the need to overanalyze everything? Is it to minimize our risk and exposure? For some false sense of security, an illusion of feeling in control, certain?

The only thing that's 100% certain, is that we are all going to die. Someday. It will happen. We just don't know when. That's the inevitability of our existence.

But while we are alive, how frequently do we allow our lives to be controlled by things we fear, most of which are not real? Do we cower and pretend there is no fear or puff up and pretend that we "have no fear"? How do you typically respond to fear?

Neither denial nor false bravado are lasting solutions. Granted I understand our need to get fired up sometimes. Enthusiasm and energy are contagious. But adrenaline is a short-term solution, especially when it comes to facing our fears. And whether we admit it or not, we all are afraid of something. I agree with Kevin and don't subscribe to the "no fear" movement.

Do it Scared®

Instead, true triumph occurs when we face our fears and "do it scared." That's where our courage is tested, where lasting confidence is built. Not from chest thumping, back slapping, rah-rah. That shit will fizzle out faster than a cheap sparkler on the Fourth of July! The lasting victories over our fears are achieved as we stand boldly before them and say to ourselves, *"You don't own me anymore."*

My problem is that if I don't begin to exhibit boldness, I will remain afraid of failure for the rest of my life. That's why I wrote this book. Because I know for a fact that I am not the only one who thinks like this. I am not the only one who procrastinates or battles with "imposter syndrome."

Something wonderful happens when we are honest with ourselves and/or another about our insecurities, we open the door for connection. When we are vulnerable and transparent enough to share our own shortcomings with those who won't use them against us, we diffuse the power our fears hold over us. Our humanness is not a sign of weakness (though in some cultures it is), rather it is a sign of great courage and strength.

Changing The Conversation With our Mind

The sad truth is that most of what we say to ourselves is negative. Yet we keep talking and listening. As a result, we have created well-worn neural pathways that have become beliefs. False beliefs. Lies we have believed far too long which are killing our dreams and sucking the life out of our souls.

When are you going to say, *enough!* and flip the script in your head?

Unfortunately for me, I am too stubborn and all too often have to hurt bad enough before I finally surrender. Like most people, I still succumb to the critical voices in my head, every day.

Voices

I'll never ever forget that summer day in 1987, in early recovery. Laying on my back, fists full of hair trying to pull the voices out of my head. *Who do you think you are? You really think you have what it takes to stay sober? Ha! Your higher power can't save you. I own your ass!*

And that moment, where I pounded the bed with my fists and screamed, "Get the hell out of my head!" That was the moment I decided that I would no longer be controlled by the liar in my mind.

When you follow and apply these simple five steps: *Identify* the problem or opportunity, clearly *decide* what you want, know *why* you want it, write a *clear plan,* and *start* working that plan consistently over time, your life will change. You will procrastinate far less and no longer be controlled by fear. You will gain confidence and courage and find that you are happier because you are actively moving forward toward something you deeply desire. That, to me, is what makes living so fun.

The opposite is also true. In the periods of my life where I felt lost or without motivation or direction, I was not a happy camper.

I must confess, this has been one of the most challenging chapters for me to write because I kept second guessing what I had already written down. I'd start writing some witty story about how I used to worry about stuff all the time and how I had this grand epiphany and was somehow cured of worry and the insidious affliction of doubt and insecurity. How I "overcame" or irradicated my fear. If I said that, I'd be lying.

Maybe what will be most helpful is to just tell the truth. To let you know that I still struggle with overthinking things. I still tend to wander off the trail and get lost in the prickly scrub brush and second guess which path will lead me home.

I just keep moving forward and trust that eventually I will manage to find my way back. And I usually do. But often not before periods of frustration, or times when I want to throw the towel and give up. But I'm too stubborn to give up so easily.

So, what did I do this time? I got my hair cut then took a shower. It helped clear my head enough to realize that I don't need some earth-shattering story to illustrate the importance of making a decision and sticking to it. That I already had more than I needed with my forty-eight-minute interview with Kevin and the hours of other interviews. Of my experiences. The struggles. All of it. I have more than enough.

And so, it is for you. As you progress, I urge you to believe enough in yourself to take some risks. To make bold decisions. To just take a chance on you and *don't keep looking in the rearview mirror*. Stop trying to compare yourself to others. And trust your own decisions more.

Avoid the Analysis Paralysis Trap

Next to procrastination, analysis paralysis is a huge problem for most of us. It's a trap. One easy to fall into because we often become so fixated on maximizing the potential outcome or minimizing the risks of a problem to solve or opportunity to gain, that we lose sight of what we are trying to accomplish and why we want to for the sake of fully understanding the minutiae of strategy.

Strategy always follows vision. But execution never happens if we stay stuck in the strategy phase.

In most cases the amount of discovery you deem important is not. At some point you need to make a decision to proceed with 80% confidence of a positive outcome, knowing that there will always be other choices and improvements to make later. Don't overthink it. Sometimes simple is better and more effective too.

So, the better question is, how can we overcome some of our self-doubt and fear-based habits like procrastination, avoidance, and analysis paralysis to improve our decision-making abilities to feel more confident about the choices we make, rather than second guessing the ones we've made?

You guessed it; *Ten Seconds of Boldness*. Be bold enough to just make a decision. Find the courage to face the truth about ourselves especially patterns that continue to reappear. Like broken relationships, or fears of failure and rejection. Feelings of codependency and control issues. Challenges with trust, anger, procrastination, etc. *We will continue to experience situations which we have not yet learned what they are trying to teach us.*

Whether consciously or unconsciously, we find ways to push them aside and pretend they are gone but like a perpetual game of "whack-a-mole," they continue to pop up until they don't.

So, the obvious question most ask is, how do we get rid of them? Wrong question. Those thoughts are like any pest—ants, rats, or cockroaches—and unless we change, they will keep coming back to steal our food and use cereal boxes as a bathroom. Change is merely a decision to take control of our thoughts, attitudes, and actions.

F.E.A.R.: False Evidence Appearing Real

Most worries and fears are illusions: false evidence appearing real.

Fear, doubt, worry, and insecurity by themselves are inert; innocuous. Like a loaded pistol, they are harmless until you hold them and pull the trigger. The problem is, we are hardwired to respond with some form of fear—fight, flight, or freeze—as a means of protection. Unwarranted fears and worries keep us in a heightened state of stress when most of the things we tend to worry about are untrue—figments of our imaginations and controllable. To those who suffer from PTSD or a host of other mental health conditions, there are solutions best addressed by a medical and/or psychiatric professional, which I am not. However, most of us suffer from some form of fear, most of which exist only in our mind.

It is those "problems" that continue to crop up, which in my experience impede my ability to feel confident.

I have noticed that when I am afraid, I lack confidence. The opposite is also true. When I worry about something that may or may not happen, I lose confidence. When I am not 100% honest with myself or others, I feel guilt or shame which also impede my level of confidence. When I worry that a prospect is going to say no, I find a hundred other distractions and pretend I am "busy" rather than finding the courage to do a little research, rehearse what I'm going to say and how I can help them, and to find that ten seconds of boldness to pick up the phone, smile, and dial.

I have been where you are. And I am still there at some point every single day. That's how this book started. I get you. The difference, however, is that I have seen this work enough in my life and, right now, my confidence bank is pretty flush.

However, in the beginning, I had to operate on courage and blind faith that it might work. My motto for years has been "Plan your work and work your plan." That motto was the harbinger of the five steps we have been exploring.

Five years later and some of the best years in my sales career to back it up and I can say without a doubt that this process works.

Are You Impatient Too?

Impatience is still one of my biggest character defects. Do you get impatient too if the results don't happen as fast as you want?

I have wanted to be done with this book for three years, but I had more to learn. More problems and challenges I had to face so I could write from a position of experiential expertise rather than merely hypothesis, conjecture or OPI (other people's ideas).

There is nothing wrong with OPI. But to me it is far more lasting and powerful when I have experienced something I have learned, rather than just paying it lip service.

For me experience carries more weight and depth than mere knowledge. I know what it's like to worry incessantly about shit I cannot control and to come out the other side with a level of acceptance and clarity that I only need to change the things I can control. In many circumstances, I have developed wisdom to discern the difference.

The bottom line is this: *if we want to be more confident, we need to make healthier decisions and take control of what we choose to focus on and do.*

Let's look at New Year's resolutions: The end of one year is a beginning of the next and a time when, according to multiple studies, more than half of us set some form of New Year's resolutions or create goals and plans for the changes we want to make in the year ahead. Some of the most common are:

- Exercise more.
- Lose weight.
- Get organized.
- Make more money.
- Save more money / spend less money.
- Learn a new skill or hobby.
- Live life to the fullest.
- Quit smoking or stop some other "bad" habit.
- Spend more time with family and friends.

Our challenge is that life, ambition, and personal growth are not always simple. We are complex beings. We know we want something but aren't always sure where to start.

What Can We Learn From a Thousand Piece Jigsaw Puzzle?

Our thoughts and actions are like putting together a thousand-piece jigsaw puzzle—corners and edges first. Then we slowly add pieces that look as if they belong together, connecting them one by one, and slowly an image begins to take shape. It may even vaguely begin to resemble the point of reference on the puzzle box.

As we continue to assemble the puzzle, the pattern becomes clearer. Soon the pieces seem to fall into place almost on their own. You step back and look at how far you've come. Maybe you even feel proud for a moment looking at all the connected pieces that form the image you are trying to recreate.

But something is off, missing. There's still a big hole in the middle of the puzzle. You look at the remaining pieces and quickly fit them where they belong, closing that hole, piece by piece. But there's a problem. You're one piece short.

You look on your lap, your chair, the floor, the sofa, but it's nowhere to be found. Then your dad casually strolls over to the kitchen table, reaches in his pocket and with an impish grin says, "I believe you are looking for this." And he places the final piece to complete the puzzle.

That is a true story my mom told me years ago when I was a teenager. She and my grandma used to love putting together jigsaw puzzles. Big ones with a thousand pieces. Often of serene landscapes or idyllic castles nestled on a verdant knoll overlooking a pond with geese. You get the idea.

They would make hot cocoa and spread the pieces out on the smooth dining room table. For a whole afternoon they methodically put it together piece by piece, while Grandpa watched football in the living room.

Even after the first time, they knew they would be at least one piece short, they didn't let it stop them. *They worked with the pieces they had and didn't worry about the missing piece or pieces because they knew where they were*—in Grandpa's pocket.

Most of us Know Which Pieces Are Missing

I believe most of us know where our missing pieces are too. But they aren't really missing, we just have to go ask our grandpa for them and decide if we're going to let him place them or if we're going to take them from his hand and put them where they belong.

When we are faced with a decision, whether something we thought of, or that which has been presented to us, we need to choose. Choosing not to decide is still a decision. However, I have never experienced any forward progress, change, or transformation by staying where I am or by not choosing what to do or not do.

If we want to complete the puzzle, we need to place the remaining pieces.

No Decisions Are Perfect. That's What Makes Life Fun and Interesting

As we wrap up this chapter, remember this: **No decisions are perfect.** If we can learn to have a little grace with ourselves upfront, we will be more accepting of our shortcomings. If we are sincere about wanting to get better, we can make healthier choices next time. We know what's healthy and not.

A simple decision-making guide I use is to ask myself these questions: Is it selfish? Honest? Kind? Helpful, to me or others? And, is it legal, moral, and ethical?

As a result of your cultural or spiritual beliefs, you may have different or deeper codes of ethics to live by. If so, I encourage you to honor them to the best of your ability and to not feel guilty when you don't. We all carry more than enough guilt and shame to last twenty lifetimes. *Let that shit go. And stop adding to it.*

Similarly, certain careers—medical, legal, judicial, etc.—have clearly stated codes of ethics and values which govern their service. Whatever those guides or rules are for you is what you must follow. Anything contrary is a breach of ethics and may have consequences.

So, to make this easier, let go of the guilt, shame, and remorse, and make healthier choices. Or don't. At the end of the day, all we can do is the best we can, one day at a time.

No matter what you choose, I know this to be true: You get out what you put in. *Our results are influenced by the decisions we make and actions we take. Period.*

Ten Seconds of Boldness will help you find the courage necessary to make a decision or begin a new endeavor. To become willing to find the desire and inspiration within to motivate you to move forward. It all starts with you honoring your own dreams and aspirations, then making a decision to become bolder one moment at a time.

> The most loving thing you can do for yourself is to make bolder decisions and stick to them.

Prompt #2: Five Confidence Building Tips

Here are five suggestions to remember next time you have to make some tough choices.

1. Make a decision even if you don't have all the answers.
2. Don't overthink or second guess it.
3. Avoid analysis paralysis.
4. Commit and be willing to take risks.
5. Follow through with <u>action</u>, *not words*.

Chapter Twelve
The Not-So-Secret Power of Prayer, Meditation, and Creative Visualization

"What you think, you become. What you feel, you attract. What you imagine, you create."
Buddha

The Secret, the best-selling book by Rhonda Byrne, is no longer a secret to the millions who have bought it nor countless others who have watched the documentary of the same name. When applied, the principles she outlines have literally transformed many lives. It's power and testimony are well documented.

For those unfamiliar, the theme of *The Secret* is based on the "Law of Attraction." Simply put, it's about mindset, intentionality, visualization, and building belief, and reaping what you sow. That whatever you think about, hope for, and dare to pursue will manifest itself in your life. That we must consciously and intentionally pay attention, not only to what we think and what we say to ourselves, but also what we do or don't do.

Once again, what we choose to believe affects who we are and what we become.

Power Tools for Success

Faith, belief, prayer, and meditation, coupled with hard work, are powerful tools for transformation. I know from personal experience that when individually and routinely practiced, these disciplines change lives.

I am not alone. There are billions of people around the globe who believe in some power of the universe greater than themselves. That this "secret" power and "Law of Attraction" in its purest form is all about suffering or sacrifice or surrender or grace or love. Or all of them.

The Secret is not about religious dogma, though for some it may be.

A Lesson from Fred Rodgers

For me, the secret is about being a good human, to yourself and others. It's about love and living by the Golden Rule: "Do unto others as you would have them do unto you."- Matthew 7:12

Or straight from Jesus: "Love one another," and "Love your neighbor as yourself."

These verses are integral to what Mr. Rodgers taught for more than four decades: Be a good neighbor and do the work necessary to reprogram our minds in such a way that we replace our obsolete, negative, and detrimental beliefs that continue to tear us down, with ones that build us up. Build our confidence, courage, and belief in ourselves. In each other.

The above verses are also about relying on tightly braided cord of prayer, meditation, and creative visualization. That when harnessed, the "secret" power within them can expand exponentially, unlocking a world of possibility, creativity, and ingenuity to enable the human spirit to accomplish great things.

That regardless of what one chooses to believe about the origin, meaning, and purpose of life, the vast majority of us have some concept or understanding of and believe in some unseen force or forces in the universe—of a power greater than ourselves. And that power is incredibly transformative for those who believe in it in their own way. It's not a secret. For many it's a way of life.

I am not going to unpack everything about what that means to me here for a couple of reasons. One, it's too big of a topic to cover in a chapter. And two, it's not necessary.

What is necessary, however, is that in order to feel confident and be successful in any endeavor, we need to grow and nurture our spiritual and creative sides and not rely so much on logic and our five senses to validate our beliefs. We need to learn to believe in that which we cannot touch, taste, hear, feel, or see. And learn to accept that we do not have to have all the answers. Sometimes all we have to do is ask, listen, and follow an inner spirit that guides us to where we need to go.

My Power Source

Prayer, meditation, and creative visualization, for me, are the missing links to connect my abilities and imagination to a giant conduit of possibility, the sum of all thought and creative energy.

So, the question becomes how can we tap into this invisible power to benefit ourselves and others? I can't answer that for you. That is a matter of personal desire, motivation, need, and belief. It's one of the great mysteries of this thing we call life.

But I don't want to leave you hanging like that.

Here are a couple brief examples from my own life about my personal discovery and the importance of this invisible power. Before I share them, I want to offer this disclaimer—this is *my experience.* Yours will be your own. Please don't misinterpret my occasional enthusiasm as religious zeal or didactic preaching about what you should or shouldn't do with respect to each of these.

Your path is your path, and I respect that. *All I ask is that you keep an open mind, have a sincere desire to improve your life, and be willing to do something about it.*

As I heard a long time ago, **"take what you want and leave the rest."**

For now, I want to zoom in to some of the not-so-secret secrets of my own life through three lenses: Prayer, meditation, and creative visualization. More specifically, I will briefly explain what they are to me and how they have helped me not only gain more self-confidence but also transform how I think about my goals, dreams, and problems in my life.

Prayer, meditation, and visualization loosen the grip of that thin wire, like the one tethered to the ankle of the circus elephant I mentioned earlier. Practicing each enables us to see a new reality and realize that the stake in the ground is not nearly strong enough to hold us back.

For me, these three are spotlights for a path forward. They release me from the stake, from the shackles of self-doubt. They enable me to see and believe, like the elephant, I can walk out of that tent whenever I choose to. Liberated to live a life of intention, meaning, purpose and significance.

But as I've mentioned earlier, knowing what to do is only part of the equation. To step out of the circus tent and graze freely, we need enough courage to walk through the open door and move forward without a map.

I find that courage in prayer: in connecting with a power greater than myself on a daily basis.

What is Prayer?

In simple terms, prayer is a conversation with God, or what you consider spiritual. Prayer can mean whatever it means to you, as long as it's not a soliloquy. We talk enough to ourselves already. It's part of why we stay stuck. Prayer for me is all about asking. Meditation is all about listening.

Prayer is asking and waiting for guidance from a source that is not our own minds. In my opinion, it can be whatever you chose to call it: Higher Power, The Universe, Mother Nature, God, Allah, Buddha, Yahweh, etc. To me, the name is not nearly as important as the act of praying.

I pray a lot, and when I do, my days go smoother. Not always, but frequently enough that it's become a habit. Why? Because I like smooth days.

Is There a Right Way and a Wrong Way to Pray?

I don't think so, but some may. Some say we should only pray for others. I don't. I pray about selfish things all the time. But inevitably when I am doing better, others get helped too.

As in early recovery when I didn't have a car and was running late for work. I prayed for the bus to be on time and if it wasn't, I thought or prayed for God to send someone who could give me a ride. In a sense, that is praying for others because if I was late, it would mean others would be inconvenienced by my tardiness. This simple routine was the start of my learning to trust in something I couldn't see. It became like a game of "go fish with God—"Hey

God, got a ride for me today so I can be to work on time?" Rarely was His response "Go fish." I believe that God was smiling just because I wanted to connect with Him.

Over time I've learned to build that trust and belief. So much so that when I need something more important than a ride to work, my faith is strong enough to pray, wait, and believe that this secret power is strong enough to perform miracles. Like the day my son was born.

Fully Trusting the Still Small Voice Within

It was a routine visit to turn a breach baby and avert an early delivery. As the doctor assessed the positioning of our son in utero my wife and I looked at the ultrasound monitor. We watched and listened. We could see his heart beating and hear the steady whoosh, whoosh, whoosh from the monitor indicating he was alive.

After the doctor successfully turned our son (palpitated) head-side down, the obstetrician instructed us to wait a bit for observation.

When we were alone, I looked out the window imagining what it was going to be like to be a dad.

Suddenly I heard the "whooshing" slow.

"Did you move?" I asked my wife.

"I just scooted up a bit," she said.

"Something's not right," I worried. Inside I felt this loud voice scream, "Ask her to stand up and touch her toes."

As she bent over the whoosh slowed to almost nothing. I freaked out. I felt my own blood pounding in my ears.

When she stood upright the heartbeat grew steadier, back to what it was before the doctor left.

"Can you try it again?" I asked, fearing the worst.

As she touched her toes again, the room grew silent.

"Nurse!" I cried out.

The umbilical cord was wrapped around our son's neck and when she bent over it was cutting off his oxygen.

The nurse got through to the doctor and shortly after, he arrived and said my wife needed an emergency C-section, immediately.

I prayed some more. Lots more.

My wife was prepped, and seven minutes later, our son Andrew emerged into this world alive and healthy.

He is now (as of this writing) twenty-six and doing very well. He's a great kid. We both love him dearly and are so proud of the young man he's become. Our marriage didn't last, but we never stopped loving our son. Never will.

What if?

The point is *what if? What if* I wasn't there? *What if* we didn't notice? *What if* we went home and dismissed it as nothing to be concerned about? It breaks my heart to even consider what could have happened.

The fact is in that moment I listened to an inner voice that screamed at me to *do something.* So, I did. I prayed and asked for help. "Nurse!" That day, my prayer was answered, and we were all blessed.

What is Meditation?

There are many forms of meditation, from transcendental and spiritual to mindfulness and focused breathing, movement, and progressive relaxation as with various forms of yoga (I am not going to explore the differences in yoga, meditation, or mindfulness here).

In essence, *meditation is about being present long enough to still our minds and allow thoughts to unfold without judgment.* It's about awareness and presence, feeling and listening to what our minds and bodies are trying to tell us, and not trying to fix anything in our meditative moments.

When it comes to meditation, I'll admit I am a complete novice. I practice yoga occasionally and have used guided meditations in the past. I often find being in nature or hiking to be relaxing and therefore meditative. But disciplined, I am not. But my wife is, mostly. She regularly makes time in the morning to sit still and listen to one of many meditation apps. She swears by "Headspace." She's told me that it helps her not feel so stressed. She's even encouraged me to meditate, but I have a hard time sitting still, even though I know it will probably do me good. I'm sure she's right. She usually is.

My problem is I usually wait until I'm stressed out then realize that I'm being too uptight. As I was the other day about some challenges at work. My boss told me to go for a walk. I followed her suggestion and it helped, some. Then I ate a sandwich, took a catnap, and felt ten times better.

A Sound Bath Surprise

Recently, seeing me get a little too stressed out, my wife gave us a surprise.

"Dress warm and wear something comfortable," is all she told me.

The day of the event, she suggested I grab a blanket and a yoga mat.

I gave her a look that asked, "What the heck are we doing?"

"Trust me. You'll love it."

Moments later, we pulled into a dirt lot at the dahlia fields near our home.

The parking lot was nearly full and people were walking through the brightly colored dahlia fields, yoga mats and blankets under their arms. Ahead I saw a massive golden gong, and several women dressed in white linen on a wooden stage with speakers all around.

What the heck is this? I thought.

We lay down and huddled under a down comforter as the program began. We were instructed to keep our eyes closed and listen. To relax and allow ourselves to *let go.*

For the next forty minutes, waves of sound resonated through my entire body as the hosts guided us through a meditation accompanied by sounds of gongs and rattles that sounded like stones being tumbled by gentle waves. It was a sound bath. An experience unlike any other, and one that you can only fully grasp by being there.

In the weeks and months following, my productivity went through the roof. That immersive auditory experience was a catalyst for hitting my sales goals at work that as of now has continued. But more than that, I felt more alive and resonant like a finely tuned violin. I highly recommend it.

Creative Visualization

The third strand in this powerful cord of this "secret" is Creative Visualization.

Steven Covey says that visualization is simply to "Begin With the End in Mind®." I agree 100%!

I first learned about Creative Visualization from Shakti Gawain in her best-selling book, *Creative Visualization: Use the Power of Your Imagination to Create What You Want in Your Life* (CV).

When I read it the first time as a teenager, I found a simplicity in her instructions that inspired me and gave me hope and began to create a vision for what my life could be. This was around the same time as I was listening to audio tapes and was deeply immersed in this phase of discovery and hope and possibility. The timing was perfect.

I learned about affirmations—speaking our truth in advance as if we already have that which we desire. I began to practice what she taught.

Like my favorite tropical paradise, Kauai, or a close friend, CV is one of those resources I return to time and time again because it frees up mental space. After a visit, I am usually way more productive.

It reminds me of the sheer power of our imagination and, with few exceptions, our ability to create something from nothing but inspired thought and focused effort; to *manifest a visualized life.* To call upon and trust in the powers of the creative universe, to clearly see and believe what we can be, have, or do, then find the courage and faith to work toward fulfilling that vison.

It also reminds me of a goal setting class I took at a community college.

Beyond Goal-Setting

My understanding of visualization, goal-setting, and affirmations increased even more in the summer of 1988, after I took a class at College of Marin, taught by John Croxall called, Beyond Goal-Setting.

John stressed the importance or writing our goals down and creating dream boards to aid visualization. He also taught us about to build belief and confidence in ourselves. Lastly, he taught us how to create action plans as a way to begin the process of achieving our goals.

In hindsight, what I learned from John, Shakti, and many others, as well as my own first-hand experience, has been worth millions of dollars. More important than the financial benefits to my family and me, and to those I have worked for, all of those principles have enabled me to build an unshakable foundation of belief that they work. **Their power is undeniable. And once that power is realized, it can never be taken away.**

Believe in That Which You Cannot Yet See

Once again, we return to the word "belief." Believing in something we cannot see. According to most studies, 65% of us are visual in nature. We tend to believe that which we can see.

This is why writing our goals down and doing dream boards are important actions. Without some visual frame of reference, of what could be, of what we want, it's hard for us to see ourselves having, doing, or becoming something we aren't yet.

These three disciplines, principles, or habits of prayer, meditation, and creative visualization are critical components which will help us reframe and reprogram *how* and *what* we *think* and *believe* about ourselves and others. They are wholistic, encompassing, connecting.

This reminds me of the conversation I had with Steve Lavin. We spent several minutes riffing on life and relationships, and he wrapped up by commenting that "everything comes back to a sphere": basketball, life, and the interconnectedness of it all; of us all.

For me, prayer, meditation, and creative visualization are three strands of a powerful cord that bring hope, healing, and strength especially when I feel I have none.

Prompt: Getting Into Action and Taking Eyes Off Yourself

Close your eyes and think of someone you know that may be experiencing some pain, hardship, or difficulty in their life. Pray for them to find the solution to what ails them.

What is the pain telling them? Is it to eat healthier? To see a doctor or seek other professional help? What would it look like from your perspective for them to be free of that pain or difficulty? Imagine what you might do or say to encourage or help them.

Next, turn your thoughts inward and repeat the process for your own difficulties.

Chapter Thirteen
Building Clarity, Vision, Mission, and Purpose

"Clarity precedes success."
Robin Sharma

By now, you should have a better idea of some area of life you would like to improve and have written down several goals you'd like to accomplish. Hopefully you are implementing what you've learned so far and already becoming a little bolder, more confident, and finding it easier to make decisions. Perhaps you can even see yourself as you would like to be and are beginning to believe in your own visions and dreams.

Next, we want to expand our scope to be more encompassing and wholistic. In other words, to broaden and clarify our vision, mission, and purpose so they aren't all about us.

A New Perspective

The purpose of this chapter is to help you build upon what you have already learned, and to transfer that knowledge into a clearer vision, mission, and purpose. To expand beyond personal ambition and demonstrate how vision, mission, and purpose are designed with two primary goals: *First* how each benefits others. And *second*, how they maintain focus and alignment with your or your company's core values.

Writing them will serve to further build your confidence and provide a framework to help ensure you or your company are moving in the right direction.

Don't expect to have 100% clarity about any this right now. But like an outline for a book or a term paper, or a business plan, it's helpful to have some frame of reference to start with.

It's likely that you won't be clear about what you want until you know what your motives are. We'll cover motivation and inspiration at length in the next section, "Finding Your Why."

For now, let's apply what we've already learned.

Take a step back and look at your life as a big puzzle. What are the key pieces that matter most to you right now? Next, consider what those mean to you. Why are they important to you, and how will they significantly improve your life? As you mull over those questions, you can begin to create vision, mission, and purpose statements from them.

When I first heard about these terms, I was like, "Huh? A vision what?" I don't want to scare anyone away, but these are not questions to be taken lightly.

Because of their gravity—their weight and breadth and depth, and often our lack of clarity—they can be incredibly difficult not only for businesses, but especially for individuals, to formulate.

Two Guys With Integrity and a Dream

Five years ago, when I was first formulating the plans for this book, I interviewed Jon Diamond: a friend I'd made at a local church we used to attend and a very successful co-owner of a multimillion-dollar HVAC company (at the time, he was thirty-eight).

What struck me about Jon is his integrity and confidence. Even though I didn't yet know what this book would become, I had a gut feeling that I needed to reach out to him. To interview him and learn how he became so successful.

Initially, I was mostly interested in his goals. In particular, how he and his business partner, Curtis, turned an idea into a multimillion-dollar company and every year under their leadership, became one of the Inc. 5000 Fastest-Growing Private Companies. But that was short-sighted of me. I got so much more. Jon gave me his key puzzle pieces.

As Jon recalls, in 2010 he "got the itch to own. I was new to faith, so I prayed." He told me that the message that came back was to reach out to his former business partner, Curtis.

Jon and Curtis had become partners several years earlier in an HVAC business and nine months later, when it failed, their relationship was strained, and they parted ways.

Jon kept feeling this nudge from above to reach out to Curtis.

He found out that Curtis had recently started his own HVAC company in his garage and finally trusted his intuition and made the call. The rest is history.

They set a goal to sell a million dollars in sales their first year as partners. They hit it—barely—closing the year at $1,000,040 in total revenue.

The next year they set a goal for three million in sales. While a bold goal, Jon explained, "When sales came in at $1.4M, it felt like a kick in the face."

So, he and Curtis met and discussed a strategy and began to look at what other top HVAC brands in their market were doing in terms of marketing and business positioning. "What were their values, and how well did they seem to serve their customers?" After a bit of market research, Jon recalled, "We wanted to be like them only better. Only one big problem: We had no clue how."

They needed more guidance about how to do that, so they attended a seminar by *New York Times* best-selling author, speaker, and sales trainer, Weldon Long.

Weldon taught them about goals, but more importantly, he taught them to "Hire for Heart." To build a team. To do what's right by each other by their clients. He taught them about values. Specifically, these three: *Character, honor, and integrity.* And to create a culture that "through every employee and to the customer is built on trust."

The three takeaways Jon recalls were:

1. To remove the friction between management and staff as well as the customer. That philosophy became their value statement and satisfaction guarantee: That any job would be **100% Right or 100% Free.** And to respond to and resolve any complaints immediately. It worked. Their complaint percentage was only 1/10th of 1%.

2. **"To hire for heart. To love on people."** During the interview [for new hires] to ask them about their dreams and goals and aspirations. What is their motivation and character? He added, "Skill can be taught, but we hire for their motivations." He also said to hire people that are smarter and better than he is. "Most companies don't do that. And they pay the price."

3. **Clearly identify industry KPI's** (key performance indicators) and track them relentlessly.

Again, their strategy worked. From 2010 to 2017 when they sold the business, they went from $1 million in sales to more than $21 million and made the *Inc* top 5,000 fastest growing companies every year!

Beware of Pride and Arrogance

That kind of growth can easily lead to pride and arrogance. Near the end of our interview, I asked Jon about humility. Happily, he was man enough to admit that he struggles with pride. He said at the time that "lack of humility is the biggest problem we face in our business." He also admitted, "I can be overconfident and cocky—it's my weak spot."

He also left me with this gem about being bold:

> **"If you're not failing, you're not fulfilling your potential."**
> **- Jon Diamond**

Let that sink in a moment. Two guys with a dream and a whiteboard in a garage, who failed their first time out, pulled themselves up by the bootstraps, made some adjustments and figured it out to the tune of building a multi-million-dollar business in a few short years.

Don't miss this: *They had clear and specific goals. They had a mission and visualized what kind of company they wanted, wrote it all down, then went out and built it.*

Unpacking Clarity, Vision, Mission, and Purpose

Let's return to the key elements of this chapter—Clarity, Vision, Mission, and Purpose—and take a moment to define each so we are on the same page.

Clarity: Being free of ambiguity. Instead, being lucid. Intelligible. Coherent. Lack of clarity, focus, or direction cause confusion and impede progress. *Clarity for our purposes does not mean certainty.* Rather, clarity should answer the *who, what, when, why, where,* and *how* questions to the best of your ability with the knowledge, experience, and resources available.

Part of our problem is that most of us are visual and have difficulty envisioning what we cannot yet see. Taking the time to clarify your wants, needs, desires, or problems you want to solve, as well as the plans to accomplish them will help bring your desired outcome into focus. Until you make a concerted effort to clarify things, your ambitions will remain a muddy mess.

Vision: A thought, concept, or object formed by our imagination. *An ideal image of what can be.*

What do you imagine your ideal life looks like? Or if that is too big, apply it to one goal or area you would like to improve.

Note: This is different than a vision statement for a business. A good vision statement should be written in present tense, be brief, and clearly identify company values and why it exists. Those reasons should not be too general but should *evoke emotion* and *connect* the organization to all it serves.

Here are a few examples:

Apple's vision statement is "we believe that we are on the face of the earth to make great products and that's not changing."

Microsoft's corporate vision is "to help people and businesses throughout the world realize their full potential."

"Our vision at Kaiser Permanente is to be a leader in total health by making lives better."

> My vision statement: I believe I am on this planet to share stories that inspire people and businesses to greatness.

Mission: A strongly felt aim, ambition, or calling. Being on a mission is undertaking a task that one considers to be a very important duty. In relation to this book, you might say your mission is to get better at solving problems and building your self-confidence.

A mission statement on the other hand is defined as an action-based statement that declares the purpose of an organization and how they serve their customers. This sometimes includes a description of the company, what it does, and its objectives. A mission statement is a short summary of a company's purpose.

Here are a few examples of mission statements:

Apple's mission statement is "Bringing the best user experience to its customers through its innovative hardware, software, and services."

Nike's mission statement is: "To bring inspiration and innovation to every athlete in the world."

"The mission of The Walt Disney Company is to entertain, inform and inspire people around the globe through the power of unparalleled storytelling, reflecting the iconic brands, creative minds, and innovative technologies that make ours the world's premier entertainment company."

> My personal mission statement: To encourage, inspire, and help people become brave and confident enough to believe they can accomplish their dreams and goals.

Purpose: The reason for which something is done or created or for which something [or someone] exists.

Your purpose answers the question why you choose to do what you do and be who you are. It is your motivation, your reason for living. **Our purpose adds meaning and significance to our lives.**

For writing: A purpose statement is a declarative sentence which summarizes the specific topic and goals of a document. It is typically included in the introduction to give the reader an accurate, concrete understanding of what the document will cover and what he/she can gain from reading it. To be effective, a statement of purpose should be:

- Specific and precise - not general, broad, or obscure
- Concise - one or two sentences
- Clear - not vague, ambiguous, or confusing
- Goal-oriented - stated in terms of desired outcomes

Note: A purpose statement is not the same as a thesis statement as it doesn't discuss any conclusions.

For business: A purpose statement is a single statement that defines the reason your company exists—beyond simply making a profit. It also illustrates how your product or service positively impacts the people you serve. Once your purpose is established, you'll need a series of goals to drive that purpose.

*The key difference between a purpose statement and a mission statement is **focus and value.*** A purpose statement reflects the values of an organization and its worldview. Whereas a mission statement relates more to the value a company provides is customers. The purpose statement is deeper and more impactful from a wholistic standpoint. In short, a purpose statement takes the focus off profit and puts it onto the benefits it provides for those it serves.

Note: Not all businesses have a purpose statement.

Here are a few examples of purpose statements:
- eBay: To empower people and create economic opportunity for all.
- Intel: To create world-changing technology that enriches the lives of every person on earth.
- Southwest Airlines: Connect people to what's important in their lives through friendly, reliable, low-cost air travel.
- United Airlines: Connecting people. Uniting the world.

> My personal purpose statement: To love and inspire people to believe in themselves.

Whether you are a business owner or want to be, or you simply want more clarity in your life, I encourage you to take time to carefully consider and draft personal vision, mission, and purpose statements. Like Jon and Curtis, they can serve as anchor points to what you value and will help you maintain proper perspective with the decisions you make and the direction you wish to go and who you will help in the process. *They are the outline of the next chapters in the book of your life.*

Prompt: Consider and Jot Down a Few Ideas

Whether a business owner or not, if you do not already have a vision, mission, or purpose statement consider what key elements you would want to include in each. Would your personal statements be different than those for your business? If so, how? If you feel inspired, write a rough draft of each.

> The primary purpose of writing vision, mission, and purpose statements is to clearly articulate your *why* to those you serve.

Section III
Find Your Why

- ◊ Finding Your Why
- ◊ Belief: Changing How You Think About Everything
- ◊ Willingness: What Are You Willing to Do to Get What You Want?
- ◊ Love: The Source of All Motivation and Inspiration

Chapter Fourteen
Finding Your Why

"He who has a why to live for can bear almost any how."
Friedrich Nietzsche.

Thus far we've looked at many of the problems that stand between us and what we want. We've also discussed the importance of becoming bold and decisive if we are to begin the process of changing how we think.

Now, let's turn our attention to *why*. To motives. To inspiration. To drive and ambition. To all the things that are going to get us off our butts and into the game of life either because we must or because we have a desire or motive so powerful that we will not be denied.

Your Why is the Cornerstone to Your Success

This is one of the most critical sections in the whole book, because without a clearly defined why, we tend to give up too soon. We quit at the first setback or consider ourselves a failure because we didn't get what we thought we wanted in the time we expected to get it. In short, there are three primary blocks to our success:

1. Unclear motives
2. Unrealistic expectations
3. Impatience

Each of these also negatively influence our belief system—about what we believe we can or cannot do and what we perceive and believe about our skill level, resources, and abilities. Part of the problem, as I have mentioned several times, is *we think too much.* Our minds are cluttered with thousands of thoughts, most of them negative, which only exacerbates our feelings of confusion, especially when it comes to establishing goals, creating plans, and finding our motives.

We are distracted by hundreds of trivial things which impede our forward progress. In some instances, the distractions are so large and prevalent that we have no clue how address them. To add to our dilemma, we don't know where to start. *We don't know what we don't know and, as a result, feel so overwhelmed that we do nothing.*

So, what are we to do? One solution is to organize our lives and minds. Start with getting rid of crap we do not need.

We Need to Organize Our Minds

Most of us have too much junk in our heads—fears, worries, doubts, appointments, obligations, deadlines, etc. Like an overstuffed garage, our minds become filled with hundreds of things we no longer use or need, like broken TVs, or outdated computers, or old clothes that no longer fit, and scores of other things that have outlived their usefulness. As a result, we feel weighed down. Unmotivated, if not downright lazy. Worse, we keep wasting time thinking and worrying about shit we can't control, which only adds more stress.

Have I struck a chord? I hope so. Because like everything else thus far, there's more work to do. Let's start by making some decisions about what we need to keep and get rid of.

Out With the Old to Make Room for the New

It's time for a mental garage sale, a few trips to Goodwill, or a dump run. Time to get rid of old habits which are not fulfilling us so we can make room for creative energy necessary to pursue what we really want and to clarify why we want it.

Why, you may ask, did I drop this in here? What does getting rid of old stuff have to do with finding my why? Didn't we already talk about this already?

The short answer is yes. We have already discussed clearing out stuff and the importance of making decisions. But if your garage is like mine, there's still way too much crap in it. Maybe it's still a cluttered mess, because you cannot yet decide what to keep, donate, or discard. So, like me, you likely procrastinate. My physical garage is a wreck, again. We remodeled two years ago and have yet to do what I suggested above for our mental house cleaning. There are bins marked "keep" and "donate" still piled high. Our backyard has a dump pile. I mention this because it's normal for us to put off things that are not a priority.

When our motives are clear and our desire or need is great enough, most of us will get into action to do what needs to be done.

The truth is most people procrastinate and are not clear about what they want or what the perceived benefits are. What's more, we also have a confidence and belief problem: We are not sure if the effort will produce the results we want or are unsure of our ability and desire to put in the effort. Instead, we keep adding to the crap that's already in our mental garage. And soon we can't find anything when we actually do need it. We are not motivated to clean it, so the garages (mental and physical) remain cluttered. We remain scattered, unsure, and that impedes our ability to feel confident or productive.

Hopefully we will wake up one day and say, "today's the day." Then make a decision to clear out our physical and or mental garage. If you do let me know. My actual garage is going to stay a mess until I finish this book.

Find a Reason That Matters to You a Lot

For my wife and me, it was Mom after she had neck surgery and had to move into the room we built in the garage. My reasons were clear: First, I needed to clear a path so she wouldn't trip and fall. Secondly, she's my mom and I didn't want to hear her nag me as if I were a teen to clean up my messy garage.

In one weekend, my wife and I cleared that sucker out and organized it enough to both be safe and to quell any potential comments from Mom about what a disaster it was.

Now I could make this story sound all altruistic about how we did all this because we loved Mom so much and it was the right thing to do, but that would be bullshit. Not the love part, but the appearance of altruism. **We did it because we had to.** We didn't really have much choice.

There's a lot more to the story, about why she needed to live with us in the first place (not just because of her neck surgery), and the family dynamic that necessitated this change. But it's too long to tell here. Suffice it to say she likes her independence as much as my wife and I do. But she needed us and was humble enough to ask for our help. So, yes, we did it out of necessity, but we also did it out of love. As I've said before, **love is and always will be the greatest motivator of all.** But love, like good intentions of cleaning your garage, (mental or physical), without effort or commitment is hollow and meaningless.

Do the Work and Ask for Help

We need to put in the work: organize the piles and properly store what we are going to keep so it's easy to find when we need it. Then we need to make the Goodwill and dump runs to get rid of everything else. We need to make the room comfortable and inviting, an expression of our love as if we were preparing a room for our mom.

Ask for help, do the rehab, and be patient for the recovery to happen just as it was with my mom recovering from neck surgery. And later moving my ninety-year-old stepfather into the garage "suite" with her, until we could find a new home for them both.

Wait

My wife and I were diligent, kind, loving, and patient. Mom got her husband back and eventually moved into an independent living home nearby. They were able to spend the next two years together until David passed in 2019. She's since moved into a smaller apartment and made it her own. Her apartment is furnished and organized the way *she* likes.

Sometimes Our Why Finds Us Before We Find it

At the time all this happened, we questioned why. It wasn't a self-driven goal. It was inconvenient, and yet caring for my mom and David gave my wife and me a sense of purpose.

It provided an opportunity for my wife to reevaluate her work situation where she was getting burned out. It allowed me to connect with both my mom and David on a deeper level than I had in many years. It allowed me to be grateful for the job I had that gave me the latitude and freedom and flexibility to care for my parents; my managers maintained a "family first" attitude that wasn't just lip service.

It also gave my wife and me a chance to work together caring for someone else. In the end, that made our relationship stronger. I mention this because we may not find our exact why by thinking about it. But, as you will learn in the next chapter, *when we approach life with an open mind and a willingness to learn and love, we discover our why or it will find us nearly every time.*

The next three chapters will take a much deeper dive into three critical topics—Belief, Willingness, and Love. And how they are integral to helping you clarify and discover your *motives, purpose, and drive*. The goal is to help you find and clarify your why so you can become more confident and thrive in all areas of your life: *finances, relationships, career, mental, physical, emotional, spiritual, etc.* You may discover as we continue that our why is dynamic, fluid. That our goals are not always an end result or destination. That would make them transactional. The lasting and, in my opinion, far greater rewards lie in our pursuit of why with a mindset and objective of transformation and becoming rather than mere achievement and acquisition. We will explore this concept further in the remainder of this section.

Chapter Fifteen
Belief: Changing How You Think About Everything

"The world we see that seems so insane is the result of a belief system that is not working. To perceive the world differently, we must be willing to change our belief system, let the past slip away, expand our sense of now, and dissolve the fear in our minds."
William James

Take a few moments to consider the reason or reasons why you want to tackle something new. Is it to add to or get rid of something you feel you are better off without? Something that you really, really want? Or is it something that is causing you pain? If so, on a scale of 1-10, how great is your pain?

Carrots and Sticks: What Moves You into Action?

Pain and pleasure are the carrots and sticks of human motivation and ambition. We either are motivated by our need to avoid pain or our desire for pleasure. But that is really an over-generalization which ignores the full complexities of human existence collectively and individually. That theory overlooks the breadth of our cultural, relational, and experiential differences, and puts us all into a binary box, even if our motives really are as simple as avoidance of pain or desire for pleasure as Sigmund Freud posited back in 1895.

Pain or pleasure as motivators remind me of the science experiments I learned in school. The ones about rats or hamsters in a cage. Sometimes they involved exercise or a challenge—a wheel, or a race in a maze. Often, they tested responses to various stimuli or rewards—a sip of water, a piece of cheese—or punishment—a shock, or locked doors in a complex maze. Still others tested the effects of addictive drugs like cocaine and nicotine, as well as survival instincts—such as an experiment with Norwegian rats to see how long they could tread water before they drowned.

These scientific experiments were conducted to test hypotheses and form conclusions about choice, drive, or motivation. Some were very revealing. I was especially intrigued by Ivan Pavlov's experiments involving a buzzer (or shock), a dog, and a treat, which led to his theory of *classical conditioning*: *animals and people can be trained to respond in the same way we would unconditionally.*

For example, our natural, unconditional salivary response to the aroma of fresh baked chocolate chip cookies can also be learned, based expectation of a reward. In other words, **we can be conditioned to respond based on the anticipation of an expected reward**. Anyone thinking "Got milk?" right now?

Pavlov's findings have influenced behavioral psychology, marketing, motivation, and so much more in our lives. If you don't believe me, consider the last commercial you saw. The one with tropical breezes, and beaches, and sunsets, and smiling faces. Were you even thinking about how nice it would be to stroll along a sandy beach with someone you love, listening to the sounds of the sea, holding hands as the sun sets? If not, you are now. You can't help it. Advertising and marketing are essentially classical conditioning.

Ironically, I am on a plane as I am editing this section, returning from a magnificent vacation in Kauai with my wife. I don't mention this to boast but because classical conditioning is closely related to visualization which we discussed earlier. Our vacation exceeded all mental images I had while planning and visualizing what it would be like. Flipping through the pictures of our trip is like Pavlov's bell; I'm already dreaming of the rewards of our next vacation: Waking up next to the woman I love, watching the last shooting stars skip across the pre-dawn sky; of easy days on a beach, holding hands, as the bright orange sun takes a bow then dips below the horizon waving goodbye.

Later we will further explore how important visualization and affirmations are to building your self-confidence and accomplishing your goals. For now, let's return to Pavlov.

Dopamine Rush and Notifications

Dopamine is a feel-good neurotransmitter often associated with food, exercise, love, sex, gambling, drugs, and now, social media. According to an article by Harvard University researcher Trevor Haynes, when you get a social media notification, your brain sends a chemical messenger called dopamine along a reward pathway, which makes you feel good. Studies indicate that on average *we check our phones sixty-three times a day. Like Pavlov's dog, most of us have become dopamine junkies.* Don't believe me? Check your reaction the next time you hear "Ding" on your cell phone.

While I'm not advocating animal or human experimentation, when it comes to my goals and motives, it is interesting how I still think in terms of black or white, pain or pleasure, risk or reward.

I can totally relate to the dopamine effect noted above. It reminds me of something my friend told me about male emotional motives. Joking, he said, "Guys basically have two emotions: They are either hungry or horny. If they are not horny, give them a sandwich."

We've already covered a lot. I hope that by now you have a better understanding of the factors which typically impede our confidence and how they are tied to our belief systems. To reiterate, our belief system is the sum of our upbringing, experiences, environment, culture, values, and drive. *Remember also, our worth is not defined by what we do or our past.*

Our self-image, attitude, and how we respond to a variety of situations and circumstances, threating or not, is greatly influenced by what we believe and how we process information.

Our belief system is like a complex tapestry: you don't exactly know which color thread to weave first. But you must start somewhere. To that end, consider what might you change or do differently to move beyond your current situation. Ask yourself: What you are avoiding? What are you denying? And more importantly, what would it look like if a) you overcame that obstacle or b) had something better to replace it. How would you feel?

> When we become willing to take an honest look at ourselves, clarify our motives, and ask for feedback from others, we will find the real areas that have been holding us back. We will then move one step closer to becoming who we want to be.

Prompt: Consider and Capture

Take some time to look at your situation. It could be how you think or how you process information. What you say when you talk to yourself. Is your inner dialogue, positive or negative? It may be pride, or something that you are not yet willing to address that continues to be manifested in a multitude of areas. In relationships for example: Are you afraid of commitment or over controlling? How do you feel about these aspects of yourself?

In your job, are you not picking up the phone because it's too scary to talk to someone? What are you afraid of? And what do you really want? Why? What will it mean to you if you find ten seconds of courage to push through whatever fear is in your way? What's the benefit of courage? What's the payoff? As yourself WIIFM? (What's in it for me?).

Take a few minutes to capture you thoughts/feelings in a journal or on paper. As you do, avoid the temptation of self-psychoanalysis by asking *why* or looking for root causes. Instead, *explore what you see, think, and feel in situations that cause anxiety and stress. How do you behave when stressed?* Monitor your reactions, look at the facts, and capture them on paper. You may also want to brainstorm solutions. What, for example could you do differently, to produce a different outcome?

We have become a culture that wants to accept only what we see, understand, and believe. None of us have all the answers. But when something is important enough to us, many will do what it takes to get it.

As mentioned earlier, part of that process, requires introspection, courage, and willingness to try something new.

There's No Need to Fear. Ain't No Monsters in There

How often do you dig our heels in at the first thought of change? Your stubbornness, which can be a positive trait or another block that keeps you locked in your comfort zones, fearing things that are not real, like monsters in your closet.

> Just because you're afraid of something doesn't mean it's actually scary.

As a kid, were you afraid of the dark? I was. I'd cry out, "Dad, there's a monster in the closet!" He'd rush in, all brave and shit. No surprise there, after all, he was a fireman. He'd flip the lights on and open the closet doors "No monsters here, just coats and shadows," he'd declare.

"What about under the bed? I thought I heard something," I'd ask him, blankets tucked under my chin.

"Let's have a look," he'd say. "Nope. No monsters here, either."

Once reassured that the monsters were more likely just shadows, and not real, I felt safe. Dad would give me a kiss goodnight and turn out the lights.

What's in Your Closet?

We are not perfect. Far from it, actually. Then why do we spend so much time trying to be? Judging ourselves for making mistakes or messing up? Being overly concerned about what others may or may not think of us, striving to belong? To feel a part of something. To be accepted. Is our worth really measured by how we *think* others perceive us? Read that again.

Attaching our identity and sense of self-worth to praise, recognition, and whether we are loved or accepted by others makes us people-pleasers, not bold and daring individuals striving to gain self-confidence.

Internal vs. External Locus of Control

In psychology, there is a name for this common inner battle we face. It's called Internal vs. External Locus of Control. This concept was originally developed by Julian Rotter in the 1950s as a question-based assessment for students. It is now a widely used tool among psychology professionals.

In an article from *Psychology Today*, Richard B. Joelson, ECW, LCSW expands on the concept of Locus of Control. To paraphrase, Joelson suggests:

"Locus of control is an individual's belief system regarding the causes of his or her experiences and the factors to which that person attributes success or failure." He separates those factors into two categories: internal and external. Joelson argues that individuals with an internal locus of control tend to credit their success to personal "efforts and abilities." They "expect to succeed and therefore are more motivated and more likely to learn." In other words, they feel in control of their own destiny and find a more direct correlation between self-effort and success.

Conversely, people with an external locus of control tend to feel their success is a result of luck or fate. Joelson adds, they are also more prone "to experience anxiety since they believe they are not in control of their lives."

Because there are many variables to be considered, Joelson does not classify internal locus of control as "good" nor external locus of control as "bad." He points out that one is not necessarily better than the other.

But psychological research has found that people with a more internal locus of control seem to be better off and tend to be more achievement oriented and get better paying jobs.

In summary, locus of control is an attempt to uncover causes and conditions responsible for our perceptions of success or failure as they relate to our belief system.

Finding Balance

We have already discussed many questions to help guide you toward becoming the person you want to be. You have also likely established that there are things you want to be different, to change.

Great news! Now is the time you get to flip the script and take control of your own future. If you have not yet used ten seconds of boldness, now is your chance. Especially if you lean heavily on the side of having an external locus of control. Because if you want to be bolder and more confident, it's your responsibility, no one else's. *Nobody else is going to take the steps for you.*

On the flipside, for those like me who have a more internal-based system of control, *a word of caution—stay in your own lane.* I have already talked about what I lost by being too self-absorbed, controlling, and at times, cocky. That's why one is not better than the other. Both have value. As with many things in life, balance is a beautiful thing.

I am mostly internally focused. But I also know, appreciate, and respect the need to be externally focused, especially in terms of my spiritual growth and development. At times, that creates friction, and an internal struggle between my will and God's will.

There are no perfect or clear-cut answers. That's not how life is. Over time, I have learned to nurture both sides of my personality as best I can at this stage of my life. And I will continue to do so until the day I die. That's just how I'm wired. That does not mean you have to be that way too.

But **I encourage you to nurture the non-dominant side of your personality.** To stretch beyond what is easy and comfortable. Build. Improve. Be diligent and intentional about your own personal growth and development. My advice is to **keep an open mind and never stop trying to become better.**

There is No One-Size-Fits-All Solution

There are a multitude of tools and techniques to help you become more confident and successful. I've already discussed prayer, meditation, and creative visualization. Other methods I have found helpful include writing, especially journaling, therapy, counselling, and spirituality. All are designed to increase my awareness and inspire me to change something— diet, attitude, behavior, etc. All have been beneficial when approached with a solution-based mindset.

All the tools in the world are useless unless you use them. None of the techniques you may learn can help you until you practice them. I like how Dalai Lama XIV puts it, *"Change only takes place through action, not meditation and prayer."*

There is great wisdom in the above quote.

Unfortunately, our natural proclivity is to excessively ruminate (replay) our past mistakes and shortcomings, or future trip (worry) about what *might* happen. What a complete waste of time and energy. It's no wonder so many of us feel stressed out and exhausted.

While there are many solutions, none is a panacea.

We are multi-dimensional, complex beings. Why would we think there is a single solution, a one and done, to fix us? Not gonna happen because a one-size-fits-all solution does not exist.

That is what makes this ten seconds of boldness concept and five-step plan so essential. The book is specifically designed as a rubric to help you tackle the multitude of problems you will face in your life. Personally, and professionally. It is a frame of reference. A guide.

Why do I reiterate that here? Because all too often the solutions to the problems we have are not as complicated or elusive as we may think. Quite often the solutions we are desperate to find are literally right under our nose. But as already mentioned, **attempting to find a solution if you don't know what the problem is, is ludicrous.** For our purposes, most of the problems we encounter are a product of a faulty belief system. We will continue to explore what that means and how you can fix it.

For now, here's a short tip that I use whenever I feel stressed or fearful: I say a prayer, often the serenity prayer, because it's easy to remember, covers most of what I am struggling with, and puts the responsibility on me to resolve. Then, as the Dalai Lama suggests, **I get into action.**

That action starts with the five-step success and habit building plan of *Ten Seconds of Boldness*.

Basic Motives: Revisiting Freud's Pleasure Principle

Let's move beyond Pavlov's dog, and locus of control and explore motivation further starting with Sigmund Freud's *Pleasure Principle*.

In Freud's psychoanalytic theory of personality, the pleasure principle is the driving force of the id that seeks immediate gratification of all needs, wants, and urges. In other words, according to Freud, the pleasure principle strives to fulfill our most basic and primitive urges, including hunger, thirst, anger, and sex.

It's clear that we are motivated to seek pleasure and avoid pain.

For addicts, studies show that the pleasure of a high is often replaced by pain (crash) and the desire to return to normal (pleasure) once addicted. Ironically, for many addicts or alcoholics, the decision to get high in the first place, on some level, is an attempt to escape pain. For many, the escape works in the short term-until it becomes a habit. An addiction.

To oversimplify, the "new normal" for an addict is getting back to the euphoria of being high. Of continuing to ride a never ending roller-coaster because it feels good, until it doesn't.

Our own habits and negative self-talk are very analogous to the life of an addict. I know that may sound harsh, but it's true. Avoiding tough decisions, procrastinating, pretending to have it all together even when we don't are the very same things I did when I was drinking. It is this destructive cycle of seeking pleasure and avoidance of pain that keeps addicts hooked. In essence, whatever substance, or behavior an individual is addicted to is both a problem and a solution.

In my case, recovery helped but, as I mentioned earlier, some issues were deeper and required professional therapy to resolve.

In five years of intense work with a therapist, I learned about many of the thoughts and behaviors that were undermining my self-esteem. To rebuild it meant that I had to change how I thought and reacted to memories and triggers. Essentially, I had to change my entire belief system.

Similarly, our beliefs and habits shape our self-image and become an endless loop until we do something to disrupt, modify, or reprogram those patterns and beliefs.

When we are in flux or indecisive about what we want or are reluctant to do anything to change our current situation or circumstances, we suffer. Our confidence wanes. And we become less effective in many areas of our lives. For addicts or alcoholics, the penalties, for reluctance to change are "jails, institutions, and death."

Beyond Pleasure and Pain

In the book, *Beyond Pleasure and Pain: How Motivation Works,* E. Tory Higgins says that what people really want is to be effective in their life pursuits. To paraphrase, he suggests *three distinct ways that people want to be more effective:* They want desired results **(value)**, which can include but is not limited to pleasure. They want to manage what happens **(control)** and want to know what's real **(truth)** "even if the process of managing what happens or establishing what's real is painful."

In the next two chapters we will further explore motivation and some effective tips to building our confidence with one goal in mind: **To inspire and encourage you to <u>become willing to change</u> as you discover your why.**

Chapter Sixteen
Willingness: What Are You Willing to Do to Get What You Want?

"Change is the essence of life. Be willing to surrender what you are for what you could become."
Reinhold Niebuhr

From a practical perspective, this chapter is about becoming willing to be willing to change.

Think of it as a pep talk when things aren't going as well as you may like or when you are having a difficult time believing in yourself. Or a half-time speech or quick huddle to get the team fired up to come from behind and win; *to remind you of what it feels like to win again.*

Willingness is like a gut check. It may seem daunting, but it doesn't have to be. It is your opportunity to prove to yourself what you are capable of.

Willingness is not the same as commitment. We'll cover that later—no, I'm not avoiding anything—I'm prioritizing. Before we can commit, we need to become willing. What does that mean, really?

Oxford Languages Dictionary defines **willingness** as: **"the quality or state of being prepared to do something; readiness."**

I would also add to that definition one of my favorite quotes: "Success happens where opportunity and preparedness meet," modified from Zig Ziglar's original quote: "Success occurs where opportunity meets preparation."

Willingness is about planning and preparation. It's also a *mindset*. To get your head in the game and not somewhere else. It's about *belief, drive, and determination.*

Willingness is the first word in the definition of boldness which I mentioned at the beginning of this book. Here it is again:

bold·ness
bōldnəs

willingness to take risks and act innovatively; confidence or courage.

> If boldness was a stepladder, willingness would be the first step.

To best illustrate willingness, confidence, and courage, consider the following fictionalized account of a true story I wrote about my son and his little league baseball team entitled, *Just Keep Swinging*. This story first appeared in an anthology entitled *Remember When*, published by the Redwood Writers in December of 2021.

Just Keep Swinging
By Shawn Langwell

I was in a slump, and I couldn't seem to shake it. No longer one of the top salespeople in the company, I had gone from "hero" to "zero" in less than a year and now I agonized over my weekly call with my manager. Fearing the worst, I took a deep breath and dialed. To my surprise, she didn't threaten or scold me. Instead, she offered a few words of advice:

TEN SECONDS OF BOLDNESS

"Just keep swinging, you can do it. I've seen you do it before."

"I know," I said. "I took my eye off the ball. I got complacent."

"I get it," she said. "We've all been there before. Why don't you go for a walk and clear you head?"

I put on my Giant's cap and went for a walk. I approached a ballfield. Shuffling my way past the weather-beaten, green bleachers to the backstop behind home plate, I laced my fingers through the chain link fence and peered onto the dusty field. I closed my eyes and inhaled deeply. The smell of fresh cut grass rekindled fond memories of watching my son, Andrew, play ball there many years earlier.

In my mind, I could hear the encouraging cheers as if no time had passed:

"Let's go one-seven, give it a rip!"
"Just keep swinging kid."
"You'll get it next time."

I drifted back to that day when…

It was the bottom of the fourth inning, and we were getting our butts whupped, losing 9-0. If the other team scored one more run, we'd lose by the ten-run rule.

I knew what it was like to have my back against the wall. In 1986 I had gone into rehab for addiction to drugs and alcohol. It was no easy feat to stop … or to stay stopped. I had a whiff of déjà vu as I stood in the dugout, feeling again as if my back was against the wall. But there had been people who helped me, who loved and encouraged me until I could do it myself. I thought of my sponsor, my mom, and Joannie, a close family friend, who hugged me with tears in her eyes the first Christmas I was sober, and said, "I am so proud of you. You can do it."

Between innings, the kids slumped into the dugout and sat on the bench with their heads hung low. I paced back and forth searching for the right words to somehow lift their spirits.

"Hey guys, guess what? We're losing ... again. Kind of sucks, doesn't it?"

"Yeah," they grumbled, eyeing the laces on their cleats.

"These guys are good, but I think we're better—we have heart."

A couple of the boys turned in my direction and I continued.

"Has anyone ever wondered what it would be like to come from way behind to win? You know, like the Giants when Duane Kuiper makes the call, 'It's the bottom of the ninth, the bases are loaded...Bonds steps into the batter's box...here's the pitch...he hits it high...he hits it deep...that ball is... outta here!'"

"All. Season. Long!" our team captain Brandon barked. "Let's do it guys!" he added, clapping his hands. "What've we got to lose?"

That got their attention. They all leaned forward; jaws set. Their eyes intent, focused, as I continued pacing the length of the bench.

"Here's the deal—we need ten runs. There's thirteen of you on this team ... and...somehow, ten of you need to find a way to get on base and cross home plate. You can do it. I know you can. But the real question is ... do you think you can?" I stopped and stared at them, letting my challenge sink in. "Joey? Matthew? Think you can you do that?"

"Yeah," they said half-heartedly.

"Stanley? Andrew?"

"Yes," louder.

"Brandon?"

"Yes!" he shouted, thumping his chest.

And all the way down the line:

"Yes!"

"Yes!"

TEN SECONDS OF BOLDNESS

"Yes!"

I felt goosebumps. Each "yes" was like a jolt of electricity, of hope; a unified heartfelt call to the baseball Gods to somehow produce a miracle comeback for these kids.

"Bring it in. On three—Win it!" We joined hands and I counted off, "One. Two. Three…"

"Win it!" we all shouted in one loud, clamorous voice that rang across the field.

"Batter up!" the ump yelled.

The first boy up in the bottom of the fourth was Matthew, our shortstop. He was also one of our best hitters. After fouling off several balls, he hit a bloop single to leftfield. On the next pitch, I flashed the "steal" sign. If we were going to come out swinging, I decided, we were going to give it everything we had. As the pitcher wound up, Matthew broke for second. The catcher's throw sailed into center and Matthew raced to third. We were still nine runs behind, but it felt like a rally in the making. Brandon was at the plate. He hit a slow roller to the shortstop, but the ball bounced off his glove and dribbled into the outfield as Matthew crossed home plate for our first run. The entire bench was on their feet cheering and their excitement sent a charge through our fans, some of whom stood up in the bleachers and shouted our name.

With Brandon on second, Joey, our clean-up hitter, came to the plate. The pitcher wound up and threw a fastball that plunked him in the shoulder. Joey glared at the pitcher, shook it off, and sprinted down to first. I heard the opposing coach call out to the pitcher, "C'mon, bud … rock n' fire!" We hadn't hit a ball hard the entire inning, but everyone in the dugout could feel something happening. And the frustration by the pitcher was clear as he slapped his glove against his thigh.

Next up was Stanley, one of my son's best friends and the smallest player on our team. "C'mon, Stanley," I yelled. "You can hit this guy." The pitcher scowled at me, taking my comment personally that such a weakling would even dare to swing the bat. He rocked and fired, and Stanley (eyes closed) took a powerful cut and hit a pop-up between the first and second basemen. As they both lunged for the ball, they collided, and it fell safely on the edge of the infield.

Suddenly, the bases were loaded for Mario. Throughout the season, Mario had struggled to make contact at the plate. Our fans roared as if we were in the World Series, and their energy crackled through the ballpark.

By now, the entire team was on its feet, hanging on the chain link fence, me included. The pitcher seemed to regain his composure and got two quick strikes on Mario. Then he missed with a pitch outside, then inside, then low. "C'mon, ump!" the opposing coach cried. "What're you lookin' at?" The pitcher took his wind-up and fired: "Ball four!" He had walked in a run and still the bases were loaded!

Nick stood at the plate. Nick had only four hits all year, all of them weak grounders that somehow found a hole.

"Let's go Nick!" His mom cheered from the stands.

The pitch was in the dirt and the ball skidded away from the catcher. Another run scored; it was 9-3. On the next pitch, Nick slapped a line drive up the middle for a clean single into center and two more runs came in to score. We high-fived the base runners as the crowd roared its approval. We were still on our feet when the next batter hit a pop fly to right field that was caught for the first out. At the crack of the bat, we all cheered as if every swing was charmed, and then reality hit me: the score was 9-5 and we still had a long way to go to get back in the game. The fear of forfeit to the ten-run rule had disappeared but the fact we had made our opponents sweat gave me even greater determination. Each run scored was like a shot of hope. The team was pumped—they had started to believe they could win—and so had I. "Let's go, guys!" I shouted. "We're not done yet!"

Zack, our next batter, took a mighty cut in the on-deck circle, like he was going to rip the cover off the ball, then stepped into the batter's box and dug in. The pitcher stared him down and went into his wind-up. On cue, Nick broke for second. The catcher's throw was high and caromed off the glove of the shortstop into the outfield; Nick hustled into third on the error. Zack roped a line drive past the diving first baseman, driving in Nick and pulling us one run closer at 9-6.

That was the score as we headed into the last inning. We had made a valiant comeback, but we were down to our last three outs, and we needed three runs to tie the game.

Rica came to bat. She was the only girl on our team, but fearless and fast. Rica smoked a high fastball over the head of the right fielder who was playing too shallow; by the time he chased down the ball, she safely slid headfirst into second for a double.

The crowd went wild.

Andrew, my son, was our lead-off hitter. He was thin and fast, a speedster in the outfield. A new pitcher had taken the mound for our opponents; as he warmed up, the slap of the ball against the mitt of the catcher sounded like a gunshot. Andrew stepped in, tapped his bat on the plate, and adjusted his helmet. "Let's go, one-seven!" I called to him. "You can do this!" His teammates joined me in a flurry of encouragement. The first pitch was high heat, brushing Andrew back from the plate; the second was right down the middle. Andrew swung and topped a ground ball to third. Rica faked like she was breaking for third, causing the third basemen to double clutch, allowing Andrew to easily beat out the throw to first.

We were back in business. The next batter was Matthew. I signaled to the third base coach for a "hit and run." Andrew and Rica adjusted their helmets to let the coach know they saw the sign and extended their leads. The pitcher checked each runner, then quick-pitched Matthew. Andrew and Rica took off as soon as the pitcher released the ball. Matthew took a wild swing as the pitch bounced on home plate. The catcher scooped the ball and in one motion fired to third, sending the ball over the third baseman's glove into left field. Rica scored easily making it 9-7. The left fielder ran the ball down then airmailed it over the cutoff man, allowing Andrew to take third on the error.

On the very next pitch, Matthew hit a weak grounder to the shortstop who held Andrew at third before gunning down the runner at first.

Brandon then hit a pop up to the pitcher for the second out. The opposing team intentionally walked Joey and Stanley to load the bases.

We were down to our final out and Mario was up next. The last time up, he had drawn a walk; just getting on base seemed to boost his confidence. I grabbed the fence and shook it: "Come on, Mario! Keep it going! You can do it!" The bench, all standing, chanted: "Mar-E-O ... Mar-E-O ... Mar-E-O." The pitcher checked the runners and wheeled home. As if in a blur, I saw Mario swing and watched the ball headed to the outfield, deeper and deeper, until it smashed off the scoreboard for a grand slam.

The collective roar sent chills up my back.

Andrew jogged home from third, pumping his fist in the air. Joey, Stanley, and Mario crossed the plate right behind him. Our players stormed out of the dugout and swarmed Mario, jumping up and down and high fiving each other. Someone in the crowed resumed the chant…

"Mar-E-O … Mar-E-O … Mar-E-O."

Soon everyone, even the opposing team, was chanting as if our team had just won the World Series. That day, for one special moment, it felt like we had.

I have replayed this story many times over the years. It reminds me that life is a lot like baseball: I've been beaned more times than I can count and struck out on more nasty curves in the dirt of life than I would like to admit. But each time I'm knocked down, I get up, brush the dust off my pants, dig in, and keep swinging. Eventually I know I'll get a hit. Perhaps even more important, I know that if I don't quit before the miracle, it may even be a game-winning walk-off grand-slam.

Prompt: Consider These Two Important Questions

Question #1: Are you willing to try and fail and keep getting back up until you succeed? Are you willing to be bolder? To change? To grow? To trust? To believe in yourself, again. To do whatever it takes to accomplish that which you seek? That's what willingness is all about.

Question #2: Are you ready to grab a bat, step up to the plate, and *Just Keep Swinging*?

Chapter Seventeen
Love: The Source of All Motivation and Inspiration

"Do everything in love."
1 Corinthians 16:14 NIV

Your Why Matters, a Lot

In fact, your why is and will be the most powerful force to motivate you to press on, especially when things aren't going the way you would like. And things will not always go according to your plans. But just like the story in the last chapter, when you begin to believe in yourself great things can happen.

Therefore, it's crucial to not only be decisive about what you want but to also have a visceral emotional attachment to the reasons why you are choosing to pursue something new. You need to feel it in your mind, body, and soul. Why?

Because your why is a means to your end. Your personal growth, your quest for courage and confidence, your dreams, goals, and aspirations. **Your why is the fuel that will keep your desire, dreams, and drive alive.**

Your why will also inspire you to be courageous enough to do the introspection necessary to make the changes you need to, so you can develop new habits that will improve and not keep you stuck or worse, destroy your life. It will also serve as a rudder to guide your trajectory toward success, whatever success means to you.

New Year Resolutions Don't Work

Studies indicate that less than 10% will actually achieve the goals set at the beginning of the year. I rarely set "resolutions." Instead, I often write out goals, or choose a word or words that are easy to remember and focus my attention and energy on them. For 2022, my words are completion and love.

Completion

I have so many projects in the works—completing this book, remodeling our master bathroom, clearing out the garage, staying on top of my sales goals for work, and planning our ten-year anniversary—to name a few. All will get done (half already are), because I've developed the confidence and determination to see many goals like these through to completion in the past. What motivates me is not only completing them but the joy that comes from pursuing them, planning, and enjoying them, especially like the epic vacation my wife and I just had.

Completion is how I create *compound confidence*—a mindset in which confidence grows exponentially upon each previous success.

The pursuit, process, and completion of any meaningful goals I set, build positive memories that will last a lifetime.

That doesn't mean that I won't face the same mental challenges of doubt, boredom, or laziness that many of us share. But I also know that to succeed I am going to need to be diligent and follow my own plans as outlined in this book. If I don't, then I am a hypocrite.

Love is the Most Powerful Healing, and Motivational Force in the World

It's been said that "love conquers fear." I agree because I've experienced it. It is also the answer to everything.

"Life without love is like a tree without blossoms or fruit." – Kahlil Gibran

"Love is patient, love is kind. It does not envy, it does not boast, it is not proud. It does not dishonor others, it is not self-seeking, it is not easily angered, it keeps no record of wrongs. Love does not delight in evil but rejoices with the truth. It always protects, always trusts, always hopes, always perseveres. 1 Corinthians 13:4-7 NIV

"And now these three remain: faith, hope and love. But the greatest of these is love."
1 Corinthians 13:13 NIV

"All you need is love." – John Lennon

I agree. How could I not?
Starting with those who loved me enough until I learned to love myself, I'd go so far as to say that love is as important to our survival as oxygen, water, food, and sleep. Love created a beautiful son. Love gave me a second chance at marriage. Love is so powerful, it saved my life in the form of a greeting form my mom to me: "Son, please get help. I love you too much to watch you die. Love, Mom."
More songs, books and movies have been written about love than any other topic in the world. Fun fact: The Beatles use the word

"love" a total of 613 times in their songs. That's more than the 514 in the American Standard Version of the Bible.

It's worth repeating what I've said several times earlier: **love is and always will be the most powerful healing, and motivational force in the world.** Today I try to do everything with love. It makes the "world go 'round."

One of the reasons I switched my annual key area of intention to one or two words is that all too often I'd get frustrated and impatient with the process to accomplish a given goal or resolution and would start to beat myself up for not sticking to a plan. I'd let life get in the way and "put off today what could be done tomorrow." I know I am not alone.

I had to accept that I would make mistakes and had to cut myself some slack for not achieving what I wanted, when I wanted it. I also had to learn how to love myself. I still do on a daily basis. I do it by treating myself with a little more kindness. By pushing through the uncomfortable feelings and trying to replace my negative self-talk when I am not doing what I think I should be doing. This may sound weird but think about this: How hard are you on yourself when you make a mistake? When you fall short of your chosen ideal, would you talk to a child or subordinate the way you talk to yourself?

I also have come to realize that all my goals will not always work out exactly as I planned. That I am not going to be confident in the beginning of anything new. I accept that. After many years of trying and failing, and many years of disappointment, I made a decision to never give up trying to be better. I never will. Today, it's just who I am. I also know that just because I have a plan, doesn't mean I will follow it perfectly. It means accepting and loving my "humanness," my inadequacies and imperfections. It means learning to love myself with all my warts and bruises. And to cut myself some slack when I fall short or decide to move in a new direction. It means giving myself permission to try, fail, and change my mind.

This also means that whatever I share from this point forward must be couched in love. I learned that from my sponsor thirty-five years ago. It's also spiritual—and the "Golden rule." "Love one another," that is the greatest commandment. And "Love your neighbor as yourself."

Sometimes that means tough love, like my mom threatening to kick me out unless I got sober. Or deep care, like the card she left for me.

When we accept that we are loved, we begin to see the world of possibility and once again have that childlike faith and hope that we can achieve our greatest aspirations. We come to understand that **courage and love are secret weapons for building our own confidence**. That we don't have to have all the answers. That willingness to change, is enough to get started. I also know that nothing will change until we do something different, uncomfortable. That requires not only making a decision to change, but more importantly developing the discipline and motivation to persist, despite any challenges.

We'll talk more about that later but for now let's look at reality.

The stats don't lie. Most people will fail on their New Year's resolutions. What typically happens is we come up with a list and are all excited to "change our lives." We join the gym or change our habits for a while. Then something happens. We try to do too much, too fast. We expect instant results. Before we know it, we slip back into old patterns. Skipping a day or two of our plan. Soon we decide that we don't really want or need _____ (fill in the blank), as much as we thought. Or we find reasons why we can't do something and fall into a habit of making excuses, or worse, blaming people or situations for our ambivalence and self-doubt, and inability to achieve what we want. We justify our decision and give up on our resolutions. When we do, nothing ever changes.

This is typical among many alcoholics in recovery. They try for a bit but don't follow the program. The next thing they know, they drink again, thinking somehow it will "be different this time." It never is. Many have reported that things actually got worse. Some never make it back alive. Sadly, when that happens, the problem is not the plan. **The problem is they failed to surrender and work the proven plan. They thought they could do it alone, their way, without help.**

Words of Encouragement

Do not despair, I love you too much to watch you not live up to your full potential. **Please take a chance on you. You are worth it!** Keep reading because the solutions are closer than you may think. It's time to make a plan and then put that plan into action.

Section IV
Plan Your Work

- ◊ Keep it Simple
- ◊ Write that Shit Down.
- ◊ Shit Happens: Expect it. Plan for it. Deal with it and Be Flexible
- ◊ Manage Your Time or it Will Manage You

Chapter Eighteen
Keep it Simple

"By failing to plan, you are planning to fail."
Benjamin Franklin

The "Perfect Plan" Myth

There is no such thing as a perfect plan. That would imply that it is and always will be the best, that there is no room for improvement. That's as foolish as digging your heels in to resist innovation. Of being a lifetime member of the "if-it-ain't-broke-don't-fix-it" club. Of not wanting to change because things are fine as they are. They're "good enough."

But are they, really? If they were, you would not have picked up this book nor read this far. Again, no plan is perfect, nor are we. If you want perfection, consider this: It's *perfectly normal to be imperfect.* It's normal to adapt our plans if they will improve our results. In fact, if we aren't adapting or innovating as businesses or individuals, we're stagnating and risk losing market share, momentum, or worse, becoming obsolete and unemployed or out of business.

This is why it is so important to be a perpetual student in all important areas of your life. This is why it's important to "plan your work and work your plan."

Perpetual curiosity and willingness to innovate and improve are virtual guarantees that you will never be bored or become complacent.

It's also worth noting that no matter how perfect you think your plan is, even if it works great, others will attempt to copy it or improve it. *To maintain your competitive advantage, you must continue to improve, developing new habits and plans. You must* **commit to perpetual innovation.**

Plans are Not the Same as Values

Rob Devincenzi, publisher and president of the Marin Independent Journal (the news organization where I currently work), often reminds his sales team and journalists that the only constant in life is change. That we must adapt and adjust our strategies and plans to the needs of our clients and subscribers. It's normal for plans to change, but, as we covered earlier, the company vision, mission, and purpose, and its core values remain steadfast.

What is a Plan?

In its simplest form, a plan is a goal paired with action steps. Where many of us get hung up, in my experience and opinion, is trying to create the perfect plan which will produce a guaranteed outcome. **There is no perfect plan. Successful plans are flexible; they always change.**

Plans are merely our best attempt at creating a roadmap to a desired outcome. Like architectural plans, schematics, or business plans, our personal plans are the blueprints for how to go from where we are to where we want to be.

Yet we are creatures of habit. *We like our comfort zones. Some of us way more than others.* But the leaders and innovators of tomorrow are the ones who are constantly looking at cultural and behavior shifts and are mindful of and intentional about creating plans to either improve their own lives or to enhance and/or better serve others.

And still how many of us have plans? I heard once that most people spend more time planning an event or a vacation than they spend on planning their life. How unfortunate.

Others invest untold hours and dollars for research, study, and analysis, trying to find and/or create the perfect plan. For what? Is it really necessary? In some industries it is. But quite frankly, that kind of expense and energy is a waste of time and money and not necessary to get the job done. It's inefficient and another form of procrastination.

The Man Who Changed the World

Steve Jobs was a genius when it came to designing intuitive, innovative, and elegant products. Along with Steve Wozniak and many other talented and creative people, Jobs changed how we communicate, connect, listen to music, and so much more. All because of his dream and plan to be the best, and because he dared to be different.

He was a master at merging technology with art and built a multi-billion-dollar business based on his plans to best serve his customers. When it came to developing new products and marketing them, he paid attention to his gut and shunned extensive focus groups and research.

Not every leader can do that—many industries rely on science and research to solve problems for everything from tangled hair to energy efficient and environmentally responsible transportation—but some may do better to follow Jobs' lead and learn to trust their instincts more.

Don't get me wrong, we need a plan. And Jobs was a perfectionist, to a fault. I think we all are to some extent, but I still don't think "perfection" is realistic nor a prerequisite for greatness.

One thing however is certain—**without a plan you will never achieve lasting success**. But even with a plan, don't expect it to solve your problem or accomplish some objective. People and machines do that, not plans.

Keep Them Simple

Simple plans make it easier to get started, and, if they are easy to execute, build momentum faster. Complicated plans create confusion and consternation, and while they may look impressive, are usually ineffective. *Unless the project warrants incredible detail and complexity, keep your plans simple.*

All plans require thought and creativity and should be designed to solve a specific problem or produce a desired outcome. *Keeping them simple increases their effectiveness.*

A Few Thoughts on Collaboration

In business, creating plans in a silo without input from others is foolish. I am not suggesting that every plan or decision needs to be run though focus groups, surveys, etc., or involve every company employee or stakeholder. It can be a big mistake if you have "too many cooks in the kitchen" because it can bog down the process and lead to nothing getting done. It's a balancing act and may seem counter-intuitive to the "keep in simple" argument.

However, studies show that collaboration—brainstorming and working with others—can fuel innovation, improve efficiency, and increase productivity. Those who are part of the plan also become part of the solution which creates stickiness, or buy-in. Involving others, *especially those responsible for executing the plans*, increases morale and employee satisfaction.

That's one of the things I love about the management team where I work: they involve us in many, but not all decisions. As a result, our team effectively serves our readers and advertisers and produces positive outcomes for all key stakeholders.

Get Started. Now.

So far, we've covered the *who, what, why, where*, and *when* questions. Starting with this chapter and the next two sections—Plan your Work and Start Working Your Plan—I will map out the *how*.

The best way to start is by using the five essential habits: *Identify* the problem or opportunity, clearly *decide* what you want, know *why* you want it, write a *clear plan*, and *start* working that plan, as frame for creating your plan and get started now.

I have to ask: How many wanted to cut to the chase and skip over all the *what* and *why* stuff, including all the prompts? I probably would have too. As I said earlier, I am impatient. I have skipped the *why* way too many times in my life. I've even skipped the planning part. I'm a doer. I like to get things done, fast. But that's not always the most effective strategy.

Glossing over the *what* and *why* steps to cut to the bottom line is not an effective strategy for success.

Failing to plan or not having the courage to implement your plan will not produce the results you want. Period. But following the suggestions outlined in these next chapters to the best of your ability will surely improve your attitude and life. It will also likely increase your income and improve your relationships as it has for me.

I know because I have spent so much of my life planning, dreaming, and putting them to use. They have become a natural part of who I am and how I think. That is not to say I follow them perfectly or practice them in every circumstance. But I will say that Ben Franklin's quote, "By failing to plan, you are planning to fail," should be a law because I've proven it to be true enough to know. I have also experienced enough success to know that *having a plan and working that plan are tantamount to accomplishing anything worthwhile.*

I've experienced the results of not having a plan, like not bringing enough warm clothes or a pot to boil water when my wife and I camped at Joshua Tree, February of 2021. We planned for most of the essentials: tent, food, ice, lanterns, flashlights, hand warmers, etc. But we forgot the pot and didn't account for the high altitude and wind and how cold it would get at night. With wind chill, it felt like twenty degrees. We made it work. We boiled water in the frying pan before making breakfast and made toast in our sausage grease, because we also forgot butter. At night, let's just say we pretended we were stranded in the Sierra and made use of our combined body heat.

Regardless, it was an amazing trip. I never knew watching the sunrise and full moon set at the same time in the high desert would feel so magical.

Three Simple Questions to Help You Get Started

I understand that every reader is at a different spot in their journey and will do my best to keep the steps in these sections practical as well as challenging. Because if they appear too easy or too difficult you won't do them. And you still may not do them.

I will focus on the key elements of planning I believe will be helpful to you now and for the future. As you feel that you master them, I encourage you to pursue other sources to further expand your knowledge and experience in each of these areas.

To get started, ask and answer these three questions:

1. What problem do you need to solve?
2. What opportunity are you considering?
3. How do you plan to accomplish it?

Don't Reinvent the Wheel

Look for existing plans to adapt and fit your needs. **Start with what you know.** Or what you don't know but want to. Like anything new, if you don't know how, ask someone. Look online if you need to. Find out what tools, skills, materials, or ingredients you need. **Be resourceful.**

Here is a simple three step process I use as a plan for anything new:

- Ask
- Follow
- Try

And another, I heard at a business event years ago about how to do effective presentations:

- See one
- Hear one
- Do one

The above, incidentally, is a highly effective way of learning because it addresses the three primary learning preferences: Visual, auditory, and kinesthetic.

Find a Recipe and Follow Instructions

Take cooking for example. *When you find a dish you like, find a recipe, and follow it.* After you've made it a bunch of times you may no longer need to follow a recipe. You may experiment and fine tune it to your taste. *It is the same with your plans: Keep them simple and practice them regularly.* Make a plan, stick to it until you feel you've mastered a process. Then be creative. Experiment. And have fun with it.

Here's a very simple example to illustrate a plan that requires no special skills. If you can boil water and crack and egg, you can also learn to poach them.

How to Make a Poached Egg

Tools/Utensils:
- Small pot, pan or poaching tray
- Slotted spoon
- Stove

- Fork
- Plate
- Napkin

Ingredients:
- Egg
- Water
- Salt
- Pepper

Optional:
- Meyer lemon olive oil (I prefer my friend's award-winning olive oil-Calolea) or equivalent as a healthy alternative to hollandaise.
- Vinegar
- Smoked paprika

Instructions:
1. Fill a small skillet or saucepan with 3" of water (1 ½ – 2 cups).
2. Add three to four shakes of salt (½ tsp.).
3. Add 1 tsp of vinegar.
4. Place pan on stove over medium high heat and bring to a boil.
5. Crack egg(s) slowly into boiling water.
6. Wait.
7. When the whites look firm and the yolk is cloudy—usually 1-3 minutes at most—turn off heat and remove eggs with a slotted spoon.
8. Serve over an English muffin or toast.

Optional:
- Drizzle with Meyer lemon olive oil and sprinkle smoked paprika, salt, and pepper to taste.

Bon Appetit!

As with any plan, there are many ways and variations of not only how to poach an egg but how you can dress it up to create eggs Benedict, or eggs Florentine, etc.

Avoid the temptation at every stage of the five habits to drift into analysis paralysis. Don't let it win. Be brave enough to boil water and crack an egg. Follow a recipe or develop a plan to get started and as you progress, don't be afraid to tweak it. **Adapt and innovate.** *Your creativity is what makes you unique. It's what makes you* ***memorable and interesting.***

Beware of Unplanned Obsolescence

When it comes to business, in today's technologically driven world, the notion of, "If it ain't broke don't fix it" is the equivalent of unplanned obsolescence. Businesses that fail to innovate, will likely be left in the dust.

Think of this book as your starter kit for the rest of your life: an *essential guide* to building self-confidence and solving problems. Also, *remember as you practice your plan, your skills improve. As a result, your confidence will increase.* And as you continue to evolve you will undoubtedly add new tools to your toolbox. More importantly, don't forget to use them.

What's in Your Toolbox?

Now think about your garage, your place of work, or your mind. What tools do you have? Which do you use most often? Which do you need to get? Which do need to get rid of?

For some problems, you don't know what you may need until something like a garbage disposal breaks. When that happens, what do you do? Search, "How to fix a broken garbage disposal" on YouTube? Then compare costs of new ones?

Perhaps you can't be bothered. Even if you can do it yourself, you search online for "plumbers near me" and start calling, hoping to get a live human to schedule a repair visit.

They quote you some amount that you can't afford. Now what? Back to YouTube and the hardware store? Or you try to replace it yourself only to realize you are missing that specialty wrench.

You eye the hammer and screwdriver in your toolbox, and for a split second, consider using them even though you know they are not the right tools and may lead to a trip to the ER.

The point is, every problem has many ways to be solved. Don't be afraid to ask for help. I have done lots of stupid shit when it comes to DIY projects at home. Some I messed up royally and ended up losing time and money because I was too proud and stubborn to call a pro in the first place.

When a problem arises, come up with a plan and find a way to fix it, with *one very important exception*: If you are a guy and your mate comes to you to express a "problem," *do not try to fix it. Just listen with empathy.* Say, "That must be really difficult," and *shut up*. Depending on the response, you may or may not want to ask, "So, what have you thought about to fix it?"

That is something I still fail at all the time, though I am slowly improving because I love my wife and I want to learn to communicate better.

My simple plan, when I remember to do it, is to pause and assess the situation *before* immediately jumping into solution mode; to *pay attention to everything she is not saying and just be there.* That is no easy feat. But it's worth it.

That same lesson is what my stepdad shared with me three decades ago. The tool I use now when facing an uncomfortable situation is also the first step of my plan—to pause and breathe and not panic or immediately jump into a solution. I am a work in progress, and that's okay. I accept that about myself.

Focus On Finding a Solution

When it comes to planning, here are a few simple tips:
- Start with a general game plan.
- Do some research. Enough to get you moving in the right direction. Remember **to stay focused on the problem you are trying to solve and why you want to solve it.**
- Be willing to start with only 70-80% of a reasonable expectation that your plan will help you achieve what you want or move you closer to your objective.
- Consult/Ask others who have experience.
- Don't get bogged down in the planning stage (avoid procrastination and analysis paralysis).
- Be willing to live with uncertainty.
- Don't sabotage your plans before you see them through.

There are few absolutes in life. A carefully created plan will not guarantee success. Learn to embrace change and develop plans that serve a specific need. **Be flexible.** Also be mindful of our tendency to use the planning process as a crutch to avoid getting started. As my wife says, "That's procrastination."

Side note: This may not be acceptable in some situations or even cultures, but do your best to let go of mistakes, pride, shame, and guilt. Learn to accept that failure is part of the process and that even the best-made plans will not always work. That **if a plan fails, it doesn't mean you are a failure. All it means is that that plan didn't work and needs to be modified.**

Prompt #1: Check Your Plan's Alignment:

- Does it align with a mission or serve a purpose?
- Does it support a vision?
- Is it challenging, realistic, and attainable?

Consider and respond, in writing.

Prompt #2: Some Questions to Ponder When Creating Your Plan:

- What tools, skills, resources do you have?
- What resources and information do you need to get started and implement it?
- Who are the stakeholders, and do they have buy-in?
- How will they or you benefit?
- Is it a good enough plan to get started?
- Is it written down?
- Is it clear?
- Are you bold enough to start?
- What's your plan?
- Do you believe it will work?
- So, what are you waiting for?

Why Plan?

Nothing will ensure your success more than a *carefully crafted plan* and the *motivation* and *determination* to execute it. You need all three. A plan without action means you're a starter not a finisher. A plan without a solid understanding of how it will benefit you or others is merely a wish or a dream. But a plan paired with motivation and the courage to put it into use will help you stay focused and make your life so much easier.

Some Plans and Benefits

Planning is a great aid to building confidence. Plans help you stay within a budget. Plans increase efficiency and effectiveness.

My wife and I take turns creating weekly meal plans for dinners, which includes shopping and cooking for that given week. And whoever cooks doesn't have to clean up. That plan works for us. Sharing this responsibility helps prevent burnout. We also eat healthier meals, plus save money and time because we don't have to make so many trips to the grocery store.

The other solutions are to be lazy and order DoorDash, eat fast food, or dine out. All of which are fine on occasion, but costly in many ways, namely our waistlines and pocketbook.

Other types of simple plans we use or have used include:
- Home maintenance/projects.
- Debt reduction and emergency savings.
- Investment plans for retirement.
- Vacations.
- To-do lists. I do these daily to prep for the next day.
- Calendars— the best planning tool of all.

- Chore plans to help minimize arguments and teach kids responsibility.
- Grocery lists on the fridge, so we don't have to make multiple trips to the store, wasting time, money, and gas, because we "forgot to write it down."

You get the idea. Can we all agree that life is easier with a plan? So ,what plans are you thinking of that you haven't made yet?

Don't plan for planning's sake. Plan because you intend to follow through with it. Otherwise you are just wasting your own and possibly other people's time.

I urge everyone to make plans and invest the time to consider not only the framework of a plan but what problems it will solve and why they need to be solved. The purpose of a plan is to provide a blueprint for what you want to build. And building a future sounds like an important plan to make.

Chapter Nineteen
Write That Shit Down

"In the absence of clearly defined goals, we become strangely loyal to performing daily acts of trivia."
Unknown

One of the most important things you can do to become more confident and successful is to set goals and create a plan of action, then *write them down*.

According to several experts in neuroscience, our brains form a stronger connection and focus better when we take the time to write things down. Some studies say that we are 42% more likely to accomplish goals that are written down, yet many other studies indicate that only 3% of us actually have goals and of those only 1% actually write them down.

So, it's not just an opinion. *If you want to achieve a goal, write that shit down!*

At the start of this project, I reached out to my friend, Jon Diamond, for my first interview. With respect to goal setting, he said you need to do three things:

"**#1 Write it down**. I don't care what it looks like, what format. Write it down. I don't care if you write in on a piece of scratch paper and you throw it away. Write it down. I heard one time that it's 1,000 times more likely to happen if you write it down… There is power in writing it down just as there is power in the spoken word."

"#2 Talk about it." He and Curtis started talking about their goal. "We weren't looking at a piece of paper, but we were talking about it. And you can call it God, or you can call it universe, whatever you want, as if it was here. Be very careful about the words used."

To clarify, Jon was referring to the *power of affirmations*, not just writing them down, but the inherent power of intentionality. Of discussing their business goals in positive terms, *creating a mindset for success. Of abundance, not scarcity.* "[Rather than saying] someday I'm going to. It's always someday away. Instead, say *I am* or *I have*, or *I did*. Guess what? Someday we get to say that for real. Say it as if it's happened."

As mentioned previously, what he and Curtis were doing worked. They grew a business from $1 million to $21 million in five short years!

"#3 Don't get held up if something else happens. Sometimes we make goals and God decides something else for our lives and for some reason or another doesn't bring that in [manifested]. We may not understand it right now, but it's okay. Just refresh your list."

He added: "I realized that once I write them [goals] down and I'm talking about them, if I'm not doing them, I feel like shit. *If I'm not doing the income producing activities or the action steps, I either need to take it off the list so I don't feel like crap anymore or get my ass to work."*

Use Your Calendar

It is easy to put off things we don't want to do. As an author, I'm especially challenged to get into the habit of writing consistently. But I write a little bit almost every day. My digital calendar pings me at 6:30 a.m. every day to remind me of my daily appointment: "Write: 500 words or for one hour." Most days I do it, especially when I'm in the middle of a project like finishing this book.

Sometimes those 500 words may be journaling or capturing thoughts or ideas for other projects, marketing, work related opportunities, or merely a blog like opinion piece on something to get shit off my mind. Most of that is for my eyes only. And most of it is pure crap. To me, it doesn't matter as long as I am writing.

The point is I write consistently. And I don't squander time making sure it's perfect. For me, it's about capturing the essence of an idea or thought before it evaporates into the back hole of space, which happens all the time. Especially when I don't write it down.

I also give myself a break. I am consistent but not my own taskmaster.

There are many new tools you can use to retain and capture important thoughts or to brainstorm. I use "Hey Siri" every day for taking notes, making phone calls, setting alarms, or adding events to my calendar. There are many productivity apps available. I encourage you to find the ones that will make tasks easier for you. Or you can be like Anne Lamott and never leave home without a stack of 3" x 5" index cards and a pen or pencil.

Anyone who is ambitious or creative should invest in themselves by taking the time to plan and write down what is important in their life. Always be curious, contemplating what you want and why. Or using your time to imagine what it will feel like to have it (visualization and affirmation). Writing is cathartic. It's healing and it will make a huge difference in your life. What's important is developing the habit and process of writing, not necessarily what you write.

Writing Goals and Plans are Like Taking Aspirin for a Headache

If you ever feel scattered or have a stress related headache, or you want to feel more productive, efficient, or effective, try writing things down. Then, as we've done with a few earlier prompts, break those lists into manageable action steps. I'll explore this in greater detail in the section, Into Action. But I want you to start thinking about it now because once you get into action and start succeeding, it's easy to forget about the basics. **Never forget the fundamentals.**

Writing Sets Solutions in Motion

The other reason you want to write things down is it gets your brain into solution mode. Because as your thoughts and ideas begin to percolate, they may lead to other connections or paths to creative solutions for some goal or problem you are working on.

Writing down your thoughts, plans, goals, ideas, and possible solutions is critical to your success to solve any problem. Remember to **focus on the solution.**

The tips and suggestion in the book are specifically designed to help you develop the skills necessary to rewire your faulty belief system and habits. They are only effective if you utilize them.

Prompt #1: Sign up for Free Resources

As you get closer to fine-tuning each of the five essential habits, you are going to want to make use of the tools in the appendices. In particular, the self-assessment tool, the *Ten Second of Boldness* Productivity Planner, the affirmation sheet, and a gratitude list found in the back of this book. You have my permission to reprint any **for personal use only**. Or you can sign up to my newsletter: bit.ly/ShawnLangwellMotivation (case sensitive). When you do, I'll send you a PDF of the *Ten Second of Boldness* Productivity Planner for free. I'll also send occasional tips, success stories, or other inspirational insights to help those of you who entrust me with your email.

And, at some point, I may make them available as a workbook or in an app. For now, if you are serious about where you want to go, start writing down the things you want and watch what magically begins to happen with each step forward.

P.S. Don't forget another critical action step: Do something!

Writing Goals and Affirmations Work

I want to close this section with a story that Jon Diamond told me about one of their installers who wanted to transition into sales and service. According to Jon, this young man had a good heart and was teachable. He was redoing his goal for the year: "I want to earn $150K+ per year." And his affirmation: "I continue to educate myself on sales and technical ability. I serve my clients to the best of my ability at every opportunity. I am a high-producing commission salesperson." Jon said this young man ended up making $200k that year. **In two years, he went from making $40k a year** to $200k, because he had a plan, wrote it down, and started working that plan.

Jon also shared this same young man's next goal, grinning as he read. "I own a beautiful home in Windsor. I consistently meet or exceed my income goals. I am responsible with my spending. And do not spend frivolously." This was one more example that **written goals and affirmations precede results.** *Affirmations are clear, present, positive statements, written or spoken in advance as if you already have accomplished your goal.*

In this instance, this ambitious employee of Jon's was specific about what he wanted, *wrote it down,* and Jon said this guy "bought a house in 2017 in Windsor. A really nice house." He also mentioned **the rep hadn't touched that prosperity plan in a year and yet what was written down came true!**

Enough said.

If something is important enough to you and you want it bad enough remember the three steps:

1. Write it down
2. Talk about it.
3. Don't get held up if something else happens.

Prompt #2: TSB & WTSD

For the rest of your life, if you want to succeed at anything, remember these two things—
Ten Seconds of Boldness and **Write That Shit Down!**

Chapter Twenty
Shit Happens: Expect It. Plan For It. Deal With It and Be Flexible.

"Sometimes things happen in life that are not part of the plan. When that happens, don't give up on your dreams, just find another way to reach them.
Ritu Ghatourey

We could spend the next two days philosophizing about justice or fairness and how good things happen to bad people and bad things happen to good people. But I won't. Why? Because it is not a productive use of our time.

> We cannot control everything and the sooner we understand and accept that fact, the sooner we can get back to working on the things we can control, such as our attitude, our plans, our work ethic and habits, our values, ideals, and beliefs—all the other internal things well within our control.

"That's Life."

When something doesn't go my way, I may pout, have a pity party for a minute, feel like a victim, or, if I am really pissed off, break bottles in the recycling bin. Occasionally, I may even recall the sarcastic serenade of my mom's boyfriend, Pat, when I was in high school.

Whenever he heard me as a teenager or my brothers or even Mom complaining about school, money, relationships—whatever, he'd get a bug-eyed grin, raise his caterpillar eyebrows, and belt out in a Frank Sinatra voice, "That's liiiiiiife… That's just the way it is sometiiiiiimes." Whenever I recall those moments, I laugh and think about another Sinatra tune, "My Way."

Ironically, I have a love-hate relationship with doing things my way. I love to be independent and feel as if I have it all together, have all the answers; that my way is usually the right way and if you don't like it, too bad.

Unfortunately, as I have already mentioned, until I learned some new skills and developed new habits, my way didn't work out so well. My self-important, selfish, and self-centered attitude cost me dearly. I lost jobs, a marriage, and nearly lost my life by being inflexible and unwilling to change. That's a high price to pay for my stubborn refusal to be open-minded, and insistence on doing things "My Way."

I have since learned that humble pie is actually quite tasty. That does not mean that I had to become a pushover and a "don't-rock-the-boat" or "go-with-the-flow, don't-make-waves" kind of guy. Far from it. That's not who I am. But it does mean I need to be more curious and less judgmental or opinionated (I'm still working on that one).

It means to build connections and relationships, I need to consider another's viewpoints, even if I don't agree with them. As St. Francis of Assisi said, I need to "seek to understand, rather than be understood." It means that I have to lighten up and not get so hung up on the petty stuff or beat myself up, especially when I make a mistake.

Bottom line, I need to be flexible, not only with my plans, but in my attitude and how I relate to myself, others, and the world around me.

In relation to solving problems or pursuing opportunities, I have learned that its prudent to have contingency plans and to be adaptable.

I have also learned to have a little more grace with myself. It's normal to have an occasional "bad-hair day." We all do. The trick is not to loiter. Don't wallow in it. Instead, feel what we need to, have a look in the mirror, talk to someone, take a walk around the block, book a therapy session—whatever we find necessary to process our emotions, cool off, and get back into the solution—back to work. No all-night pity parties. No playing the victim card. No blame, shame, guilt, or remorse. In private, take the time you need to sit with your feelings. Don't try to deny them, avoid them, or pretend they do not exist. Then get back on your horse, grab the reins and boldly declare, "Giddy-up!"

As we accept and take responsibility for what we can control and let go of all that which is beyond our control, our confidence begins to soar. Things seem to flow easier. We don't feel so stressed out or get rattled as easily. **With acceptance and personal responsibility, and by letting go, we find inner peace.**

It comes back to the Serenity Prayer:

> "God, grant me the serenity to accept the things I cannot change, courage to change the things I can, and wisdom to know the difference."

It really is that simple. Don't complicate it.

Chapter Twenty-One
Manage Your Time or It Will Manage You

"It's not enough to be busy, so are the ants. The question is, what are we busy about?"
Henry David Thoreau

The last time I checked, we all have the same twenty-four hours in a day. Some of us use our time wisely. Others are so busy being busy they barely have time to think.

We've all played the hypothetical "what if" game with money. But what about time? How many have heard the stories of those final words as someone's life comes to an end. Rarely if ever does someone say they wished they watched more TV. Or had more money. Or had no regrets. No, **most wish they had more time.** More time with people they love. Time to travel the world. Or like the famous poem by Nadine Stair, "If I had my life over —I'd pick more daisies." To live with more joy.

And still, some die with deep regrets, wishing they hadn't had to work so much or were there for their kids' soccer and Little League games. Or that they were happier and loved more. Or they yearn for a mulligan, a do-over so they could take back all the things they did wrong.

As long as you are breathing, it's not too late.

Let me ask you a few blunt questions. If time were not an issue, what would you be doing right now? How important is that to you? What's preventing you from doing it?

Now flip it. If you knew you only had five more years to live, what, if anything, would you do differently?

Time is not the problem. How you manage it is. What you do with your time is your prerogative but understand what you chose to do with the limited time you have on the face of this planet will shape your future.

Will you manage your time and invest it in things that are meaningful, important, and lasting like friendships, and experiences, and connections, events that you will remember for a lifetime? Or will you continue to squander it on an empty quest to keep up appearances, staying busy, pretending that you have arrived because you have so much stuff that you need to rent a storage unit to store more stuff? Will you continue to put off today what can be done tomorrow and keep repeating the "someday-I'll", "if-only" cycle like a hamster in a cage?

I hope I pissed you off a little bit, angry enough to change. Why? Because I have lost so much in my life, and I know that time is the most valuable commodity we all have. No amount of wealth or things can ever buy you more time. So, I have to ask, *what do you do with your time right now and what will you do with the uncertain quantity of time you have left?*

I said at the beginning that a chief motivation of writing *Ten Seconds of Boldness* is that I don't want to die with the regret that I was too scared to follow through with it.

It's far deeper than that.

I have for most of my life had this gnawing feeling and vision of what I want to do. Ever since listening to those early cassette tapes as a teenager, I knew I wanted to inspire others to love and live the life of their dreams.

TEN SECONDS OF BOLDNESS

For the past four decades I have been figuring out what that means to me. And I am now at the crossroads. I have a decision to make. To continue working hard to make others wealthy, or to put every tip and suggestion I have outlined in this book to the test and take a chance on myself by doing what I can to help you.

This is my "Olympic-donut moment." I'm going for it and can see that future unfolding before my eyes in a relatively short amount of time. I can see myself walking away from my "day job" at the top of my career and spending the rest of my life in pursuit of much bigger dreams and goals of helping others believe in themselves.

As I write, I can look back at all the subtle shifts that have happened in my life to bring me this far and I've never been more excited about the next five years of my life. With every step forward, every presentation, conversation exchanging words of encouragement, all of it, I am moving closer to fulfilling my childhood dream.

Each step builds my confidence and belief and keeps me motivated to keep moving forward. To not quit before the miracle.

So, I ask again, *what will you do with the next five years? Do you have a plan? Is it written down?*

Can you see it? Do you say it? Are you working to change your old belief system so you can believe whatever you want is possible? Or are you still hesitant. Afraid?

We are all afraid at first. The difference between those who are and aren't is courage—*Ten Seconds of Boldness,* repeated moment by moment day in and day out. *Now is the perfect time to stop letting your life be ruled by a belief system that is broken.*

As I mentioned earlier, it's time to upgrade your hard drive. Time for a mental reboot.

Three Common Truths About Time and Life:

1. We all start in the beginning.
2. We all have twenty-four hours in a day, 168 hours in a week.
3. We choose what we do with the time we've got. That includes work.

Time is Relative

In his theory of special relativity, Albert Einstein determined that time is relative—in other words, the rate at which time passes depends on your frame of reference. That in everyday activities, its impact is basically unnoticed (unless you are "running late" or "don't feel like there's ever enough time"). But as one approaches the speed of light, time seems to slow down.

We have not yet even come close to approaching the speed of light, though I often feel as if I am going a hundred miles an hour being busy. When I finally slow down, I'm often amazed at how little I accomplished. Those moments usually happen when I am scattered and not focused. Other times, when I follow the same five-step plan I have mapped out in this book and stay focused, time slows down. Nor do I feel the need to move at the speed of light.

Our minds are capable of way more than we may realize, and we have the ability to slow time by focusing on one thing at a time.

If you have ever been in an accident or experienced some trauma, you know what I mean. When I was seven, the brakes on my bike went out as I was riding down a steep hill.

A car was approaching and then I saw a brick wall. In a flash, I weighed the possible outcomes, none of them good—*Car. Wall. Car. Superman.* I vividly remember those few seconds like they were yesterday. And at the same time wished I was like Superman and could let go of the handlebars and just fly away safely.

Too late. The brick wall won. I smashed my face into it and lost my two front teeth.

I didn't have a whole lot of options in that situation. Even if I did, I wasn't a superhero and could not fly away or freeze time. Nope. I paid the price with my face.

The same feeling of suspended time has happened several other times, most were accident related. Each has given me greater insight to what happens when that fight-or-flight rush of adrenaline courses through my bloodstream; to how much sharper I can think and process information.

The same results without the roller coaster high and crash can occur when I stay on point and focused on what I am trying to accomplish. It's like being in the "Flow," which usually happens when I am fully engaged in something, listening, doing, being—fully present.

These intentional periods of concentration have proven to lift my productivity dramatically. Often, I am able to get a full day's work completed in two-thirds the time when I am focused and not distracted.

In summary, lack of time is not the problem, our decisions and habits are.

I am not going to spell out a time-management system in this chapter or even this book. Instead, let's look at a few examples you may find helpful.

Examples: Practical Application of Time Management Tips

To give you a sense of practical application, let's use my college experience as an example of how I effectively managed my time while working twenty hours a week and taking nine to fifteen units at San Francisco State University.

Looking back to our five essentials, *identify* the problem or opportunity, clearly *decide* what you want, know *why* you want it, write a *clear plan*, and *start* working that plan, we need to identify the problem or assess the situation.

Potential Problems:
- Competing priorities.
- Limited resources; time, money, transportation, and friends. I had to pay for school myself, which meant I had to work, study, and commute by bus, and have some semblance of a social life.

Time commitments and limits:
- Work schedule: Wed-Sat evenings 5:00 pm – 10:30 pm
- Class schedule: either mostly T-TH classes or M,W,F. Times varied
- Commute: at least ninety minutes each way from Marin to San Francisco
- Study and homework: rule of thumb is one hour of reading and study per unit per week.

Blocking: Taking Control of the Time You Have

To make this work, I had to use any cracks of time between work and class. I made a calendar— on paper. This was before smart phones. I mapped out every waking minute of the day, creating blocks of time where I could focus on studying, reading, writing, working, or participating in class. One of the most efficient uses of my time was to complete my reading homework on the bus or by the pool before work.

When I could, I also blocked out time for a nap between studying and work so I could stay fresh. After work, depending on what the current project deadlines were, I would go out dancing or stay up studying. I made it work because I was determined to finish what I had started years earlier.

Between work and dancing, I was not only getting exercise, but I was also connecting with people and filling my social needs.

I continued to pray that I would meet someone I could fall in love, with but I got tired of going to the dance clubs/bars after work, "looking for love in all the wrong places." Plus, as a newly recovering alcoholic, hanging out in bars was stupid.

I gave up. No more bars. No more dancing.

Several months later, on a whim, a voice inside whispered, "You need to go dancing." I listened and, long story short, that's where a friend introduced me to my first wife who became a wonderful mother for our son.

The point is, even when we manage time to the best of our ability, I believe there is another powerful invisible spiritual force that has a bigger plan for us. It is my job to stay tuned into that higher power, ready to listen and follow the subtle or not so subtle prompts so I make better decisions.

Often, I have found when I let go of my vain attempts to make something happen in "my time," the miracles of the unknown and unseen forces of this world seem to get together, assess a situation, and miraculously say, "Yeah, I think he's ready. Let's give him what he's been asking for. It's time."

We can only manage what is within our control. That is what we think, do, say, and believe with the twenty-four hours of each day. The rest of it, I leave up to my higher power and trust that when it's time, I will receive what I've been seeking. For now, I do my part and wait for the results.

Prompt #1: Block and Tackle Practice

No, I'm not talking about football practice. You don't need shoulder pads or cleats for this exercise.

Take ten minutes to write down everything you want or need to do today (be sure to include the things you've been procrastinating over).

Look at your list. Are the important things on your calendar? If not put them on it. Next, organize your list into things that can be done in blocks of time. For example: I am sharpest in the morning, so I will put anything that requires creative thought, such as writing or working on marketing proposals, on my calendar for a one-to-two-hour block in the morning. Then I get to it.

Next, on a separate piece of paper write down everything you want or need to do this week. You get the idea. Repeat the process for a month, year, or longer. For "to-dos" with a deadline one year or longer, I recommend using the productivity planning sheets in Appendix II. We'll also explore more tips and tricks, in the next section, *Into Action*.

Prompt #2: More Time Management Tips

Things are easiest to remember in groups of threes. I don't know why. But they are.

In addition, or separate from the example above in prompt #1, I like to make at least two separate lists with three items each. One for work. One for personal stuff. Usually I write them out daily, before bed or as soon as I sit at my desk in the morning.

There is a method to my madness—on any to do list, item #1 is the one thing I don't want to do or the thing I want to do the least. I do my best to tackle that thing first. Item #2 is one thing that needs to be done. Item #3 is the one thing I want to do that is either easy or fun.

In less than two minutes, I have my priorities in order. Simple, right? That doesn't mean that I don't add more number 1's, 2's or 3's. But at the very least I write a three-item daily to-do list, nearly every day.

This habit is one of the easiest ways I know of to build confidence and feel successful, one day-at-a-time.

Here are examples of two recent lists:

Work:
1. Contact three prospects or inactive accounts to arrange a meeting.
2. Weekly 1:1 meeting with my manager.
3. Complete quarterly review assessment.

Personal:
1. Write for at least one hour or five-hundred words.
2. Prep for Redwood Writers meeting.
3. Get a haircut and a massage.

See how simple and easy it is? And, in case you're wondering, I did everything on both lists except prep for the Redwood Writers meeting.

I put that off until today because I wanted to write more. And I didn't lose sleep over not doing it, yet.

What are your three things? Remember, *write them down, then do them.*

What's the Point?

The point is to get you into a habit to stop procrastinating so you can enjoy life more. Or at least change the date of your goal *before the deadline passes*, but don't put it off indefinitely.

Whichever method you utilize—grouping tasks and processes by time and/or type of energy and effort required (blocking) or writing three item to-do lists—both methods are efficient and effective. If you like, you may also organize your lists in a way that works for you. For example: I have lists for grocery shopping, home projects, yardwork, goals, etc. Also, don't forget what Crissi said, *"Don't confuse process with productivity. That is a form of procrastination."*

Another key to building your confidence is to not only write the things down but to block out the time for them and commit to doing them for that period of time, *without distractions.*

As you do so, you will not only be more productive and feel better about yourself, but will also become more confident and may even enjoy getting things done so you have more time for all the other things you say you don't have time for.

Ambitiously Lazy and Guilt-Free Living

List making, goal setting, and blocking may not be for you. I get it. But I am ambitiously lazy and like to get as much done in as short amount of time as possible. Especially the things I don't want to do like laundry, dishes or scrubbing toilets. When I do, I have more time to relax, or write, or go for a hike or whatever I want, guilt-free.

Prompt #3: Take a Day to Be Ambitiously Lazy

Make a list of one to three things that you know ought to be done but you have been putting off for far too long. **Get them done, now.**

One at a time. Once completed, pay attention to how it feels to actually get them off your back. I bet you feel less stressed, maybe even giddy. Often when I do this, I realize that completing the task was much easier and took less time than all the wasted hours worrying about doing it.

If you want less stress in your life, **do it now. Then go have some fun. Be ambitiously lazy.**

Section V
Start Working Your Plan

- ◊ Getting into Action
- ◊ The Power of Association
- ◊ Practical Steps
- ◊ Progress Not Perfection
- ◊ Persistence, Practice, and Patience
- ◊ Visualization: Using Your Imagination to Create the Life you Want
- ◊ Affirmations: Inspiration from the Inside Out
- ◊ Building Confidence is a Balancing Act

Chapter Twenty-Two
Getting Into Action

*"A dream is just a dream until you find the courage within
and decide to do something about it."*
Shawn Langwell

Life is too short to sit on the sidelines with a head full of dreams but a mind full of fear. Far too many of us allow the voices in our head to determine our sense of worth, never fully trusting our own abilities, or becoming confident enough to take the first steps toward accomplishing our dreams. Or worse, we finally muster the courage to pursue whatever we want and must deal with the disappointment of rejection and failure. I know how all that feels, it sucks.

In high school, I was the last player cut from the boys Varsity Basketball team that went 32-0 and won the California State Championship in 1982. My dreams were crushed. Once again, I felt left out, abandoned, and "not good enough."

That was a bitter pill to swallow, but compared to my competition, it was the truth—or so I believed at the time. Though I could shoot the lights out then—I still can, even in my fifties—I didn't have the ball handling skills to play point, or the bulk to play shooting guard or small forward. It wasn't meant to be, and I had to accept that (though recently, my best friend Joe, who was one of the last guys to make the team, told me, "You shoulda made it." It was nice to know that someone else believed in my ability and worth even four decades hence).

In hindsight, getting cut was a blessing in disguise. Instead of cheering on my friends while warming the bench, I did so from the stadium bleachers. Sure, I was pissed. It stung a lot to get cut, and rekindled feelings of rejection and abandonment and lack of self-worth. Just like when my dad left.

Soon I began to withdraw more and used drugs and alcohol to mask my anger. But below the surface something else started to simmer—an inner drive to prove to the world that I was worth it.

I became obsessed with learning about the psychology of winning, and devoured books and tapes on personal growth, inspiration, and motivation. Any topic that would help me discover who I should be, could be. That senior year, I became a cheerleader for my friends and never stopped loving the game of basketball. More importantly, I became my own best cheerleader, more determined than ever to become great at something. To become the best player on my own team, even when I felt like shit. Even when I wanted to give up. But *I learned a long time ago that it's never too late if we stay in the game and don't quit before the miracle.*

Be Part of Your Own Solution

This may sound harsh, but it's the truth. If we are to learn and develop new habits, we must be part of our own solution. All the knowledge and understanding in the world will not result in any meaningful personal growth. Transformation and change require action. As Thich Nhat Hanh says, "Knowing can be a crutch, we stay with what we know and shut the door to grow and evolve inner understanding."

This is the turning point. Your decision to act or not act will determine your future. All too often this is where most of us stop. We invest hours reading, learning, studying, and trying to "figure out" what we need to do differently. But when it comes time to take the first step, far too many of us hesitate in the starting gate or never commit to finishing the race we started. Or worse, kick back on the sofa, watching life pass us by, our dreams held hostage by all-too-common fears and worries—"what-ifs" and "if-onlys"—instead of jumping in and saying "what's next?"

Three Truths About Personal Growth:

1. Knowledge is not exactly the same as experience.
2. Meaningful and lasting transformation can only come by doing.
3. Your life will not change until you do something different to change how you think and act.

Remember not to confuse good intentions with knowledge and experience. They are not the same. The key differentiator is action.

Simply put, knowledge is both theoretical and practical understanding of a skill or topic. Knowledge can be based on hands-on experience. For example: As a kid, my dad warned me not to put metal objects in an electrical outlet. He had knowledge that it wasn't safe. I wanted to know why and what would happen, so one day I stuck a fork in the outlet. When sparks flew, I learned what it felt like to have a 110-volts of electricity shock me. I now have *knowledge and experience* that putting metal objects into an electrical outlet is pretty f-n stupid.

Lesson learned. I never did that again.

The point is, knowledge by itself is not as impactful as knowledge and experience.

Without application, all the knowledge in the world will change nothing. Knowledge never ends, but neither should our desire to innovate. Just because we discover one solution doesn't mean it is the only one, or even the best. Nor, as I said earlier, should we fully resign ourselves to the mindset of "if it ain't broke don't fix it." To grow we must continue to evolve, innovate, and challenge the status quo.

The same is true for attitudes and beliefs. As we continue to be curious and open-minded to new possibilities and put that knowledge into practice, we create lasting value and build confidence as a path toward mastery. *Mastery and greatness are not products of being comfortable or complacent.* As I said earlier, *they are the products of* **courage, conviction, commitment, motive, and effort.**

The Time to Act is Now

Any worthwhile endeavor or change requires a bit of courage. Not reckless abandon, but meaningful, purposeful, and intentional action to move one step closer to that which we want to be, have, or do. Now is that time.

We are all actors in the movie of our lives and the director has just barked, "Action!"

Everything we have done to this point has been a dress rehearsal. We have already begun to take small steps toward shifting how we think about ourselves and the world around us. Now is the time to put it all together and step onto the stage, under the bright lights and to shine—to become the star of our own lives.

Not in a self-indulgent, pompous ass way. Rather, in a humble and confident way that not only increases our self-worth but more importantly, our value to others and the world.

Now more than ever is when we need to summon our courage, to know why we have chosen a particular path, to have enough grace with ourself, knowing that every single step is not going to go exactly as we plan. As we do, we will begin to trust our instincts and be confident enough in our ability to improvise when necessary. *We will begin to understand that the creativity of facing unexpected problems while we are in action is where some of the greatest insights and breakthroughs occur.* But we must not retreat at the first setback and throw in the towel.

> True greatness happens in the face of challenges, not in the absence of them.

Why? Because **each time we combat fear or adversity with courage, grit, determination, and boldness, we win.** The outcome may not be exactly as we hoped, but we win because we did not cower. Because we never give up. We must *do* or we will never know that we *can*.

The Four Keys of Boldness

Essentially there are four key ingredients to becoming bolder and more courageous:

Belief: Have hope, faith, and belief that God's got your back. Whatever that means to you.

Willingness: Be willing to do whatever it takes to accomplish what you seek.

Action: Do something. Get started, knowing that courage and confidence only expand when you *stop thinking* and *start doing.*

Detachment or Surrender: Simply put, this means doing the work and letting go of the results. Think of it as a spiritual hug that says all will be well when we do our part. Or putting a Post-it note on your mirror as I did in early recovery. It read:

> *Shawn:*
> *Thanks, but I won't be needing your help today.*
> *Love,*
> *God.*

We can't bullshit our way into becoming more confident. We've done enough of that already, which is why we are where we are. And we can't solely rely on individual will power to face all our challenges. **We need help from others.**

It Takes Courage to Believe in Something you Cannot See

"Now faith is confidence in what we hope for and assurance about what we do not see." – Hebrews 11:1 NIV

For many asking for help or believing in something we can't yet see is a huge leap of faith and courage. As I have said, a higher power to me is a guiding spiritual force that gives me hope and confidence. One I have come to believe in and trust. It is my secret weapon. My superpower.

Complacency is the Graveyard of Unrealized Potential

The transformational power of increased confidence comes when we *intentionally become uncomfortable*. Like the cliché "no pain no gain," confidence is built through repetition and practice. *Doing*, not thinking, or saying what you're going to do.

If we are not stretching ourselves, pushing our boundaries and limits, or dreaming bigger, we risk becoming average. Worse, if we are overconfident, being too reliant on our own abilities and willpower, we risk becoming lazy and complacent. And I don't want that. To me, complacency is the graveyard of unrealized potential.

Get Your Hands Dirty

Lasting transformation, courage, and confidence come through sweat, tears, pain, and perseverance. In other words, you've got to feel it in your gut, roll up your sleeves, and be willing to get dirty in the trenches of life if you are to realize your full potential.

I love how Theodore Roosevelt says it:

> It is not the critic who counts; not the man who points out how the strong man stumbles, or where the doer of deeds could have done them better. The credit belongs to the man who is actually in the arena, whose face is marred by dust and sweat and blood; who strives valiantly; who errs, who comes short again and again, because there is no effort without error and shortcoming; but who does actually strive to do the deeds; who knows great enthusiasms, the great devotions; who spends himself in a worthy

> cause; who at the best knows in the end the triumph of high achievement, and who at the worst, if he fails, at least fails while daring greatly, so that his place shall never be with those cold and timid souls who neither know victory nor defeat.

One thing is certain, your life will remain the same until you commit to change. The same problems will continue to haunt you until you become willing to find the courage within to move through whatever is holding you back. Once you commit, you will then know firsthand what it means be fully alive and to thrive.

Does Anyone Really Like Change?

Let's face it, most of us don't like change or doing things that are boring or unpleasant, yet we want the results. I get it. I don't like change either. I am a creature of habit. I like my routines, structure, and the predictability of my life. It's safe. But safe can become boring. And, if we're not careful, playing it safe can lead to apathy. Personally, I like a little drama, a little tension, and stress. It makes me feel alive. But not too much change or stress or I get burned out.

Be Ambitiously Lazy

As I mentioned in the last chapter, I am ambitiously lazy by nature and like to get things done as quickly and efficiently as possible, especially things I don't want to do. I make a game out of doing those unpleasant things, like laundry, or cleaning, or shopping, or cold calls, or completing reports at work. I tackle my to-do list as fast and efficiently as possible, so I have more time to do what I want to do like read, write, hike, or simply to do nothing that requires thought.

Change will always be uncomfortable at first. Expect to struggle and make mistakes. It's part of the process. That doesn't mean we are going to necessarily enjoy it. It takes time to get used to it, like breaking in a new pair of leather dress shoes. At first, they are tight and may rub our heel or pinch the top of our foot causing a blister, but once they become pliant, flexible, and supple, we will not only like how they feel but how they make us look (it's true, even if it sounds like a George Zimmer commercial for Men's Warehouse).

Be Clear and Resolute. But Don't Trip About the Details, Yet.

This section is literally where the rubber meets the road. Be clear and resolute, but don't get hung up in the details. Meaning, don't feel as if you need to figure everything out before you can act. As we've already discussed, that's an excuse and crutch for too many people and only perpetuates the cycle of fear that our inner critics love to feed on. Instead, don't feed the beasts in your mind.

Prompt: Be Bold. Do it Now.

If you are determined, you will figure out *how* as you get started. Resolve to *do what needs to be done, especially when you don't feel like it.*

Build upon your new habits as you progress and beware of your tendency to drift into old patterns, especially your tendency to procrastinate. Procrastination is like mastication, everyone does it. The difference is one satiates hunger, the other causes unnecessary worry, doubt, and anxiety, and commonly erodes confidence.

The good news is you get to choose what you want to do. It's all up to you.

Chapter Twenty-Three
The Power of Association and Perpetual Curiosity

"Be like a five-year old. Never stop asking what and why."
Shawn Langwell

Nobody is "Self-Made"

While I am a huge proponent of drive and ambition, I believe that lasting success and happiness are achieved when we aren't lone wolves. Every successful person or organization thrives when the collective creativity and skills of many are harnessed toward a common objective.

Look at team sports, for example. No team wins a championship because of one player. Our life is no different. If you want to be a champion, get around champions. Learn, study, ask questions. Associate with those who have what you want.

Be like Coach Lavin, soak up as much knowledge from legends like John Wooden, Bobby Knight, and Coach Keady. Pick their brains and sit on the bench. Ask questions, observe, listen, learn.

Most of all, **be humble and a perpetual student of life. Greatness is earned and learned, not a gift from God.**

Yet, as one of the most "advanced" cultures in the world, I wonder why our thinking is so self-centered? Why do we insist on being self-reliant, thinking that asking for help is equivalent to shame? That we should know or have all the answers or if we don't know that we shouldn't let others know we don't know. And when we do know, do we offer to share or help others? Or is life just a dog-eat-dog world—a Darwinian reality show called "survival of the fittest?"

Is Success Really About Individuality, Independence, and Greed?

Throughout the worlds of entertainment, marketing, in social circles and groups, and in business organizations, there is an overriding message and cultural paradigm that stresses the importance of individuality, independence, and greed. It's no wonder so many of us have low self-confidence or are afraid of failure.

If we aren't on top, we feel like we're failing. At least many of us do, even if we don't talk about it. How can I say this? Because as I have already stated, there are millions of people who are just one paycheck away from being broke, and millions more drowning in debt. Good hard-working people trying to get ahead but stuck in a cycle of debt and poverty because they are chasing their dreams with a credit card. It may not be as deadly as the COVID pandemic, but the cycle of debt is a killer of hopes and dreams that will keep you enslaved forever unless you change your mindset about money, wealth, success, and debt.

Are Our Priorities Wrong?

As a culture, the United States is one of the richest countries in the world. Yet, we still have more than 500,000 people every night who must find shelter or sleep in the streets. According to estimates provided by the United Nations in 2020, approximately 690 million people worldwide go to bed hungry every night.

TEN SECONDS OF BOLDNESS

In 2016, I went through the San Rafael Chamber of Commerce Leadership program. As a class we were tasked to come up with a project that could benefit the community. Our class theme focused on Busting the Myths of Homelessness.

The primary misperception about homeless people we quickly discovered was that all homeless people are not bums and drug addicts. Some are, but that stigma is just another myth.

During the project, we interviewed and interacted with several homeless people in San Rafael, California. We organized a community clean-up day where our class and elected officials worked alongside them picking up trash in East San Rafael.

What I discovered in the course of the interviews and impromptu conversations during the clean-up day was that most in fact were not bums or drug addicts. Many were successful before becoming homeless. In most cases, some life event—a job loss, a divorce, a diagnoses of mental illness, etc.—was the trigger that inhibited their ability to provide for themselves or their families. As a result, they lost the place they called home.

We also discovered that, contrary to other misconceptions, many do want to get out of the poverty cycle and are taking full advantage of the social services available to them, including meals, training, jobs, and housing. And most are not afraid to ask for help, to get the mental health and training to rebuild their confidence, self-image, and self-esteem.

Seven Simple Suggestions for Success

1. **ABC – Always be Curious.** Never stop learning about ways to improve or seeking out others who have what you want. Be bold ask questions. You will be amazed at

how many people love to talk about themselves if they think they will help you. Seriously.

2. **Don't be afraid to ask for help.** It's okay to say, "I don't know." Don't be shy about saying what your purpose is or afraid to ask for help. Most people enjoy helping someone who is passionate. **Be passionate.**

3. **Associate with "winners."** Be around people who are where you want to be, or have the success you'd like, and gather input from them. Take a page out of Coach Lavin's book and spend time immersed in the environment you think you want to be in.

4. **Do what it takes to live your dream.**

5. **Never lose sight of your why.** Your enthusiasm and passion alone will open doors of opportunity and help for you. Let your why shine bright.

6. **Be bolder.**

7. **Never give up on yourself.**

Seek. Ask. Find.

Here's what some of those tips look like on a practical level:

If you want to be _____, read, and seek out material and people who can help. Ask for help. Associate with them. Learn, practice, and fail fast. As you do, your confidence will grow.

Want to become better? Hire a coach, therapist, trainer, find a mentor, or register for a seminar or school to learn from experts.

I find it is more efficient to first get an idea of what I think I want, *then* ask others who have either already accomplished that goal or who may offer me some insight to point me in the right direction. But be careful who you ask. Even experts have opinions, and sometimes getting advice from too many sources creates more confusion because you are not confident whose advice you should trust or follow. The same thing can easily happen when surfing the web, trying to find accurate advice or information from a reputable source. Even if the source is reliable, *you will not always find a singular right answer.* Unless it's math, there usually isn't one. So, it's going to take some trial and error. The point is don't expect to do it all yourself or become self-made.

True joy—as all five people I interviewed, (Cara Wasden, Steve Lavin, Jon Diamond, Kevin Miller, and Aaron Locks), confirmed—**is in sharing with others.** They all teach, lead, coach, and counsel others on how to improve, achieve goals, and overcome obstacles.

Our joy is magnified exponentially when those we encourage step forward with boldness and confidence as a child taking their first steps or learning to ride a bike. Or in my case, as an author finding unexpected joy from the stories shared by all those I interviewed, further validating the vital importance of collaboration and connection.

I don't know of any doctor, lawyer, salesperson, educator, or any leader or person of influence who does not rely on peer input or advice to remain relevant and competitive.

Why would you think you are any different?

One of the easiest ways to learn what you don't know you don't know is to sign up for a masterclass, podcast, or attend an in-person event on a subject of interest to you.

You will quickly get a feel for the types of questions to ask and usually walk away with helpful tips and guidelines on what to do next, to get started.

As we wrap, here are a few basic reminders:
- Be perpetually curious.
- **Be bold.**
- Be focused.
- Don't be afraid to try and fail until you succeed.

This is nothing new. Surround yourself with people who believe in you. Those who will lift you up, encourage you, and challenge you. Those who will be your advocate and cheerleader and tell you the truth with love.

If you want to write a book, study the authors of books you like. Join a writing club, or critique group. If you want to overcome your fear of public speaking, consider joining Toastmasters or a similar group. Watch YouTube videos, podcasts, etc., and read the books that may help you become a more confident speaker. You might also consider hiring a coach.

No matter what area of growth you want, seek out and pay trained professionals and experts. It's one of the best investment for your future you can make. Plus, it's incredibly efficient and way more effective than relying on your own thinking, which can only get you so far.

Prompt: Find Those Who Can Help You

Step #1: Research opportunities to learn about and associate with those who have expertise in an area you want to improve. *Seek. Ask. Find.*

Step #2: Watch for and learn from people and opportunities to improve when they come your way. Wait and remain ready to act.

Key Takeaway: Find the Courage to Ask for Help. Be Coachable.

The next chapter will give you some practical tips for further practice.

Chapter Twenty-Four
Practical Steps

"To know just what has to be done, then do it, comprises the whole philosophy of a practical life."
William Osler

New Will Always Be Awkward at First

Whether learning to walk, ride a bike, starting a new job, switching careers, dating someone new, becoming a parent, etc., all of these are awkward at first. But we figure out how to do them anyway. If you take a moment to look back at all of your "firsts," at least those you can remember, it's easy to recall how uncomfortable you felt in the beginning.

Look at where you are now. Do you have to spend a lot of time psyching yourself up to drive a car? What about brushing your teeth, mowing the lawn, or making love? I'm fairly confident that you know how to do each of these. True they were probably awkward at first. Most things are. But you likely have done them enough times to be confident in your ability without much mental preparation. That's true with any learned skill—**practice and repetition build confidence.**

In addition to all the other strategies and suggestions we've discussed thus far, becoming bolder, more confident, and accomplishing any worthy ideal or goal will require some effort and at least these seven simple steps.

Seven Steps to Accomplishing Anything Worthwhile:

1. Be honest with yourself.
2. Decide what you want to be, have, or do.
3. Know your why.
4. Write down your goals.
5. Develop an action plan—baby steps—to accomplish them.
6. Get into action. Do something every day that moves you closer to their attainment.
7. Believe in yourself.
8. Do the work and leave results up to the universe.

Your action plan is simply a series of steps you take to accomplish an objective.

Ideally you develop a plan, routines, and habits that, repeat consistently, will produce positive changes in your life over time.

Each of the simple changes you make, not only in the way you think but the way you act and what you believe, soon becomes a perpetual feedback loop driven by your personal motives and your willingness to find the courage to change.

Change is inevitable. The sooner you stop trying to resist it, the sooner you will grow. I would argue that a life without change and some sort of goal is not going to be very fulfilling. The energy and sense of being *alive* that comes from pursuing a dream or vision builds confidence and brings meaning and purpose to an otherwise flaccid life.

Every Innovation Starts with a Vision or Dream: Imagine the Possibilities

Throughout history, all endeavors start with a dream or a vison, usually in response to a problem or opportunity.

Years ago, I had a dream and a vision to write this book. Initially it was going to be all about goal-setting: how to set and attain them. A brain dump of all the challenges and personal triumphs in my life and how goal-setting had become deeply ingrained into who I am and how I live. As I began to write, I had a gnawing feeling inside that something was missing, and I didn't know what. Not knowing drove me crazy. No matter how hard I tried to figure it out, the answers eluded me. So, I let it go.

I didn't give up on the project. I just put it aside for a bit.

As I mentioned earlier, life happened.

I was in a sales slump at work. My mom and stepdad were battling health issues. My wife was also frustrated with her own job. At that time, it felt as if the whole universe was conspiring against me. I'd been in slumps before. They happen. But this one was different. I felt there were some very important lessons I needed to learn but grew increasingly impatient waiting for clear answers.

"Maybe That's How it's Supposed to Be."

The ah-ha moment never came. Instead, my wife and I turned our attention to caring for our family and for each other. We did what needed to be done, even though at the time neither of us really wanted to.

Four years hence, I feel butterflies in my stomach as I write this. This morning, out of the blue, I recalled the day of my youngest brother's funeral. (He died in a car accident at twenty-eight-years-old).

It was a sunny summer day in a meadow flanked by redwoods. As I approached the meadow, my (first) wife holding one hand and my young son holding the other, an old family friend greeted me with a hug. "Is your dad coming?" he asked.

I wondered, *Why did he ask me that question, in that moment? Did he somehow know three days earlier I had ripped the phone out of the wall and thrown it across the room when Dad said he wasn't coming?*

My jaw set. Angry tears welled in my eyes. "No. He said he's 'made his peace'," I said. "I'm pissed. How can a man not show up for his own son's funeral?"

He looked at me, bushy eyebrows raised. And in a soft, compassionate voice replied, **"Maybe that's the way it's supposed to be."**

How simple, yet deeply profound.

When I put this project on the back burner, I still beat myself up, thinking I let life get in the way of my dreams and goals. Perhaps all of that happened for a reason. I had something else to learn. Perhaps I still do. What I have learned so far, though, is how much of my identity is still attached to accomplishment. Of being the best. Of feeling as if I need to have all the answers. Of wanting to be loved and accepted. Of wanting things to go according to *my* plan. Of the incessant battle in my own mind between my inner critics and the excuses I continue to make when I try to do it all by myself.

Perhaps to fully value what I had, I needed to lose myself in helping my mom and stepdad. Perhaps I had to let this project go and ask the universe to teach me what I still needed to learn and to give me the strength and courage to persist even when the path remained hidden. I now understand and believe both my dad and friend were right—**to be at peace, sometimes we must accept things the way they are supposed to be.**

In a nutshell the practical steps to any significant and lasting change to accomplishment can be distilled down to three words. These are the same fundamental insights of *The Secret*, by Rhonda Byrne.

- Ask
- Believe
- Receive

The only other necessary component is a four-letter word: Work.

Are you willing to do the work necessary to change the way you think and act so you can be, do, and have that which you want need, or desire?

Prompt: Three Action Steps

Choose one of your goals or areas of improvement you want to work on and *write down **three actions steps*** you will take this week. If you like, use the *Ten Second of Boldness Productivity Planner* in Appendix II.

Chapter Twenty-Five
Progress Not Perfection

"You are your own worst enemy. If you can learn to stop expecting impossible perfection, in yourself and others, you may find the happiness that has always eluded you."
Lisa Kleypas

We all make mistakes. They are part of learning and life. Why then do so many of us beat ourselves up when we do? Do we have some unrealistic expectation that we should be perfect? That if we forget where we left our wallet, phone, or car keys, we are stupid? That if we forget an anniversary or birthday, we are a bad person. That if we rear-end someone on the freeway because we dropped our phone or were texting and driving, we are foolish? That if we have to cancel a family vacation to Hawaii because our puppy broke its leg while playing chase with my stepson, it's his fault?

No. Shit happens.

Mistakes are natural and part of what makes life interesting. That doesn't mean there is something wrong with us or others. All it means is something happened and the outcome was not what we expected in that moment. That's it. *It is what it is.*

One of the keys to quieting the nagging voices in our minds and building self-confidence is to let go of our need for perfection. To accept our humanness when we make mistakes, or when something happens to us or to someone, we love that we had no control over.

Instead, we need to learn to objectively evaluate the outcome or situation and consider what we might do differently next time. Life is not perfect. It's messy and sometimes ugly and painful and that's what I love about it.

Many times, I have failed, yet I am still alive. Many times, I've even sabotaged my own success because I didn't feel deserving, worthy. Some mistakes I have made dozens of times. I am a work in progress, not perfect. Today I accept my imperfections, more than when I was younger.

In some areas, the consequences of my behavior such as drinking, gambling, anger, or spending more money than I made became so painful to me and others, that I finally made a decision to change. *The insanity had to stop.* I had to ask for help.

I know I've harped on this many times in the book but I am going to repeat it again because it's a huge problem and belongs in this chapter more than any other: *Asking for help is normal, not a sign of weakness or failure. Rather, it's a sign of humility and maturity.* Things might be easier if you stop trying to do everything by yourself.

All pro athletes have coaches to help them with their shot, their swing, their defense, etc. If we want to be great at whatever we choose to do, we must train and practice. Building self-confidence is no exception. Nobody is perfect. All those we consider great put in the time to progress, to get better. I have never met anyone who is perfect. If you do, please let me know. Why then are so many of us obsessed with trying? Isn't that setting us up for failure before we even start?

Greatness and The Law of Averages

A baseball player is considered great with a career batting average of .300. That means they make an out seven times out of ten. They have a failure rate of 70% which may be good enough for them to be inducted into the baseball Hall of Fame in Cooperstown, New York.

Stephen Curry is a great shooter. His lifetime free throw percentage is over 90%; he consistently makes 45-50% of his two-point shots and 35-40% from behind the arc. Many call him the greatest shooter of all time. I agree. The best part is he's not done yet. And he's not perfect—he misses more than half his shots. In basketball, making 50% of your shots inside the three-point line field is considered great.

We all have off days, even Steph Curry. Side note: As of this writing, Steph went 0-9 on three point shot attempts in game five of the NBA Finals. His playoff streak with at least one three-pointer ended at 132 career postseason games, and the Warriors still won the game. In fact, the next game the Golden State Warriors defeated the Boston Celtics to win the 2021-2022 NBA Championship.

Even on an off night, Steph's body language may show frustration and disappointment, but I have never seen him give up. Instead, he does other things to help the Golden State Warriors win. He sets picks for his teammates or dishes a no-look lob to a teammate for a dunk or gobbles up rebounds like a hungry lion. **He does what it takes to win.**

Because that's what winners do. We press on, despite the obstacles in our path. **We find a way to go from where we are to where we want to be.**

Sometimes that means letting go. For a basketball player, that may mean not forcing bad shots. For a baseball player, to stop chasing bad pitches out of the strike zone. For a salesperson, to stop selling and start asking better questions, actively listening for needs, *then* offering solutions to solve our clients' problems.

For the rest of us, when we get frustrated and impatient, we tend to listen to and believe the "itty-bitty-shitty committee in our head." To break free from our negative self-talk bad habit, we may need to hit the pause button and take a step back or do nothing for a moment. Or take a walk around the block or do something good for someone else—anything to take our minds off ourselves for a while. It works, I don't know how or why, but it does.

Practicing What I Teach

Before the pandemic hit, I decided to join a gym. I wanted to get back into shape so I could play basketball. At fifty-four, it took longer than I expected.

As a teenager and young adult, I could play for hours at a time. I was a good defender, could rebound well, and could shoot the lights out from distance. But I was no longer a young lad, far from it. There was a huge gap between the player I used to be and where I was mentally and physically. I still thought I could keep up with players less than half my age, until I stepped onto the court. I often had to guard kids who currently played basketball in high school or junior college. They were way better than I was, even when I was their age.

At first, I sucked. My youthful opponents would give a quick pump fake then drive to the basket, blowing by me like my feet were stuck in cement. It was frustrating to say the least, but I didn't give up. I kept showing up—shooting, playing, even lifting two to three times a week to get stronger.

After a year of getting into shape I began to feel more confident on the basketball court. I finally believed I could hold my own on defense. One game I chose to guard the best shooter on the other team, "E." At the time, E was a fifteen-year-old guard for a local high school basketball team, who had a quick first step and great shot from deep. Before the game started, I looked him square in the eye. "Last game you were on fire. Just so you know, you're not going to score at all this game," I teasingly trash-talked.

"We'll see about that, grandpa," he quipped.

My strategy was simple: deny him the ball. It worked. I played him so tight, he only got the ball two times. Both times with my hand in his face, he forced a shot and missed. We won the game. More importantly, for that moment, I won an inner battle with my own lack of self-confidence, I started to believe in my abilities on the court once again.

The other team wanted a rematch. I guarded E again. After four defensive stops in a row—he never touched the ball—E stomped off the court, grabbed his gym bag and left shaking his head in frustration. But the story doesn't end there. I felt bad, I had let my own ego get in the way and rattled this young teen's confidence. While fun in the moment, it was not too cool. I'd be pissed too if someone older did that to me when I was fifteen.

In the following months I would often go down to the gym at off-peak hours to practice shooting. E was often there, at the far end of the court, by himself, practicing his shot off the dribble. We usually didn't talk. Until one day, instead of working on my own shot from various spots on the floor, I walked to the end of the court where he was practicing and asked, "Wanna rebounder?"

"Hell yeah," he exclaimed, then quickly put his game face on—focused, intent.

For the next forty-five minutes we ran pass-and-cut drills; him cutting and shooting, me rebounding and dishing two-handed chest and bounce passes so he could catch the ball in rhythm, make a move, then set his feet and pull up.

"Money!" he'd exclaim, before launching a high arcing shot from behind the three-point line, making that glorious "thwap" as shot after shot snapped the net, a sound every shooter loves. I was in awe. This kid was good, really good.

That day inspired me to practice even more. Soon my stamina increased, and I was able to do more of the fun things I love about the game, like behind the back passes, pulling up for deep threes, or boxing out the biggest dude on the court then throwing a perfect pass to a cutting teammate for a fast break layup. More than re-building my self-confidence at basketball, I rediscovered my joy and love of the game. And I can still rebound well, hit 35-50% of my threes, and shoot 80% or better from the free throw line. At my age, that's a win.

The Courage-Confidence Paradox

Many believe they need to have confidence before they can be or do X. That's not how it works. **Confidence is a product not a prerequisite.** And the path to confidence starts with making a bold decision to take the first step. And another. And another.

As you move away from fear and toward your goals, an interesting thing happens—your destination becomes clearer and the past or where you came from slowly fades away, as long as you don't go backward. And the best part is it only takes *Ten Seconds of Boldness* and a visceral reason *why* for you to take the first step. And once you've taken the first, the next one is even easier, and so on.

Here's what that looks like in terms of a formula, which I call the *Confidence Quotient.* And while I said earlier "there is no magic formula for success," this formula is about as close as I have come to finding one that consistently works for me with respect to building the confidence necessary for success.

> **The Confidence Quotient:**
> (M x C+W)/Time = C
> (Motivation x Courage plus Work)/Time = Confidence

It may seem simplistic, but its impact is life changing. As you have already discovered, these basic traits, attitudes, and actions do not require any skill. They are characteristics which when used frequently, become very powerful instruments for change.

Skill comes from using the tools we have, our learned and God-given abilities, to create the life we want—one that truly motivates us.

Compound Confidence

As you continue to become more adept in one area of your life, it's not uncommon to feel more confident when approaching the next problem, goal, or opportunity. I refer to this as *compound confidence*: building on your successes, your wins, to create positive forward momentum. We'll explore this further in the next chapter.

Prompt: Memorize and Use the Confidence Quotient

> **The Confidence Quotient:**
> (M x C+W)/Time = C
> (Motivation x Courage plus Work)/Time = Confidence

Chapter Twenty-Six
Persistence, Practice, and Patience

"Patience, persistence and perspiration make an unbeatable combination for success."
Napoleon Hill

Practice does not make you perfect, but it always makes you better. Those who consistently practice, and are patient with their progress, eventually can become great at a chosen skill, craft, or vocation. Research the work habits of any successful athlete, entertainer, salesperson, speaker, business owner, parent, teacher, employee or student and you will easily see the relationship between practice, study, and rehearsal with their personal levels of achievement.

For example, the late Kobe Bryant, Hall of Fame guard for the Los Angeles Lakers basketball team, practiced six hours a day, six days a week, for six months out of the year. The rest of the time he put those skills to use on the court.

Stephen Curry, the greatest three-point shooter of all time and starting guard for the Golden State Warriors, practices three to six hours a day in the off season. And his practice isn't all about shooting drills even though he is one of the greatest shooters of all time. His longtime trainer, Brandon Payne, has created a balanced workout routine that includes flexibility, conditioning, and weight training to maximize his performance on the court.

If we think about it, anyone who is employed is "practicing" six to twelve hours a day. But are we practicing the right things? Are we getting better, or have we developed bad habits, like doing just enough to keep our jobs? There's a huge difference, and it always comes back to attitude, work ethic, and your motivation.

As I have mentioned many times, to develop the self-confidence necessary to succeed and thrive in any endeavor, we must be coachable and humble. To become adept and confident at something new requires practice. Lots of it.

"You've got to get your reps in," as Coach Lavin says. Trial and error. Making mistakes, stumbling, and falling. Accepting that you're gonna suck at first. But most of us want to be good out of the gate. Greatness isn't a magic wand. Neither is confidence. As Aaron Locks said, **"Expecting results without effort is ridiculous."**

The good news is most skills are learnable. Coach Lavin added that, you "can teach skill but you can't teach character." You can model it. You can encourage it and the development of healthy work habits. But **ultimately, the motivation to succeed rests with the individual.** In other words, how hungry are you? Hungry enough to hustle? To put in some extra time? Do you accept and understand that all greatness and transformation takes time?

When we persist and invest the time to do what needs to be done, whether we feel like it or not, we will become better, more confident, and perhaps even master that which we seek.

It's important to be patient and kind to ourselves as we progress. When we have the discipline to maintain focus, effort, and energy toward our aim, we will likely build momentum and get into a state of "optimal experience" Mihaly Csikszentmihalyi calls "The Flow." If you've never read his book, *Flow*, I highly recommend you do, especially if you're ambitious or competitive, like me.

You Can't Move Forward With One Foot on the Brake

By now it should be 100% clear that we can never become more self-confident without practice, persistence, or patience.

And yet, most of us still tend to give up too soon. We allow ourselves to be distracted on what we really want because we aren't 100% clear on *why we want it*. We never really develop any momentum because we stop doing the things we know we need to do to achieve the results we want. The work is harder than we thought or the results are taking too long to materialize. We may get in the car to go to the store or movies, but we keep braking for imaginary squirrels crossing the road. If you want to go anywhere, take your foot off the brake!

Soon, we drift back into laziness and complacency convinced there are just too many squirrels to make it safely across town.

This story may seem like an exaggerated tale but it's not. For most of my adult life, I have vacillated between ambition and laziness. In work. In exercise. In relationships. And with finances. Like a perpetual game of red light, green light. I go a hundred miles an hour, then burn out and don't want to do anything.

But when something really matters to me, like finishing this book, I persist. I don't brake for imaginary squirrels. Instead, I block out the time on my calendar, and just keep writing.

In the Beginning, We All Suck

Anne Lamott says it's normal to suck in the beginning. Her advice to anyone wanting to write a book is simple: "Almost all good writing begins with terrible first efforts. You need to start somewhere. Start by getting something—anything—down on paper.

What I've learned to do when I sit down to work on a shitty first draft is to quiet the voices in my head."

Anne's advice for writers can be applied to any endeavor. The premise is simple, you are going to suck at first. We all do. Be like a kid with a fresh box of Crayolas and **color outside the lines.** Get out of that comfort zone. Let go of your need for perfection and color more.

> Practice, persistence, and patience are three primary crayons to bring your vision to life.

Perfection is a Myth

I know I will never be perfect. So, I stop trying to be. That takes the pressure off and allows me to get the thoughts out on paper or screen and just keep writing. No editing, No judgment. Instead, I put a muzzle on my barking critics and just keep writing or practicing. One thought at a time. One word at a time. One step at a time.

Take writing this book, for example. At some point, I have to let it go and trust that it's good enough to send to my editor. And that after I implement his suggestions, the end-product will be good enough to inspire a few folks.

Practice Until You Create New Habits

The next level of progress is to develop healthy habits, disciplines, and routines. I am not going to spend time outlining what those are for you because they depend on what you want to accomplish. But I encourage you to consult with a professional who can help you map out a plan to meet your needs. If you are considering hiring a coach, visit my website: shawnlangwell.com to see if there is a fit.

Again, confidence is earned as you keep making bold decisions to solve problems in your life. Momentum develops when you begin to believe in yourself and your abilities. Success happens when you keep adapting and making adjustments to find what works for you.

That is the goal. Not the outcome or championship. Not the trophy. *The prize is for those who, despite their shortcomings, learn to believe in themselves. Who develop the confidence to keep getting up one more time.*

Prompt: One Baby Step to Overcome Procrastination

What is one thing you have wanted to do but keep procrastinating about because you are worried you will suck at it? Practice *Ten Seconds of Boldness* and do it, now.

Once completed, write down how it felt. What came up? Was it easier than you thought it would be? Perhaps you realized you need more practice. Do you feel better now that you finally did it even if the outcome was not what you expected?

Resolve to keep at it until you become confident in your ability. With each trial, successful or not, make a mental deposit in your confidence bank. Even for the failures. Why? Because mistakes are the fertilizer of wisdom. The more you make, the wiser and more confident you become.

Chapter Twenty-Seven
Visualization: Using Your Imagination to Create the Life You Want

"See it. Say it. Believe it. Then, do it."

Effective visualization has three parts: *See it. Say it. Believe it.* Achievement has one: *Do it.*

I don't know where I first heard that catchy phrase, but it sums up everything I know about using the power of our minds to create the future we want. Which is really an affirmation—*speaking the truth as we want it to be in advance.*

We'll cover affirmations in the next chapter which will also include some specific examples of visualization and affirmations. For now, let's further expand upon our earlier conversation from chapter twelve about creative visualization.

Think of visualization as a purpose-filled, judgment-free, brainstorming session. This is the time to let your imagination run wild. The only limits are those you impose upon yourself. Do your best to think big. Then think again, bigger.

I have to admit, I get a little fired up about visualization. Why? Because I have used it and seen the incredible power it has in making dreams come true, especially when you actively surround yourself with people who are where you would like to be (power of association).

As you begin, something magical happens. You are doing it. Whatever *it* is. As you write down a goal of something you want and begin to polish that grainy image you see in your mind's eye. Cut pictures from magazines, create a dream board, immerse yourself in everything you can that will help you frame a new image of the new you or what you want to manifest in your life. Choose meaningful words that help tell a story.

Visualization can also include associating with the people you want to be like or the person you want to become, just like Coach Lavin did in his quest to become a head coach. Get around others who exemplify the qualities, characteristics, and skills you want. Read about them, study them. Obsess if you want. It's your dream. How bad do you want it?

As you find the courage to take one more step, your belief increases, and you gain confidence. Your mindset will shift. What used to seem or feel like a pie-in-the-sky dream becomes more tangible and believable as you continue to fine tune your vision.

As you get closer to realizing whatever it is you set out to accomplish, it is critical that you remain confident and feel deserving of your success. *Don't sabotage your success. Step into it. Own it. Wear it like a new dress and matching shoes or a tailor-made suit.*

Like a new pair of shoes that need to be broken in, the new you will take a while to get used to. And doubt will always be there, usually when you least expect it, like a call from a telemarketer, or spam. When it does, ignore it. Don't respond. Don't sabotage all your hard work just before you're ready to breakthrough.

Expect setbacks and mistakes but don't take them personally. Remain steadfast, keeping your motives top of mind. Most of all, don't quit before the miracle.

Building a Positive Self-Image

For visualization to be effective, it's necessary to change how you see yourself. That means putting on a new pair of glasses, to **stop seeing yourself as you are and start picturing yourself as you want to be, as you can be.** And believe it. As you do you unlock the invisible forces of the universe to move you closer to your dream.

Also, when you find yourself avoiding the next step on the plan you have created, cut yourself some slack, take a walk and come back to it. As long as you keep procrastinating you will never advance. *Be bold and take one more step closer to the life you want.*

Don't constrain yourself to your initial plan. *Be flexible, creative, and adaptable.* As you progress, it's okay to dream bigger.

Right now, this whole vision thing may seem too big, too far out of reach. You may just want to have a little more confidence and courage in one area of your life. Great, start there.

Prompt: Visualization Exercises—Creating Your Ideal Image

To help you focus, start by asking yourself a few questions: How would you like to be? What does that look like to you? What would it mean to you? Can you begin to visualize who you want to be?

Start painting that picture and surrounding yourself with people and information that will enhance your ability to feel more courageous and self-confident. **Stop thinking about what you don't want and start seeing what you do want.** Unless, of course, there are things, behaviors, or habits you want to get rid of. Then visualize what your life will look like without them. *Visualization is* *putting on a new pair of sunglasses to keep the glare of negativity out of your eyes.*

For more ideas on how to bring your goals and dreams into focus, refer to the *Ten Second of Boldness Productivity Planner* in Appendix II and the specific section in it about visualization. Look for images and words that reflect what confidence looks like to you. Paste them on a dream board or in the visualization section on the *Productivity Planner*. Have fun with it. No dream is too small or too big. Let your imagination soar.

Chapter Twenty-Eight
Affirmations: Inspiration From the Inside Out

"I am happy, healthy, wealthy, and free."
John Croxall

The above quote was the first affirmation I memorized. John Croxall gets the credit because I heard it from him first. His "Beyond Goal Setting" class and, in particular, that one affirmation literally changed my life. As I went about my day, it became a mantra. It had a beat that worked well with every step I took on the way to the bus stop. While walking to class. While approaching new customers when I waited tables.

It put a smile on my face. It gave me hope. Even though, at first, I thought it was hokey, I said it out loud anyway. Soon, I started to "act as if." To "fake it until I made it." And an interesting thing happened; I began to feel better about myself, even when things weren't going the way I wanted.

I started to make more money, I did better in school, and rarely got sick. I began to dream and set goals and visualize a promising future. A career. A family. Owning a car. I wrote down my goals and created affirmations for them as if I already had them. And one by one they started to come true.

Here's an example of a goal and affirmation I vividly remember because I invested the time to write down virtually every detail and affirm it to be true before it was. Hokey or not, this stuff works.

The Goal:

"I want an affordable top-floor apartment next to open space with a view of Mount Tamalpais. It will have vaulted ceilings and a fireplace, a balcony or deck, a big master bedroom, and separate room to be used as an office. A pool, a recreation room, and a workout room. It also needs covered parking."

The list of features and amenities was a collaborative effort between me and my girlfriend who would later become my wife and mother of our son.

I then wrote down an affirmation of how great it felt to share meals with family and friends, with the silhouette of Mt. Tam in the background. How nice it was to have a clean, well-lit, comfortable home close to work that was also affordable.

I thought about it every day. We spent a week or two looking at several places, but most didn't measure up to what we wanted; one had brown shag carpet and avocado green Formica counters. When we saw this one, I knew. This was it. We got exactly what I had written down.

I have since set many goals and written them down with affirmations.

Here are a few more affirmation examples, just for fun:
- Today, I am one of the richest men alive because of love. I love and am loved. And that is worth more than anything money could buy. More than a million dollars in the bank, a mansion by the beach, or a Lamborghini in my garage.
- I am happy most days when I decide to be.
- I am healthy because I exercise and eat moderately well.
- I am wealthy because of love.
- I am free today because love set me free.

What are Affirmations and How Do You Make Them Work?

As mentioned earlier, affirmations are positive statements of your intentions, written in present tense as if you have achieved them. They are incredibly powerful. They work best if they are:
1. Believable.
2. Important to you.
3. Easy to remember and repeat.

They can also be
1. Prayers, thoughts, and meditations.
2. Natural extensions of visualizing your goals written in a way to help you believe them to be true.

If you have never heard of or used affirmations before you may be inclined to consider them hocus-pocus, mumbo-jumbo, bullshit. Not true. I have used them for decades and can attest to their power in making my goals and dreams come true. Plus, they are fun and easy to use if you stop thinking of them as weird and believe they will work for you too.

Here are a few examples of affirmations I wrote in 1988:
- I am honest in all my affairs. I express my feelings openly and freely. I am at peace with myself.
- I am kind. I am loving. I am patient. I am tolerant. I am considerate. I am understanding. I am compassionate. I am sincere. I love myself unconditionally.
- I have paid off all my back bills.
- I have earned better than a 3.2 GPA this spring semester.
- I have recovered from Alcoholism. Prayer is natural and comfortable.

You get the idea. The key is to not write them as if you "would like to or someday I'll." Write them as if they are true right now.

> **Nearly every single thing I wrote down more than thirty years ago has come true!**

The Secret Sauce to Success

Along with prayer and meditation as previously mentioned, visualization and affirmation, coupled with action, are the "secret sauce" to manifesting your own reality. Affirmations help replace, reboot, and reprogram your mind. Over time, they have the capacity to build belief and confidence because they replace tired, unproductive, negative thinking by forming new neural pathways for your mind. By learning to change your focus and how and what you think about you effectively change your mindset. This is referred to as Neuro Linguistic Programming (NLP).

Neuroscientist, Steven Campbell, adds: "Positive affirmations are very powerful because they release you from negativity, fear, worry, and anxiety. When you lock onto these affirmations, they can take charge of your thoughts, slowly changing your pattern of thinking and ultimately changing your life."

Once Again, Write Down Your Goals

I stopped writing affirmations for a while until I was reminded by a speaker at a business seminar. He validated what I had learned from John Croxall years earlier and suggested we write down affirmations or scribble positive maxims, sayings, or affirmations on post it notes and place them in clearly visible spots where we will see them frequently such as on a mirror, bulletin board, or the dashboard of your car. He said they were powerful reminders to counter our tendency to drift into worry, doubt, or insecurity. I took his advice and have been a positive Post-it note madman ever since.

Here are a few more recent examples placed in my office. I can't not see them and read them many times each day. Like the goal book from way back, their power is remarkable. They help me stay focused and fully present, especially when I am feeling anxious or unsure about myself or a new situation.

- Don't sabotage your own success. Embrace it.
- Let it go.
- Accept the things you cannot change.
- Find the courage to change the things you can.
- Be bolder.
- Ten Seconds of Boldness
- Feel the fear and do it anyway.
- Love God, Self, and Others.
- I believe in you. Love, God.
- Pause. Breathe. Smile.
- Do your best, always.
- Don't Quit Before the Miracle.
- I will…until.
- Do it Now.
- Don't Overthink it.
- Focus on what you can change, not what you can't.
- Ask. Believe. Receive.
- Be Bold. Be Brilliant. Be Gone.

Prompt: Affirmation Practice

If you've never written affirmations, I encourage you to give it a try. Or at the very least, memorize a few inspirational quotes that are meaningful to you: that inspire and motivate. At first, when you say them out loud, it will probably feel weird.

Take five minutes to write down a few affirmations. Refer back to the examples above if you need to.

I also encourage you to memorize your affirmations and say them aloud throughout the day.

You may not want to say them in public places like the bus stop, or airplanes, or in meetings because you may get a few weird looks or raise a few eyebrows. But then again, you're becoming bolder now, so if you start talking to yourself in the grocery line, it may not seem weird. If you do, wear earbuds, and nod a lot, nobody will ever know who you're talking to.

I say them in the shower or in front of the mirror in the morning. Sometimes out loud, sometimes in my head.

I used to say my morning prayers and affirmations during my morning commute because Bay Area traffic is a mess and it felt like a good use of my time instead of showing up to work uptight and stressed out.

The point is there is no wrong way to do them. Play with them, create categories. *Have fun.*

I cannot explain how affirmations, prayer, and meditation work, but I know if I follow up with some type of action, that they do. Contrary to Woody Allen's famous quote that, "90% of success is just showing up." I think it's more like 40-50%. The other 50-60% is doing something or being still enough to listen.

Affirmations can be like the focus word(s) for the year I mentioned earlier.

With spaced repetition, awareness, and practice, my affirmations become intentions moving from the recesses of my subconscious mind into my conscious mind, and in most cases, come to fruition. At the very least, they are attitude-adjustment tools that help me feel more positive, present, and confident in myself.

My challenge for you is to repeat them frequently enough to believe them and make them a healthy habit. Just like anything, it gets easier with practice.

And they come true when we *write them down*.

Chapter Twenty-Nine
Building Confidence is a Balancing Act

"Self-confidence is very important. But without compassion and humility, it's just arrogance."
Anonymous

In 2007, I had just earned not only Employee of the Year but also Salesperson of the Year from the New York Times Regional Media Group, which owned our local newspaper at the time. I was on top of the world. My ego was the size of Santa Rosa. But, as most salespeople can attest, "You're only as good as your last sale." The rush of success was short lived.

Hero to Zero Syndrome

After winning the award I became cocky and complacent. I stopped doing the things that earned me the awards, commission, and accolades up to that point. I took my eye off the ball. I thought I learned a hard, but valuable lesson: **arrogance and apathy are not conducive to lasting success.** I didn't. Quite the opposite, in fact. My sales started to slip. Soon I was failing to hit quota. Unrelated, but to make matters worse, my marriage of fifteen years had just ended. My life was turned upside down. *It felt like I was riding a rollercoaster without a seatbelt in a hurricane.*

In a matter of months, I had gone from "hero to zero" and felt like I could be fired any minute. On top of that, the economy tanked.

There were cuts, downsizing, and a frenetic push by management for the sales team to increase revenue and improve the company's bottom line.

Silver Lining

In the midst of all this turmoil and chaos, Crissi and I started dating and fell in love. Our infatuation was a silver lining on the dark skies of a mostly self-imposed shit storm. I began to feel a sense of hope. My confidence returned. I got my swagger back. And once again had a bounce in my step. As mentioned earlier, I even found the courage to ask her to marry me.

At work, I redoubled my efforts and came back strong, growing my territory by 25% in six short months. I was back on top again.

And then I coasted.

Once again, I became complacent. Repeating the self-defeating pattern of success and failure I swore I wouldn't. One would think I would've learned my lesson by then. Not me.

I began to question everything: my career choice, working for this company, my worth. But what else could I do? Go back to waiting tables? I had already done that—twice.

Before they could fire me, I was recruited by a partner company to sell digital advertising. The opportunity sounded promising with a small draw against commission as compensation and huge upside potential. Even though I was scared of jumping ship, I was desperate and accepted the job after the first interview.

It wasn't long before I second guessed my rash decision to switch jobs for the promise of more freedom and income potential.

The requirements for success at that job were much harder than I anticipated. It required lots of cold-calling. And just like Indiana Jones hates snakes, I hate cold-calling.

Yet, I found the guts to pick up that 10,000-pound phone and make the calls anyway. Not because I wanted to. Because I *had* to. I did what it took to survive and it all worked out, until I found a better job after the wedding.

Up to that point, those few years were some of the most trying and humbling I had experienced in my career. I wish I could say that I don't make those mistakes anymore. I still do, but the difference today is that I recognize the pattern before it becomes a problem. Plus, when I get too full of myself, my wife will quickly knock my ego down a peg or two just to keep me humble. And that is one of many reasons why I love her.

Why "I Got This" is Dangerous and Often Doesn't Work

I don't know where you are on your own path. But I have seen this scenario played out many times with those who want to get sober. After a point, they stop going to meetings. They don't finish the steps. Full of ego to mask their insecurities, they say to themselves "I got this" just as I did in early recovery. Soon, they are right back into their addiction.

Similar scenarios are played out every day with those who struggle with self-confidence, or any other host of problems they claim they want to change. Unfortunately, most lack a plan and the courage or motivation to act.

Besides a tendency to be complacent and lazy, most of us are also impatient. Because most of us expect immediate results, it's easy for us to become disappointed at the pace of progress and give up way too soon. We make excuses and justify what we did. But in most cases, as already mentioned, the real reason success continues to elude us because we don't have a strong enough reason why we want it. Our motives are unclear. Plus, too often we believe that the expectation and probability of accomplishment is not greater than the effort we think it will take to succeed. We weigh risk vs. reward and respond based on our expectation and confidence of reward.

Rather than redouble our efforts or change our thinking or approach, we choose to do nothing. We quit before the miracle.

As we have discussed throughout this book, it doesn't have to be that way. You can change if you want to and are willing to put in the effort. Remember the five-step process:

1. **Identify** the Problem/Opportunity
2. Clearly decide what you **want**
3. Know **why** you want it
4. Write a clear **plan**
5. **Start** working that plan

These five steps are your footbridge to becoming more confident and successful. As you practice them, they become essential habits. Keep your eyes focused on your dreams and goals, and *why* you want them. Then create as clear a picture as you can of the person you want to be or what you want to have or do. Keep stepping forward and you will not only fully understand patience and progress, but you will gain confidence with each new step.

Most importantly invest the time to *find your why*. Identify and understand your motives for change, then develop a plan to get what you want, and put your plan into action.

That's it. Never forgetting, of course, to use all the precepts of *Ten Seconds of Boldness* until this process becomes a habit.

Lasting transformation is a result of stringing together a series of incremental adjustments to develop "micro habits." one step at a time. Remember: *all meaningful progress and change begins with a first step.* Resolve and decide to take the first one. Then another. One step in front of the other.

Don't Forget to Celebrate Your Success Along the Way

Lighten up. Give yourself permission to experience joy. Celebrate your success and victories along the way. Take time out to recharge.

The same holds true when things happen that are out of your control or when you make a mistake. Accept that they happened, change what you can, and move on. Memorize the "Serenity Prayer," even if you don't believe in God: *"God, grant me the serenity to accept the things I cannot change, the courage to change the things I can, and the wisdom to know the difference."*

If you need to, throw yourself a short "pity party," but don't bake a cake or invite too many guests. They may not want to come back. Instead, stand up, pick the stickers off your thrift store suit, and keep moving forward.

Confidence Doesn't Happen in a Vacuum

Confidence is built as you stay engaged in the process of continuous improvement. Being willing to try and fail. And it certainly won't happen if you do nothing.

Beware of Complacency and Other Confidence Killers

When you succumb to complacency, all the success of your hard work begins to evaporate. Soon you lose momentum and quickly spiral back to your previous state of equilibrium, or worse. *If you are going to strive for anything, strive for progress, not perfection.* Do your best always. And leave the results up to the universe. That is how you build confidence: **one bold decision and action at a time.**

Remain mindful of and beware of these confidence killers:

- Judgment
- Comparison
- Pride/Ego
- Overconfidence/Cockiness
- Blame
- Denial
- Victim mentality
- Rejection
- Self-Sabotage
- Feeding your Inner Critics

I've already talked about the hazards of each of these. But I want to spend a few minutes talking about judgment and comparison because they are sneaky-dangerous.

Comparison, self-criticism, worry about others criticizing you, or your own judgment of others are all poisons to building healthy self-confidence.

Most of us tend to judge ourselves and our own inadequacies harshly, which keeps us in a state of low self-worth: not good enough. As we have discussed throughout the book, these negative thoughts and beliefs can paralyze us from pursuing something we really would like to do or become. Similarly, judgment or gossip is merely a smokescreen for our own inadequacies. Both are terrible habits. We put others down to build ourselves up. And it's not healthy. In fact, all that type of thinking does is reinforce any currently belief systems that have not been serving you well. As difficult as it is, I encourage you to avoid talking smack about others or yourself.

And how often do we worry about what others will think of us? Of being judged. That if we make a mistake that we somehow are a failure. Not true. Color outside the lines. Try something new. If it doesn't work tweak it. *Embrace your mistakes because once you know all the ways that don't work, you will feel a sense of confidence when you find the ways that do.*

The other silent killer of hopes and dreams is comparison. We all do it. Comparing our success to others who have already paid their dues and feeling like we deserve to be where they are without effort is ridiculous. Unless we are trying to emulate the work habits and experience that has led to others' success, comparing what they have after years of experience is not going to add anything positive to your confidence bank.

If we believe that we could never "Be like Mike." Then we never will. The problem is most of us place too much weight on the results of others without considering what it took them to become successful. We become enamored with the shiny symbols of their success: the cars, houses, fame, fortune, and lifestyle. And there is nothing wrong with wanting to be successful. Unfortunately, most of us aren't disciplined or courageous enough to discover and do what it will take to get what we want. To develop some new ways of thinking to overcome the deep ruts that the inner critics have created in our lives.

But *you can overcome all that stands in your way.*

Be patient with yourself, it's going to take time.

It's really simple but takes dedication and practice.

To increase your confidence and belief in your own abilities and develop the courage to act requires three things:

A dream. A decision. And *Ten Seconds of Boldness* to act.

Final Prompt: Reminders to Memorize and Do Until They Become Habits

Here are some reminders as you tiptoe the tightrope between confidence and humility:

- Remember do the best you can and appreciate what you have—**be grateful.**
- Ask for help/advice especially when you don't think you need it—**be humble.**
- Find courage within from whatever invisible force inspires and motivates you to change what you can—**be courageous.**
- Tame Your Inner Critics: Don't feed the beast!
- Don't judge yourself or others.
- Don't compare others' success to where you are now.
- Be patient with yourself and others. Remember, progress takes time.
- Stay in your own lane.
- Be curious and humble, yet focused and bold.

- Don't become cocky or complacent because it will undo all the work you've done faster than a fire on a windy day.
- Think Less. Do More.
- Resolve to do a little bit every day. Whatever it is; Something significant to help you grow in courage and belief.
- Keep your why alive in your heart and mind.
- Never give up your dream.
- Never stop learning.
- Never stop improving.
- Don't quit before the miracle.

Remember you can be, have, or do *almost* anything if you want it bad enough and are willing to get out of your comfort zone to work for it. When you find what you're looking for, offer to help others. It will make someone else's day and prevent you from becoming overconfident.

Conclusion
The End is Just a New Beginning

As we close, I want to thank you. Thank you for being vulnerable enough to take a chance on you. To come this far. I truly hope some of this sinks in and helps you feel braver and a little more confident. Brave enough to take whatever next step you need to so you can feel confident enough to believe you can be, have, or do, virtually anything you choose to.

I'll leave you with a few more words of encouragement and two short stories.

Remember always, living your dreams is only ten seconds of boldness away. **Decide today to be bolder and to live your life fully, without regret.**

Mom and Dad

My life started with my mom and dad, so it's only appropriate to end the book with them. I am very grateful that I had parents who loved me even when I didn't know how to love myself.

Mom

In my first year of recovery, I was having a hard time processing my feelings. So, I called my mom for wisdom and support.

No surprise, it was over a woman. My wanting a family and being down on myself because none of my relationships were working out.

Basically, I was impatient and was wallowing in self-pity, because I desperately wanted a family but had not yet found the "right woman" to marry.

Even though inside I was lonely, I still felt entitled. Because I had stopped drinking, I thought that everything else would just come to me overnight. That I deserved it all. The wife, two kids, a house, a great job. All of it. What a joke. Success doesn't work like that. Never has. Never will.

In hindsight, I realized I had a lot more growing up to do. I was only twenty-two and had the emotional maturity of a pubescent thirteen-year-old. It's no wonder I struggled with relationships.

And yet, my mom always knew when something wasn't right. Sometimes she'd call me out of the blue just to check in. And whenever I needed a bit of encouragement—usually after wandering off into the weeds and scrub brush of life—I'd call her. That's one of the things I love about my relationship with my mom. We're honest with each other, sometimes to a fault. But we've always been there to support each other.

Nearly always, I felt better afterward. Mom had a knack pointing me in a direction to help me find my own way home. Later, when she'd offer unsolicited advice about a problem I shared, we'd butt heads. But that's what most moms do. I learned it from her and still have to catch myself doing the same thing.

Shortly after that phone call, I got a poem from her in the mail. It would become yet one more mile marker I'd return to whenever I felt lost or alone. It always helped get me back on the right path home. Still does.

Life is serious. Life is fun.
In many ways, you've just begun.
Sometimes we stumble, sometimes we fall.
Even when backed against a wall.
Remember always when in your plight,
At the end of the tunnel, there is always light.

Love,
Mom

Dad

I don't want you to think that my dad was a villain. Yes, he abandoned us, and that hurt, a lot. But my dad had a heart of gold. He was incredibly intelligent and had a perpetual curiosity about life and the spiritual world that in many ways shaped who I am today. When he wanted to do something, he figured out how to do it. He read, studied, asked others for advice or help, and was a very humble man. And he wasn't afraid to be bold and take risks. After all, he was a fireman and compassionate courage are part of that job.

Despite many lost years I spent being angry and resentful at him, even after the multiple times I tried to forgive him, something still wasn't right. In hindsight I realized that I had unrealistic expectations of who I thought he should be, of how I felt he should relate to me and my brothers. And I know it's not unrealistic to expect a father to be there for his kids. But I knew I had to forgive him. Not just as a step in my recovery, but to free myself of all the silent rage still bubbling beneath the surface until things got tough. When they did, my fear and feelings would erupt like a volcano. My anger cost me a marriage, jobs, and fractured my relationships. For years, it was still one of my biggest demons. It still rears its ugly head on occasion.

The Cathartic Power of Love and Forgiveness

At nineteen years sober, I was still battling some inner demons. I'd been put through the wringer and had recently lost a ten-year job. But I remember that balmy fall day in 2005 as if it was yesterday. It even inspired me to write a short story called "Milkshakes in Heaven."

I've included a portion of it here to leave you with an image of hope.

This story encapsulates so much of my life journey about trying to become better, resilient, and to mend a broken relationship with my dad. To heal and find a sense of inner peace and learn to love again. To me, it's the best way I can think of to end our time together, for now.

Milkshakes in Heaven
By Shawn Langwell

It was a good day in Sonoma County.

The air was warm, almost balmy. Nearby vineyards, pregnant with Chardonnay and Pinot grapes, filled the air with the pleasant fragrance of fall. Maples stood like paintbrushes, bursting with crimson and gold leaves waiting for a new canvas. In the distance, the jagged silhouette of Sugarloaf Ridge and Gunsight Rock offered a picturesque backdrop to the fertile valley below.

I smiled, grateful to be surrounded by such natural beauty, before turning onto Highway 12. I wound my way down Montgomery Drive, through the tunnel of oaks, past Spring Lake,

TEN SECONDS OF BOLDNESS

flying around the corners, windows down, blasting Santana's "Oye Como Va!"

It had been a great day so far. My crew and I had just completed a flawless wedding banquet for a wonderful young bride and groom at the country club I managed. I checked my shirt pocket. Inside were three crisp hundred-dollar bills, an extra tip from the father of the bride.

I was flying high.

On top of the world.

Euphoric.

It had been a while since I felt that way. The past decade had been marked by the joy of living the American Dream: I graduated college, got married, bought a home, and had a son. That pink bubble finally burst in 2001 when I lost my job. Fear consumed me as I worried about making my mortgage payment and being able to support my young family. I was forced to find anything to make ends meet. Miraculously, I ran into an old friend who offered me a job at a local country club as a waiter. He left unexpectedly, and I was promoted to Food and Beverage Director.

Once again, I was making good money.

Once again, I was on top of the world.

"Oye como va!"

I sang out loud, still zipping past the boutique shopping center of Montgomery Village, pounding my steering wheel to the signature explosive drumbeat and guitar riffs of Santana.

"Oye como va!"

My cell phone buzzed, jostling the change in my center console. I glanced down.

"Mom," the display read.

I reached for it, briefly swerving into the other lane, narrowly missing an oncoming car. Frazzled, I still picked it up.

"Hey Mom, how are you? What's new?"

"I'm okay... I just got off the phone with your aunt."

Something was wrong. She never says "okay" like that. I pretended to be cool.

"How *is* Aunt Nellie? You guys gonna go to the casino with Grandma again for your birthday?"

"She's good...yeah, we're planning to go in a couple weeks, but that's not why I'm calling... It's your dad...he's in the hospital."

"Wait. What? What happened?"

"Your aunt says he's got some kind of infection...it's not good." I could hear her swallow hard. This news was like a gut punch.

My knuckles white as I processed what my mom was saying. All the old wounds I thought had disappeared rose to the surface again in an instant.

I pulled over and parked in front of a fast-food restaurant. Distracted by a poster of a big thick milkshake, I did my best to finish my conversation with my mom. I told her I'd visit him the next day and hung up, then started weeping.

The next day I kept my word. As I turned to enter the dimly lit room, my jaw dropped. I saw my emaciated father in a spotted gown, salt and pepper stubble on his gaunt face, his eyes distant and turned toward a gnarled oak outside the window.

"Hi Dad! What's going on?" I tried to sound as upbeat as I could.

He turned toward me, flashing a wide-toothed smile. "Ha! Shawn! How are you? I've missed you!" he said.

It had been three years since our last visit— Christmas, two years after my youngest brother Seth had died in a car accident.

"You don't look so good, Dad. What happened?"

"It all caught up with me, Son." He sighed yet didn't seem remorseful. "The years as a firefighter...partying...living fast and hard. It all took a toll on me."

I took a deep breath and said what was on my heart.

"Dad, I want you to know I love you. It hurts to see you like this."

"Aw Shawn, come here," he said, extending his thin arms. I leaned in to hug him. His rough stubble scratched against my smooth face, just like the times he kissed me goodnight after chasing away the monsters in my closet.

I began to rub his head the same way he used to rub mine. I especially loved when he would vigorously dry my hair with a towel after a bath when I was little.

We talked for twenty minutes or so, reminiscing about the fun trips to the cabin in Mariposa, how excited I was when I got to slide down the firepole at his work, and the time I got to see him drive away to a fire. The sirens were deafening, but I loved it!

It made me proud watching him speed off to save someone's home, or life. I told him how much it meant to get paintings from him every Christmas, and how I was glad he got to meet my son.

"We had some good times, Dad. I wish we could've had more."

"I know, Shawn. Me too." His face briefly looked forlorn. "I'm sorry about Seth. I really am. It's sad that he died so young..." Dad closed his eyes for a moment and swallowed hard, "but he's in a better place now," he continued softly. "I always thought of you boys. Even though we never got to see each other much...I never stopped loving you."

My lips pursed as tears began to trickle down my cheeks. "I know Dad, I know. It was just hard to accept it after you left. I'm glad I'm here now."

"Me too, Shawn." His eyes drifted back to the mighty oak outside.

"I'm not ready for you to go, Dad." My voice shook. "Is there anything I can do? Is there anything you'd like?"

He turned back, and with his charming grin said, "A milkshake."

"A milkshake? Okay—What kind?" I asked, puzzled at his request.

"Chocolate!" he blurted out like a kid going to an ice cream store with *his* dad.

I chuckled. "You got it! I'll bring one next time I come back, okay?"

"I'd like that."

I leaned in to hug him goodbye, feeling his warm embrace linger before finally letting go.

Three days later he passed. I felt bad that I never did get him that milkshake. It's okay. I'm at peace with it, now. Besides, I'm sure there will be plenty of time later for us to share milkshakes in heaven.

Love is both the beginning and the end of this magnificent journey we call life. Whether it's confidence, courage, belief, a million dollars, or learning to forgive your father and yourself so one day you, too, can share "Milkshakes in Heaven," I hope you find your *Ten Seconds of Boldness* and learn to live and love deeply. Because when it's all said and done, that's all that really matters.

Here's to your success, whatever success means to you.

And remember, *don't quit before the miracle.*

Love,
Shawn

Acknowledgements

So much of what we struggle with in life seems to come back to belief and willingness or lack thereof. Of humility, focus, and awareness—to pay attention and ask for help when necessary. Life is a team sport, a collaboration. This book is no exception.

I am extremely grateful for all who have had integral parts in its completion.

First off, thank you to my smart and beautiful wife, Crissi Langwell. You know how much I love you. I doubt I would've had the confidence to see this project through without your expertise with everything from cover design and formatting to proofreading and publishing. The best part is being able to celebrate our successes together. We are truly living the dream.

To my award-winning editor, Jim Baldwin. Jim and I clicked immediately. His style is 100% collaborative. Jim, I appreciate how you let me know what was working and what wasn't with the original manuscript and offered suggestions for improvement, with kindness and encouragement. Working with you has made me a better writer.

To Malena Eljumaily for not only another set of discerning eyes as a proofreader, but also your unexpected high praise for the project. Your compliments mean the world to me and gave me the extra jolt of confidence to get me over the finish line.

I especially want to extend my heartfelt appreciation to all those who offered their time, expertise, and insight, and key contributions to the book:

To Kevin Miller, thank you for your encouragement and critical contributions about overcoming doubt, finding what drives us, and valuable advice as a parent of many kids. I must admit, connecting with you and actually getting an interview set up took a lot more than ten seconds of boldness on my part. But I am so happy with the results of our conversation. I can't wait until our next one. Keep doing what you're doing. You have a massive platform to positively influence millions and are a living example of what humility looks like. Thank you!

To Stephen Campbell for an invaluable perspective on brain science and belief. Stephen, I knew you had something important to offer from the presentation you gave to our sales team several years ago. It was a no brainer (pun intended) to include your expertise as a neuroscientist in the book.

To Coach Steve Lavin for offering a broader perspective about life, humility, coaching, values, and joy, and the power of practice, determination, and being coachable. Steve, we've come a long way since guarding each other in summer camps at Drake. Glad to call you friend. Thank you for the magnificent conversation. In many respects it felt like Cap was on the fringe, in a green recliner, listening in with a cherubim grin.

To Aaron Locks for being vulnerable enough to share his story of building confidence as a young lad, and how that critical moment as a seven-year-old would later become a cause and calling to teaching confidence to over 300,000 kids. Aaron, you are making a difference in the lives our youth one kid at a time, teaching them to "Play Hard" and "Have Fun." I can think of few callings more noble.

To Cara Wasden, my speaking mentor and an enigmatic human with a heart for building confidence in many. Cara, I am proud to know you and so glad you shared a piece of yourself in this book.

To Jon Diamond, my first interviewee and brother from another mother. Jon, your clarity, succinctness, grit, and determination are admirable. But more important is the value of your leadership—leading with your heart and hiring for heart. That is a lesson for any who choose to lead. I am so appreciative for your insight and willingness to "keep it real."

To Jason Lam for critical insights on ambition. Your wisdom and willingness to debunk three critical myths about personal ambition from a biblical perspective are a valuable and thoughtful contribution to the book. Thank you!

To my boss Lori Pearce, publisher, Rob Devincenzi, and CRO Michael Turpin who have shown me what it's like to lead by example. I am so appreciative that each of you trust me enough to do what it takes to meet my own work goals while also understanding that life is not all about our jobs. Thank you for your encouragement and support with this project.

To my brother Kelly who taught me at an early age what courage looks like by climbing trees and diving off high rocks into cool pools as a teenager. You exemplify courage and determination and continue to amaze me with your resilience to overcome life's challenges. I love you.

To my youngest brother Seth, who lived a life out loud and feared little. Your heart of gold will remain with me forever. I miss you, Bro.

To Marleen Cullen, John Abbot, and my fellow Redwood Writers for editing my work over the past four years and encouraging me to be vulnerable enough to share tough stories in a way that readers can relive them. Thank you for living up to the Redwood Writers' Mission: "Writers, helping writers."

To Peter Byrne, who always keeps it real. I value you as a friend, sounding board, and cheerleader. Thanks for the awesome pull quote.

To all those who will remain anonymous, your hearts of service are making a difference in the lives of many, including mine.

To my English teachers: Albert "Cap" Lavin, Marc Bojanowski, and Johnny Saraff, from prose and poetry to creative writing and critical thinking, thank you for pushing me to become a better writer.

To David O'Connor, for wisdom, integrity, and encouragement. If you were alive today, I am confident this book would make you proud.

To my dad, Jim Langwell. My only regret is that I didn't let go of my resentments and forgive you sooner. I wish we could have spent more time together before your passing. I now realize just how much you gave me as a young child. I will keep all that I love about you close to my heart and am so grateful for all that you gave and taught me. I know you are at peace and smile knowing you can have all the chocolate milkshakes in Heaven you want! And when my work in this lifetime is complete, I look forward to sharing many with you.

To my son, Andrew, and stepkids, Summer, and Lucas. Being a dad and stepfather is one of the greatest gifts in the world. I am so proud of the fine adults each of you have become. I love you.

Last and certainly not least, to my mom, Joan O' Connor. Who has been there with and for me every step of the way. Loving me when I couldn't love myself. Nurturing me, listening to my rants, and teaching me how to survive and encouraging me to be bold enough to pursue my dreams. Mom, I love you for all of it. I am blessed to call you Mom. And, I have not forgotten what you said when I was a teenager and listening to all those inspirational tapes building my dream: "Remember your mom when you're rich and famous." Fame, or fortune aside, you taught me values that have no price tag, such as honesty, humility, integrity, kindness, compassion, and most of all, love. I will forever remain grateful for all you taught me. And I have not forgotten you, the dream is still unfolding.

Thank you all, for being a part of this project and my life.

Appendix I
Self-Assessment Sheets

Instructions

Start by answering these five important questions:

1. What do you think you want and why?
2. What are you good at?
3. What do you like or not like?
4. What is really holding you back?
5. What are you grateful for?

Other questions to consider:

What do I say to myself? What do I hear? Am I listening to what I say to myself? What do others say about me? What would you like to improve? What are your greatest fears? What do you think you want and why? Add any thoughts, behaviors, attitudes, or beliefs that you want to change.

For any or all of these questions write down your responses in a journal, notebook, word doc or binder paper. Do not just mull them over.

Your ability to overcome or build upon your assets and liabilities hinges upon clearly identifying them. Don't try to short cut the process. Take the time to write them down.

We will build on this list later to address specific areas of what you want, and why you want it as well as creating a gratitude list. For now, review and start filling the columns below. Don't think too hard just write.

Assets and Liabilities

What do you like?
- Everything I like about myself, do well, or enjoy.
- Everything I do well—My strengths
- What interests me?
- What I am grateful for?
- What brings me joy?
- What are my wins?

What don't you like?
- Everything I don't like about myself and wish I could do better.
- Everything I don't do well—My weaknesses.
- What do I not enjoy doing?
- What I am ashamed of?
- What do I feel guilty about?

SWOT Analysis

Strengths:	Weaknesses:
Opportunities:	Threats:

Why Do I Need to Do This?

The point of this exercise is to become comfortable looking inside and facing some of the things that are easily dismissed or swept away. The time you invest in honestly completing a rigorous self-assessment without judgment or criticism will do two things:

1. It will help you feel good about the things you do well or like about yourself.
2. By honestly looking at all the things you don't like or would like to change, it will diminish their power over you.

Appendix II
Ten Seconds of Boldness Productivity Planner

These sheets are prompts for you to create your personal action plan and your bridge to move from *what if?* and *if only*, to *what's next?* From where you are to where you want to be.

Writing down your dreams, ambitions, goals, intentions, plans or whatever you want to call them is tantamount to manifesting them. They are *your action plan* to write the next chapters of your life. What type of story will it be? What will happen? Will it have a happy ending? What obstacles will you face? How will you overcome them? You won't know until you dive in. And that's what makes this all so exciting.

While the fundamentals of goal setting have not changed in ages, there are some insights and nuances, I believe you will find helpful. Think of these planning sheets as your outline, roadmap, and game plan for solving your problems and accomplishing that which you seek. They will help you stay focused, if you use them.

As I mentioned earlier, I owe a huge debt of gratitude to John Croxall for what I learned in his *Beyond Goal Setting* class at College of Marin. Over the years I have expanded upon several of his ideas and strategies about goal setting and, as mentioned earlier, have experienced tremendous results.

With respect to personal growth and achievement, the biggest "ah-ha" realization I've had over the past four decades is this: When I clearly decide what I want, write it down, then visualize and affirm that which I want as already being a reality and actually trust and believe it to become so, then develop a plan and start working that plan, that the creative powers of the universe somehow align and guide me to its successful consummation. *It works nearly every time when my motives are clear and larger than mere personal gain.*

Remember the story about Jon Diamond who wrote down a few ideas and actually forgot about the piece of paper. Regardless of that paper being buried in the bottom of a desk drawer for a few years, his subconscious mind began to work toward making that plan a reality.

As mentioned, it all started with a "prosperity plan" which he wrote down on a piece of paper. Together, he and his business partner Curtis, set a goal to sell a million dollars in their first year as partners; the company sold $1,000,040. Four years later they sold $21 million. The company has made Inc's top 5000 for the fastest growing companies every year since 2009.

I intentionally repeated that story to reinforce and circumvent any doubt you may have. To assure you that **planning paired with action works.** Make it work for you by using these planning sheets as your guide.

Feel free to categorize, color-code, or customize and break down these steps as you like to fit your needs. Do whatever makes it easier for you to stay focused.

If you like, read and review them often or toss them in the bottom drawer of your desk. It doesn't matter, as long as you **write them down**. Put Post-it notes on your mirror, create dream boards to put on your wall. Do whatever will keep your mind focused on what you want and increase your belief that you can actually have it.

That's how it works. It's really not any great secret. It's creating a consistent pattern of effort and success; a habit of ten seconds of courage, clarity, and focused effort using the five-step plan in *Ten Seconds of Boldness*.

Do a little something every day to move closer to resolving your problems and creating or discovering the solutions you seek. To repeat what my wife says, **"Don't let process get in the way of productivity. That's a form of procrastination."** In other words, don't get hung up on strategy before you know what the heck you want.

Do the work and leave the results up to the universe.

Here are keys for you to consider:

- What's the Problem/Opportunity?
- What do you want?
- What's your ideal solution, outcome, or goal?
- Why do you want it?
- What will it mean to you and how will you benefit?
- What does that look like?
- Visualize the new situation.
- Create a "Dream Board."
- Use the *Ten Seconds of Boldness* Productivity Planner
- When do you want it?
- What's your plan to get it?
- Follow Anne Lamott's advice: "Keep your butt in the chair" and write.
- Do it now.
- What are you doing, or can you do today to make it happen?
- Affirmations: Faking it until you make it. Acting as if. How does it feel now that you have accomplished what you wanted?
- What's next?

- (ABI) Always be improving.
- (ABP) Always be prospecting (as a tool for salespeople).
- Be creative.
- Work hard and smart. But most of all have fun. Joy will follow.

Seven of the most common areas for setting goals:

- Finances/Future
- Work/Job Security
- Relationships
- Health
- Beliefs, Attitude, and Worldview
- Family
- Education

Ten Seconds of Boldness
Productivity Planning Sheets:

The Five Essential Habits, Questions, and Decisions to Solving Problems and Building Confidence to Achieve Most Any Goal

The Five Essential Habits

1. **Identify** the Problem or Opportunity.
2. Clearly decide **what** you want.
3. Know **why** you want it.
4. Write a clear **plan**.
5. **Start** working that plan.

The Five Essential Questions

1. What's the problem/opportunity?
2. What do you really want?
3. Why do you want it, and how bad?
4. What's your plan to get it?
5. Are you ready to get started?

The Five Essential Decisions

1. Decide to identify and admit there's a problem.
2. Decide what you want and what you're going to do about it.

3. Decide to find out why you want it.
4. Decide what you're willing to do to get it.
5. Decide to get into action and to never give up.

My Goal(s) and Plan(s)

Problem/Opportunity
A five to ten word, honest and specific, description of what I want to change or accomplish. The focus here is on the problem or opportunity not your ideal situation or goal.

_____

_____

_____

_____

EXAMPLES:
- I worry that I am not going to have enough money to survive in retirement.
- Even after years of experience, I still struggle with self-doubt when making cold calls for my job.
- I have a tendency to interrupt others, even though I hate it when others interrupt me.

Affirmation: "I am honest about what I want and need."

What I Want and When: My Goal

A five-to-ten-word description of what I want to be, have, or do. And when I want it.

_____

_____

_____

_____

EXAMPLES:

I want to be one of the best personal development authors and speakers of all time and become financially wealthy by inspiring others to pursue their dreams.

Seven of the most common areas for setting goals:
- Finances/Future
- Work/Job security
- Relationships
- Health
- Beliefs, Attitude, and Worldview
- Family
- Education

My specific goal and when I want to accomplish it:

_____

_____

_____

_____

Affirmation: "My goal is simply a dream with a deadline."

Why I Want It

My list of motives and benefits to me.
What will this mean to me? How will my life improve? How will I feel?

_____

_____

_____

_____

EXAMPLES:
- I'll be able to quit my day job and fund my life with things I'm passionate about.
- I'll be able to help other reach their goals.
- I'll have time outside my job for the people and things I care about most.

Affirmation: "My motives clearly drive me to keep going. I am richly rewarded financially and spiritually as a result of helping millions become bolder and more confident."

My Clear, Written Plan in Five Easy Steps

1. Keep it simple.
2. Start with what I have and what I know.
3. Find out what I need and don't have.
4. Ask for help and find out what I need and don't know.
5. Write my plan down!

_____

_____

_____

_____

EXAMPLES:

My plan is to leverage three decades of experience in sales, recovery, and leadership, to encourage and inspire others to become more confident, courageous, and prosperous. Specifically, to train, coach, and equip individuals and businesses through seminars, webinars, podcasts, and books.

Affirmation: "I plan my work and work my plan."

Visualization: What Does Success Look Like to Me?

Specific pictures, collages, dream boards, etc., to help me visualize what I want.

_____

_____

_____

_____

Affirmation: "I see it. Say it. Believe it. And do it."

TEN SECONDS OF BOLDNESS

Mental Rehearsal/Association:

Visualize some action that is moving me closer to my goal.
See, hear, and get around the people and things that will enrich my mental image. And opportunities for success. Specifically, watch videos, attend seminars, or hire coaches to guide and clarify my goals, images, and belief.

_____

_____

_____

_____

EXAMPLES:

My books are perennial best sellers.
#1 *New York Times* Best Seller list for 104 consecutive weeks.
#1, 2, or 3 in respective categories on Amazon.
I have multiple titles in the top 100 best-selling books on Amazon.
I have taught, trained, or inspired more than ten million people worldwide.
Opportunities come to me as a result of practicing what I teach.
I just completed my interview on the Zig Presents, Self-help(ful), podcast with Kevin Miller and Tom Ziglar and feel fantastic. It was a major catalyst to selling my first one million books and has led to many paid speaking engagements and countless benefits I could not even imagine.

Affirmation: "I love helping others become bolder and more confident."

Write Positive Affirmations for Each Goal:

A statement of thoughts and feelings as if I already have that which I seek.

_____

_____

_____

_____

EXAMPLES:
- I am a perpetual best-selling author who has sold millions of books.
- It feels amazing to see my books at the top of so many best seller lists.
- More important are the lives that are being transformed and the financial freedom for my family and me as a result of helping others learn to believe and help themselves.

Affirmation: "I am. I have. I did."

Getting Started

EXAMPLES:
- Action Steps (Tasks)
- Start with an idea about what I want to write, who I want to reach, and what I want to say to them.
- Due Date
- Date Completed

TASK	DUE DATE	COMPLETED
Start writing		
Outline		
Research		
Interviews		
Edit		
Format		
Publish proof copies		
Proofread		
Publish		
Market		

Affirmation: "I do it now!"

Daily To-Do List, Three Things:

EXAMPLES:

Work:
- 1:1 With Boss
- Close Deals
- Send Reporting to Clients

Personal:
- Finish this Planner
- Take Mom to Bank and Lunch
- Relax.

Other:
- Cages for Tomatoes
- Trim Edges of Lawn
- BBQ for Father's Day

Words of Encouragement:

By others. And to myself.

_____

_____

_____

_____

EXAMPLES:
- I finish what I start and it feels terrific.
- Others say I am an inspiration to them and I love that.

Affirmation: "Don't quit before the miracle."

Gratitude List:

What am I grateful for today?
Here are the top five to ten things I am grateful for right now.

_____   _____

_____   _____

_____   _____

_____   _____

_____   _____

EXAMPLES:
- I am grateful for my health, mind, body and spirt.
- I am surrounded by people who love and support me despite all my shortcomings.
- I am grateful for my sobriety, family, food, clothing, and more income than expenses.

Affirmation: "A grateful heart is a happy heart."

Appendix III
Affirmations

As mentioned earlier, affirmations are positive statements of your intentions, written in present tense as if you have achieved them. They are incredibly powerful and work best if they are:
- Believable.
- Important to you.
- Easy to remember and repeat.

They can also be:
- Prayers, thoughts, and meditations.
- Natural extensions of visualizing your goals written in a way to help you believe them to be true.

Affirmations Are the Secret Sauce to Success

Along with prayer and meditation as previously mentioned, visualization and affirmation, coupled with action, are the "secret sauce" to manifesting your own reality. Affirmations help replace, reboot, and reprogram your mind. Over time, they have the capacity to build belief and confidence because they replace tired, unproductive, negative thinking by forming new neural pathways for your mind.

As Stephen Campbell mentioned in Chapter Twenty-Eight: "Positive affirmations are very powerful because they release you from negativity, fear, worry, and anxiety. When you lock onto these affirmations, they can take charge of your thoughts, slowly changing your pattern of thinking and ultimately changing your life."

Here are a few of the examples I mentioned earlier:

- Today, I am one of the richest men alive because of love. I love and am loved. And that is worth more than anything money could buy. More than a million dollars in the bank, a mansion by the beach, or a Lamborghini in my garage.
- I am happy, most days when I decide to be.
- I am healthy because I exercise and eat moderately well.

If your affirmations are specific to one or more of your goals, I encourage you to include them in affirmation section of the *Ten Seconds of Boldness* Productivity Planner for that particular goal. Please note, while affirmations are an important part of building your mindset around a goal or objective, they also work on their own. In other words, affirmations can be a goal or intention without being attached to some master plan.

Use this space to write out any affirmations that feel important to you. Write as many or as few as you like. Just remember to keep them focused on what you want as if you already have it. Be creative, have fun.

Appendix IV
Your Personal *Ten Seconds of Boldness* Agreement

I _____ agree to get busy becoming less busy. To make time for things important to me. *To find the courage to start and the discipline to finish, regardless of internal or external obstacles. To focus on what I can control and let go of what I can't.*

I believe I can develop greater awareness and self-confidence over time. I will always look for things I can do today to move me one step closer to becoming the kind of person I want to be. And I will boldly, consistently, and persistently pursue the things which are important to me even when I don't feel like it.

I _____ promise to do what it takes to_____. (Fill in the blank with what you want to be, have, or do). I will apply these tools to the best of my ability, so I may become more confident by taking bold action to follow my dreams and earnestly live a life as I imagine.

I resolve to do a little bit every day toward whatever I am working on.

To the best of my ability, I will routinely apply and develop the Five Essential Habits for Solving any Problem or pursuing any opportunity in all important areas of my life:

1. **Identify** the problem or opportunity
2. Clearly **decide** what you want
3. Know **why** you want it
4. Write a clear **plan**
5. **Start** working that plan

I will consistently pursue areas of interest to me and strive to find and know my why.

I understand now that the process is the goal; the journey is the destination. When I feel stuck, I will be humble and bold enough to admit it and ask for help. I will keep an open mind and develop the habit of becoming insatiably curious use Ten Seconds of Boldness™ as often as I can especially when I am feeling anxious or afraid.

Most importantly, I will never give up on myself or my dreams.

I promise to never quit before the miracle.

Signed: _____

Date:_____

Appendix V
Gratitude List

"Walk as if you are kissing the Earth with your feet."
Thich Nhat Hanh

Instructions:

List everything you can think of that you are grateful for. Consider these questions as prompts:
- What are you grateful for?
- What makes you happy?
- What brings you joy?
- What feels good?

EXAMPLES:

I am grateful for:
- My health.
- My sobriety.
- Having more money than month.
- My family.
- Being loved and accepted as I am.

Notes

Citations:

Adamczyk, Alicia. "Americans' Savings Rates Hit Great Recession–Era Lows." *Fortune*, 27 May 2022, fortune.com/2022/05/27/americans-savings-rates-hit-great-recession-era-lows. Accessed 15 June 2022.

"Ambitious" *Lexico.com*, www.lexico.com/en/definition/ambitious. Accessed 28 May 2022.

"Belief" *Lexico.com*, www.lexico.com/en/definition/belief. Accessed 28 May 2022.

"Boldness" *Lexico.com*, www.lexico.com/en/definition/boldness. Accessed 28 May 2022.

Covey, Stephen R. *7 Habits of Highly Effective People*. Simon & Schuster Ltd, 2013.

Csikszentmihalyi, Mihaly. *Flow: The Psychology of Optimal Experience (Harper Perennial Modern Classics)*. 1st ed., Harper Perennial Modern Classics, 2008.

Cullen, Marlene. *The Write Spot: Writing as a Path to Healing*. M. Cullen Enterprises, 2020.

Davis, Chris. "Kobe Bryant Workout Routine: 666 Workout." *Pop Workouts*, 23 Feb. 2016, www.popworkouts.com/kobe-bryant-workout-routine. Accessed 15 June 2022.

Economy, Peter. "This Is the Way You Need to Write Down Your Goals for Faster Success." *Inc.Com*, 6 Feb. 2020, www.inc.com/peter-economy/this-is-way-you-need-to-write-down-your-goals-for-faster-success.html. Accessed 15 June 2022.

Eurich, Tasha. (2018). *Insight: The Surprising Truth About How Others See Us, How We See Ourselves, and Why the Answers Matter More Than We Think* (Reprint ed.). Currency.

Eurich, Tasha. "What Self-Awareness Really Is (and How to Cultivate It)." *Harvard Business Review*, 4 Jan. 2018, hbr.org/2018/01/what-self-awareness-really-is-and-how-to-cultivate-it. Accessed 25 May 2022.

"Fear of failure - APA Dictionary of Psychology." *Dictionary.apa.org*, dictionary.apa.org/fear-of-failure. Accessed 28 May 2022.

Goins, Jeff. *The Truth behind Natural-Born Talent*. 9 May 2016, goinswriter.com/talent-myth/. Accessed 21 March 2022. Adapted from Goins, Jeff. *The Art of Work : A Proven Path to Discovering What You Were Meant to Do*. Nashville, Tennessee, Thomas Nelson, 2015.

Goleman, D. (2005). *Emotional Intelligence: Why It Can Matter More Than IQ* (10th Anniversary ed.). Random House Publishing Group.

Jiang, Jia. "What I Learned from 100 Days of Rejection." *www.ted.com*, www.ted.com/talks/jia_jiang_what_i_learned_from_100_days_of_rejection?language=en. Accessed 18 March 2022.

Haynes, Trevor. "Dopamine, Smartphones and You: A Battle for Your Time." *Science in the News*, 4 Feb. 2021, sitn.hms.harvard.edu/flash/2018/dopamine-smartphones-battle-time. Accessed 5 July 2022.

Higgins, E. Tory. *Beyond Pleasure and Pain: How Motivation Works (Oxford Series in Social Cognition and Social Neuroscience)*. 1st ed., Oxford University Press, 2013.

Isaacson, Walter. *Steve Jobs*. 1st ed., Simon and Schuster, 2011.

Joelson, Richard. "Locus of Control." *Psychology Today*, 2017, www.psychologytoday.com/us/blog/moments-matter/201708/locus-control. Accessed 16 May 2022.

Langwell, Crissi "How the Question Was Asked." *Wine Country Mom*, 17 Oct. 2011, winecountrymom.com/2011/10/17/how-the-question-was-asked/. Accessed 28 May 2022.

Langwell, Shawn. *Beyond Recovery: A Journey of Grace, Love, and Forgiveness*. United States, Drooling Dog Press, 2016.

Langwell, Shawn, "Just Keep Swinging." *Remember When: Fiction & Memoir Tales of Memories and Times Past, edited by* Langwell, Shawn and Crissi, Redwood Writers Press, 2022, Pages 45-52.

"Pavlov's Theory of Classical Conditioning: What You Need To Know." *Very Well Health*, 31 Mar. 2022, www.verywellhealth.com/classical-conditioning-5218361. Accessed 14 June 2022.

Personal Income and Outlays, April 2022 | U.S. Bureau of Economic Analysis (BEA). (2022, May 27). Https://www.Bea.Gov/News/2022/Personal-Income-and-Outlays-April-2022. Accessed 14 June 2022.

Rogers, Simon. "Beatles Lyrics and the Words They Used Most." *The Guardian*, 16 Nov. 2010, www.theguardian.com/music/datablog/2010/nov/16/beatles-lyrics-words-music-itunes. Accessed 14 June 2022

Schwantes, Marcel. "Science Says 92 Percent of People Don't Achieve Their Goals. Here's How the Other 8 Percent Do."

Inc.Com, 5 Jan. 2021, www.inc.com/marcel-schwantes/science-says-92-percent-of-people-dont-achieve-goals-heres-how-the-other-8-perce.html. Accessed 14 June 2022.

"TR Center - Man in the Arena." *www.theodorerooseveltcenter.org*, www.theodorerooseveltcenter.org/Learn-About-TR/TR-Encyclopedia/Culture-and-Society/Man-in-the-Arena.aspx. Accessed 28 May 2022.

"Willingness" *Lexico.com*, www.lexico.com/en/definition/willingness. Accessed 15 June 2022.

Interviews:

Diamond, Jon. Personal Interview. 18 August 2017
Lavin, Steve. Zoom Interview. 23 September 2020
Locks, Aaron. Zoom Interview. 18 August 2021
Miller, Kevin. Zoom Interview. 9 September 2020
Wasden, Cara. Zoom Interview. 17 August 2021

Email Contributions:

Campbell, Steven R. Email to Langwell, Shawn. 21 February 2022.
Lam, Jason. Email to Langwell, Shawn. 19 January 2022.
Wasden, Cara. Email to Langwell, Shawn. 15 August 2021.

Suggested Reading/Listening List:

Albom, Mitch. *Mitch Albom's Tuesdays with Morrie*. New York, Dramatists Play Service, 2008.

Alcoholics Anonymous Big Book. 4th ed., Alcoholics Anonymous World Services, 2002.

Blanchard, Kenneth, and Spencer Johnson. *The One Minute Manager*. Glasgow, Scotland, Fontana, 1985.

Brown, Brené. *Daring Greatly : How the Courage to Be Vulnerable Transforms the Way We Live, Love, Parent, and Lead*. New York, N.Y., Gotham Books, 2012.

Byrne, Rhonda. *The Secret : The 10th Anniversary Edition*. New York, N.Y., Atria Books ; Hillsboro, Or, 2016.

Campbell, Steven. *Making Your Mind Magnificent : Flourishing at Any Age*. Lake Placid, N.Y., Aviva Publishing, 2009.

Cardone, Grant. *The 10X Rule : The Only Difference between Success and Failure*. Hoboken, New Jersey, John Wiley & Sons, Inc, 2011.

Carlson, Richard. *Don't Sweat the Small Stuff-- and It's All Small Stuff : Simple Ways to Keep the Little Things from Taking over Your Life*. New York, Hyperion, 1997.

Carnegie, Dale. *How to Win Friends & Influence People*. New York, Pocket Books, 1990.

Clear, James. *Atomic Habits*. Penguin Publishing Group, 2018.

Coelho, Paulo. *The Alchemist*. New York Harper Collins Publishers, 1988.

Covey, Stephen R. *7 Habits of Highly Effective People*. Simon & Schuster Ltd, 2013.

Csikszentmihalyi, Mihaly. *Flow : The Psychology of Optimal Experience*. New York, Harper and Row, 1990.

David Joseph Schwartz. *The Magic of Thinking Big. (Revised.)*. Preston, A. Thomas & Co, 1967.

Doerr, Anthony. *All the Light We Cannot See*. Rock Island, Il, Rock Island Public Library, 2014.

Dyer, Wayne W. *Change Your Thoughts -- Change Your Life : Perpetual Flip Calendar*. Carlsbad, Calif., Hay House, Inc, 2008.

Dyer, Wayne W. *Transformation : The next Step for the No-Limit Person*. New York, Simon & Schuster Audio, 1995.

Dyer, Wayne W. *Your Erroneous Zones*. New York, N.Y., Quill, 2001.

Frankl, Viktor E. *Man's Search for Meaning*. 1946. Boston, Beacon Press, 2006.

Gawain, Shakti. *Creative Visualization Meditations*. New World Library, 1996.

Kahlil Gibran. *The Prophet*. New York, Alfred A. Knopf, 2018.

Goleman, Daniel. *Emotional Intelligence*. London, Bloomsbury Publishing, 1995.

Goleman, Daniel. *Social Intelligence : The New Science of Human Relationships*. New York, Bantam Books, 2007.

Hill, Napoleon. *Think and Grow Rich*. 1937. S.L., Simon & Brown, 2019.

Holy Bible : New International Version. Grand Rapids, Michigan, Zondervan, 2017.

Isaacson, Walter. *Steve Jobs*. S.L., Simon & Schuster, 2021.

Johnson, Spencer. *Who Moved My Cheese? 2004.* Andrews Mc Meel, 2003.

Kingsolver, Barbara. *Flight Behavior : A Novel*. New York, Harper, 2012.

Manson, Mark. *Subtle Art of Not Giving a F*Ck*. HarperCollins, 2017.

Maxwell, John C., and Jim Dornan. *Becoming a Person of Influence ; Talent Is Never Enough*. Nashville, Tenn., T. Nelson Publishers, 2007.

Maxwell, John C. *Failing Forward : How to Make the Most of Your Mistakes*. Thomas Nelson Publishers, 2000.

Nepo, Mark, and Jamie Lee Curtis. *The Book of Awakening : Having the Life You Want by Being Present to the Life You Have*. Newburyport, MA, Red Wheel, 2020.

Nightingale, Earl. *Lead the Field*. Shippensburg, PA, Sound Wisdom, 2018.

Owens, Delia. *Where the Crawdads Sing*. Little Brown, 2020.

Ramsey Solutions. (2021, September 24). *The State of Debt Among Americans*. www.ramseysolutions.com/debt/state-of-debt-among-americans-research. Accessed 1 June 2022

Sinek, Simon. *Start with Why: How Great Leaders Inspire Everyone to Take Action*. London, Portfolio/Penguin, 2009.

Strayed, Cheryl. *Wild: A Journey from Lost to Found [Paperback]*. (2018). Knopf.

Tracy, Brian. *Eat That Frog! : 21 Great Ways to Stop Procrastinating and Get More Done in Less Time*. Oakland, Berrett-Koehler Publishers, Inc., A Bk Life Book, 2017.

Waitley, Denis. *The Psychology of Winning : 10 Qualities of a Total Winner*. Melbourne, Brolga Pub, 2002.

Wooden, John, and Steve Jamison. *Wooden : A Lifetime of Observations and Reflections on and off the Court*. New York, McGraw-Hill, 1997.

Warren, Rick. *The Purpose Driven Life*. Chagrin Falls, Oh, Zondervan, 2006.

Ziglar, Z. A. M. (1979). *See You at the Top: Formerly Entitled Biscuits, Fleas, and Pump Handles*. Pelican Pub. Co.

About the Author

Shawn Langwell is a leader, author, speaker, coach, and an award-winning salesperson for the Bay Area News Group, and past salesperson and employee of the year for the New York Times Regional Media Group. He has over three decades of sales experience and thirty-five plus years of continuous sobriety. In recovery, he has shared his personal story to thousands of people in more than twenty countries around the world.

He is the past President of Toast of Petaluma, and past President of Redwood Writers, a branch of the California Writers Club, the largest writing club in California. Shawn is the author of the memoir *Beyond Recovery: A Journey of Grace, Love, and Forgiveness*.

His personal mission is to add value to people and businesses everywhere. More specifically, to encourage, inspire, and help people become brave and confident enough to believe they can accomplish their dreams and goals.

Shawn lives in Northern California with his wife, adult children, and gorgeous Maine Coon Cat, Cleo.

You can find Shawn at shawnlangwell.com.